# CORAL REEF BONES

## A Practitioner's Experience With the Body

### Poetic Weavings of Patience and Practice

By

M. English, C. Denhart & L. Bennett

## Our Team

**Michael English** - CMT, Body Gardener, Interviewee, Co-Author, Editor

**Christie Denhart** - Interviewer, Co-Author, Editor

**Lisa Bennett** – Contributing editor

First Edition
First Printing 2024

Cover Designer by K. Santiago

This is a work depicting interviews with a client and is based on the transcription and review of those interviews. This is not an endorsement of any particular bodywork modality. The opinions expressed by Michael and Christie are not intended to represent any but their own.

Paperback ISBN-13-979-8-9913385-0-9
Published in the USA

# Table of Contents

# Before You Begin

Imagine that you could have a conversation with your body. What would that sound like? What would it *feel like?* What could you better understand about the current state of the well-functioning areas, the areas where trauma has settled, or even where emotions are buried? Some of the answers to these questions may be found in the pages to come.

In the following pages, whether it is an introduction, exercise, or part of the poetry that Michael and Christie weave around analogies, playful banter and curiosity, you will find a profound sense of humble respect and a view of the human body garden that is unique. The language ranges from practical anatomy, comedic self-effacing descriptors, symbolism, and imaginative playwriting. What you may not find is a purely academic approach to how your body functions, or academic writing where all of your questions are answered in full, with citations and references. The approach is intentional, and the gaps are designed to allow you the room and space to experience, first-hand, both the cognitive dissonance and the curiosity that drove the creation of this book.

Why cognitive dissonance? Cognitive dissonance, the mental stress people experience when exposed to information that is inconsistent with their beliefs, is often a precursor to learning. Your brain stops, hits the brakes, and you can take that pause to consider current state versus a new state or thought/belief/idea. You will be exposed to several new ideas, such as the idea that your brain is a Jellyfish and your bones are coral reefs, that may cause you to re-evaluate how you view yourself. *EXCELLENT!* If reading this book causes you to have a few "brain breaks", renew your relationship with your body, then we've all done our jobs.

The book closely reflects the original language of both Michael and Christie during their interviews. The thoughts and experiences expressed here are personal and represent years of

1

experience, flavor, music, between the two of them and independently. When the discussions of meeting clients 'where they are at' occur, remember that the intention is to understand the client developmentally, physically, and even emotionally, rather than 'meeting them where they are' physically in the world. There are many verbal fillers included as well; *'right'*, 'um', *'so'*, and other fillers allow space to feel the pacing and flow of the conversations as they occurred in real time. Poetry, rather than academia or fiction. The grace of opening your mind for this spacing will allow you to steep deeply and flow with the rhythm of the dance of their conversation.

To get the most out of reading this book:

- Read the Introductions from Christie and Michael.
- Take part in the exercise in Chapter Two.
- Space out your reading of the interviews – give your mind time to 'break', reform, and incorporate what you are learning.
- Make the recording recommended in "Creating Your Self-Facilitated Session".

Now, take a deep breath, get comfortable and enjoy the journey!

# Chapter One: *Beginning with Christie*

Welcome to the world of Michael's therapeutic soul work. His blend of Craniosacral work and other Western bodywork modalities with his training as an acknowledged practitioner of indigenous Earth medicine wisdom has resulted in a unique 'gardening' bodywork practice. He gardens human bodies.

You might wonder what that means and how he could do so. The sharing made with this book invites you to explore, along with him and by his example, how he begins to answer those questions and why it's important to even consider relating to our bodies in this way.

My name is Christie Denhart. I have been a client/student of Michael's work for almost two decades. I came to him in my mid-fifties having worked with my Chronic Fatigue Syndrome (CFS) for 20 years with a goodly number of bodywork practitioners, using many different modalities to try to help my physical-emotional-soul issues that were all at play in my health challenge. I also spent my adult life working as an intuitive counselor and teacher of different meditation and movement practices, so I was picky. It was a relief to find that Michael's work turned out to be an extremely fruitful exploration for me, in which I grew and changed in so many different deep and rich ways that I can hardly recognize the woman I was when I first started. I credit Michael, and later his wife, Jodi, who is a Somatic Experiencing practitioner, for teaching and holding me within their respective practices through many very difficult yet powerful transitions for me on my way to living with my body/being as well and potently as I am today.

In my long and varied experience with therapeutic work, Michael's offering in particular I found to be unique and helpful. Over time with him I kept wanting some way of writing down the understandings I was getting from his world view. I wanted more! I also kept thinking that it would be very helpful to others, particularly practitioners, to somehow have access to his work. I asked Michael if he was interested (more about this later), and this project was born.
Now to get back to some of the reasons why his work is interesting and helpful, especially with embodiment issues.

I found that Michael's language and practice has an unusual and potent capacity for naming what is needed for organic life to flourish. This organic life first means the 'livingness' of your own body, your own 'earth'. Since your body is the ground structure of your existence, your 'earth' is your particular pattern of aliveness among the others of our planet Earth. When you learn to garden and be gardened, or to even begin to think and imagine in this way, you actually can begin to discover how to literally nurture and embody yourself outside of just thinking about your body or using your body as a vehicle in the pursuit of getting things 'done'. You can begin to explore how this shift in orientation affects not only your relationship with your body but also your relationship with the ground of life you are embedded in within our planet Herself.

Often people turn to bodywork as a way to address and ease pain, usually pain in the body, although some come seeking to explore how physical pain can be linked to emotional pain, and some are seeking the source of soul pain, which might be described as a form of disconnection/fragmentation/dissociation from the body and movement of Life Itself. Michael's cross-cultural blend of Shamanism and Western bodywork is really a teaching and a facilitated exploration of the underlying unity of the roots of discomfort and how to begin to relieve those.

Michael considers himself first and foremost a gardener, using his unique talent for kinesthetic sensitivity. Making contact – through subtle and rich touch, sound, words, movement (all arising out of body 'feel') – he invites his clients/students to soften deeply into occupying and becoming more fully themselves within the neighborhoods of their body. Along the way over time pain softens, old trauma can ease, emotions can release, mind and understanding can expand and shift. In partnership with Michael, his 'people' learn to open the doorway to inhabiting their own 'feeling' sensitivity, to self-facilitate using their developing kinesthetic, intuitive perception and to experience further their own understanding and practice of ways to ease and grow. He teaches them to garden themselves, within cycles, seasons, with receptive listening and attention to their system's particular organic movement.

Their relationship to the living earth of themselves, their own bodies and being, can change, becoming more integrated, more inclusive, more creative in the expression of their particular dance of Life. As they shift and change, of course, this also reforms their relationships with others, both personal and communal, including their human and non-human communities.

The hope is that this book, what Michael has learned in his teaching and earthy focus, will interest different groups of people. There are those who may not have considered bodywork as a fertile ground for self-growth in addition to the physical relief of pain. Others may be intrigued by the taste of indigenous understandings through Michael's shamanic ground, which is to say holding to one's soul and its relationship to self and place. Some may simply enjoy Michael's way of expressing and encouraging the use of their imagination as they follow his way of exploring. More experienced body workers may be intrigued with Michael's gardening metaphor and his way of teaching and responding using sensation and the felt sense. Spiritual explorers find they are working literally with their own embodiment as they explore Michael's earth orientation and practical 'gardening' skills and suggestions.

This sharing is an experiment in translating Michael's kinesthetic world into words/marks/deer tracks on a page. The hope is that the reader will be able to begin to enter Michael's world of 30+ years of experience... and use that entry to begin to touch/feel the possibilities coming from contact with their own body, with the 'earth' of their existence, that he is cultivating and offering here.

Over the years, many clients have wanted Michael to write down what he teaches and says in sessions. It's a difficult task, given the highly kinesthetic nature of his work, and yet in talking to Michael about this, we finally started by me interviewing him over a year's time. The six interviews that form the core of this book are the result.

## Suggestions for Reading Michael

This book is an attempt to point to what Michael offers. This love story is also (and technically) a song of transmission. What Michael is teaching invokes body intelligence that is not primarily based in the brain or even the nervous system. A book by its very nature is a mental verbal process...so how to use language on a page so that it evokes the organic fluid movement of tactile understanding and creative flow that gives a sense of the movement of body intelligence.

The book has thus become a prose poem more than a logical linear explication. And... there is still a need for the verbal dance that communicates and bridges the intuitive with the more rational, linear instructive, didactic that we have tried to honor.

In my experience, when Michael works, session is more like jazz. He improvises always, using touch and language, often moving with his own body to literally, spontaneously, dance his language. There are different rhythms, tempos, voice modulations, moods, slang, made up words... a mix that is unique to that person and that particular session. Ultimately, he is inviting, seducing, reassuring, demanding, allowing, encouraging his client/his person to soften into their body and ease off control of their brain. Then the manual work that he does can perform its magic. This can then serve as an invitation for the person to drop into their experience of a unique kind of perception based on organic integration that is different from our more normal, less connected habits of perceiving reality.

The language here is punctuated a bit outside of the norm, and the style includes repetition and 'stops' to slow the speed of the reading down, such as the allowance of *ums* in the dialog. There are cycles of logic and places of apparent discontinuities. Michael is 'singing' the 'song' that is the work. This book is a libretto that points to that song, to a way of working in real time that includes the dance of touch, sound and fluid language in the movement of the jazz, of that 'song'.

This is also an attempt to 'explain' in a more traditional way many of the concepts and understandings behind the language and the work that might be used in a session. Most often, after a session with Michael, people report not being able to retain what he says in session. His words actually arise out of his body's experience in the moment, rather than in a 'brain down' way of thinking and speaking. He is talking to the client's body, not their brain.

Bodies take a long time to shift and change, unlike thought process. Michael is not as concerned with the brain's understanding... if it can't remember or retain, that's fine. He is concerned more with the slow, gradual softening and opening of the body so that through being met and nourished, whole neighborhoods of the body can ease into change as needed or as is possible. Along the way, a client learns to trust the intelligence of the whole, not just the intelligence of the brain/nervous system.

The sharing in this book is a taste of what some clients who work with Michael over time learn, which is to say that in the book he teaches definitions of the work, including his blend of using a 'meta' view from the Peruvian lineage he is trained in coupled with processes from Craniosacral Therapy and other body modalities. These all point in different ways to the cycles of work that initiate a process and then circle back, over and over, as the softening of the body happens over time. Trauma, an injury or overwhelming event, or both, take time to unravel. As Michael will explain in many different ways, the process of softening, releasing, shifting and actual change requires ongoing periodic integration in order to take the next step into what can move more fully, more wholly. There is a dance, a music that has an entry, exploration, insight, reaction, retreat, stillness, and then the next move forward... the next inquiry... the next willingness to explore again.

This writing project moves in somewhat the same way. There are definitions slowly dropped in, and then repeated again and again, each time adding a new facet of the work, a new understanding of the ground of possibility. There are times of understanding and then times of not knowing what Michael is talking about... times that require suspending the need to know, tolerating confusion, and the vulnerability of 'not knowing', and to simply keep going, learning the process by feeling your way along.

Through the interviews, there are a series of repetitions as the 'practice' and the process of communicating builds slowly over time, over the duration. By the end of the book, the fabric of the work has been fleshed out in a way that allows for the possibility of a deeper understanding of the living process of the tissues... insight into their consciousness and a taste of the unfolding of a direct experience of intimacy inherent in the wholeness of body/mind/spirit integration. Hopefully reading this sequence of interviews also builds trust in the reader's own cyclical process of coming into understanding of a different way of being with body processes.

## Ways of Playing with the Book as You Read

You may or may not want to read the book from start to finish in a literal way. In fact, I encourage you to put the book down in between interviews or whenever you get tired or flooded with information. This will help you slow down (a main tenant of the work) as well as to contemplate. This kind of 'stopping' is essential to the ongoing integration of the book. In fact, it really is a requirement.

You may find yourself skipping through the different sections, trying things out, and then you may find yourself wanting to come back to an interview in order to now get a deeper understanding of what meanings and context Michael is unfolding over the duration.

Throughout, you will get your curiosity piqued, which can then prompt you into using an inquiry process that can be very helpful. My own training in this kind of exploration has taught me to frame my curiosity into open-ended questions. This leaves room for intuitive answers or directions to bubble up into consciousness. Those are often surprising, fruitful and/or meaningful in taking the 'next steps' in the ongoing discovery process.

Some of these open-ended questions that arose for me with this work include the ones I have listed below. They may reflect your own questions, or they may stimulate other questions for you that piggyback on mine. The questions may not have a known answer. Most of the time the goal is not really to answer them at all, but to open exploration. Most often this becomes a way to train yourself in body feeling as a guide... how to literally 'feel into' the next step of this current thought or emotion or action being evoked.

Some examples of questions might be:

How do emotional and physical knots ease, unravel and absorb/melt into the depth of present-time body experience?

How does the 'opera'/the story of my trauma become liquefied into present time and thus ease my walk in the world?

How do I self-facilitate this process?

What is body gardening? How do I learn time and timing of the seasons, repetitions, tempo of body gardening?

How do I actually listen to the body?

What are the levels of engagement Michael is teaching and how do I play with them/use them to inform my 'way'?

How does this tangible, tactile learning process inform the whole of my experience differently than a solely conceptual process?

Bottom line... *how does love and respect for this body, the mystery of this human form that I am, learned from the ground of cellular experience up, cultivate and inform love and respect for myself and for all of us nested within the larger body of the planet, all of this Life Itself?*

With this first chapter, and on into what's offered here, I am inviting you to slow down, savor and allow your curiosity to lead you into exploring this account of Michael's work and the possibilities it brings up for following his lead into a different relationship to your own body and life. I definitely encourage you to try some of the resources mentioned by Michael and myself in the conclusive parts of the book to keep exploring on your own.

**Before you dive into the interviews, some strong recommendations!**

In order to get the most out of this offering, be sure to read the sections in this chapter, *"Reading Michael"* and *"Ways to Play"*. The suggestions in those pieces will make it much easier to understand and absorb the non-traditional punctuation, style and language the book uses.

It's also very helpful to read through Chapter 2 twice, putting it down in between the readings, and giving yourself plenty of time, particularly when you are going through the experiential section of that chapter. In doing so, especially in that section, you may be able to drop out of reading mode into experiencing how it might feel to be guided into a beginning session with Michael using your intuition to evoke a sense of this physical experience. Throughout the book, keep remembering to notice your body's responses as you read Michael's words.

# Chapter Two: *Beginning with Michael*

Dear Reader,

Welcome to this conversation between myself and Christie, a remarkably patient person whose willingness to walk through this process with me has changed a part of my life.

But first, let's start with an idea, my experience really. There's this dialog/monolog that's been happening with those in my life for 33+ years (actually much longer), that this dialog could be expressed in a way other than verbal just doesn't occur to me. Many of these dear people would say, "Hey... You should write this down."

Of course, my response was always, "Sure – you write, I'll converse." I'm an oral tradition kind of guy with somewhat of a writing phobia (not just somewhat!). Well, Christie is the first brave soul to take the challenge and sit me down and ask her questions. She wanted to get underneath and behind what it takes for me to do 'my practice', the umbrella of which falls under the title of Craniosacral work. This title allows me to use all my skills in an attempt to meet people 'where they are'. This is to say, not where I think they should be or where they think they should be but where 'they' are, at the time of contact. Sounds easy enough?!?!
It's made for a fully engaged 33+ years of trying to practice what one preaches which makes for a very lively engagement with my fellow beings.

So, Dearest Reader,

This is roughly the 452nd version, and also the amount of tentacles I have needed to feel and find my way through a chaotic and chess-game-filled first half of my life. Those tentacles were steadily retrieved over many years of my therapeutic process.  Also, in this version I attempted to give up on naming every person and creature responsible for 'ME' being here and able to do this conversation, this sharing, this endeavor. Soooo, if you recognize my name or any of this sounds familiar, Thank YOU!

Here goes my intro. I handle language tactilely and kinesthetically. I find the feeling and begin to wrap the words around it like verbal collage, the words have to feel right, have the right taste, texture, sound and musicality. For myself, I need it to be a living dialogue akin to the conversation that happens in good Jazz, not pop music piped into an elevator. This feeling of language must be musically responsive, tactically responsive. It doesn't work academically, that's not my kind of Jellyfish brain. How my brain works is on the abstract choreographic end of the spectrum and wants to find ways to engage the body of roots, underneath language, that encompasses our beautiful bag-o'-bones. This allows for a living conversation, akin to jazz, which is where I found myself these days rooted and supported by the all too many to be named inferred people along my taproot through time! Thank you Grannies! And everyone else!

Speaking of which...

At the ripe old age of 22yrs, after being posed a question, "What educational process would I be willing to commit to for 6 years?" After discovering college was very overwhelming, I decided on the vocational route towards massage therapy. See, I'd been working since my early teens, always finding a sense of self in working with my hands, opposed to the chaos in the homes I would find myself in. So, one week after my junior year in high school I left home, went to Colorado where I had a job lined up and my sense of life waiting. Then during that summer, a journey sent me into discovering I was headed towards becoming something I didn't want to become, my narcissistically slimy, manipulative father (yup lots of therapy on that one!) So dear reader, I found myself finagling back into my senior year of high school. Still not gifted yet in gab, I would find my hands working on people as a way to connect. With so many years of different manual labor jobs, literally feeling my way through life, this was how I communicated. Then after getting my first professional bodywork session at the age of 18 (it was a horrible experience!), I became quite upset, "IT DOESN'T HAVE TO BE LIKE THIS!!!!" Well, with that idea and a handful of strong feelings, I set out to explore my future.

In 1986, I'm in a small massage school back in California, the only school out of a dozen, the only one who actually asked me questions about my experiences and the directions I wanted to go. The training was held in a small school at a Korean Buddhist temple, remarkable!

A month into a two-year training, in our first movement class, in walks this small statured, fierce, demanding our attention woman who proceeds to ask one of my classmates about what we've been doing. She was Miss Vivian Jaye, one of the Rolfing Movement program teachers for the Rolf Institute. In response to Vivian's question the classmate went on and on about how massage should be done with the right music, candles, mellow atmosphere, etc., etc., etc. Very groovy, very healing. Well, Vivian paused my classmate and said, "NO! This work could be done in a bus depot!!!'

Well, dear reader, had this been directed at me, I would have piddled my pants, walked out and moved back to Colorado. Back to playing music and cabinet making! Oh, dear me, thank goodness for the facets in one's character! This sharp, strongly delivered challenge did its job! Not for my classmate, of course, but for the street kid in me. This statement woke 'em up. That little voice said, "Yup, she's right!" Simultaneously, within a few months I was working in a Physical Therapy office as an aide and doing tissue work for a Physical Therapist. The PT was a remarkable practitioner of her trade. She said I did very nice work, but it was a very expensive aspirin and began guiding me into the clinical aspect of tissue work. I stayed in PT offices for 9 years. Meanwhile, back at the massage school, they encouraged me to finagle my way into everything I could which included cleaning, being a front office desk jockey, assisting classes, filming most of the demos, just about everything, it was all wonderful labor for me. Then, eventually finding my way into teaching, 20+ years' worth, as well as sliding in with a Cranial institute for 10 yrs. Phew, all the while under foot with Vivian! Remarkable! 33years! How does one write about that? It's such a thick root for me!

So, underfoot, Vivian was trying to get me to become a Rolfer and finally gave up after 10 years, though not for the lack of trying. There're good reasons she'd become my mentor, we were both determined, or is it stubborn! Anyways, she threw out another Vivian statement, "Well, you know, I Rolf like a cranial practitioner and you do cranial work like a Rolfer!"

Anyways, I'm going to attempt to drop you into a summary of all these years with Vivian as my mentor...

Try to imagine my time with Vivian as a feeling, a living metaphor with an amazingly curious and tenacious educator who loved open-ended questions.

This would encourage dialogue, not just between peoples but also within ourselves and if that didn't work, she would redirect and ask, "So, can you walk for me?", this was her being a Rolfing movement instructor. Then to deepen her and the person's experience she would ask, "Say more about that."

Now we find ourselves 33 years later, just 4 days before she passed, April 27th, 2018. I had just paused at the end of her session, my hands resting on either side of her head, as was my habit over the last 20 years of working on her. This was an engaged, hands-on educational process for me, a very slow but steady tactile learner (her words by the way). Well, she opens her eyes and says, "Have you ever considered looking through other people's eyes?". Yup, 33+ years of invitational questions, but wait, she continues, "not just their eyes, the color of their eyes?" This was how we dialogued with each other. She went on, "I was just looking, feeling, seeing through amber eyes, never considered how other eye colors would 'see' the world. Whad-ya-think?" Oh yes, this continues to sing within my soul, this was my mentor and my friend. I'm such a fortunate fellow! She passed 4 days later. (should be its own book if I'd only had that kind of brain!)

Aright, let's just pause. Let's take this sharing, find the feelings that get stirred and then turn them into a tea, a palpable metaphor. This experiential tea is what I've been very privileged to steep in! Not just for the time with Vivian, but also thanks to my many instructors, teachers, and practitioners. I now can look back and see my past and say, "I've been very fortunate!" But I'll tell ya, I really miss being underfoot with that beautifully cantankerous, kind, thoughtful, humorously feisty and exquisitely thought-provoking little Jewish biddy (respectfully said, of course)! Oh, I know that wasn't much, but this is just the intro which thank goodness she's not here to read! She would roll her eyes, I think, thanks to me(Yup, still some inflation, darn puffer fish boy) she had the healthiest of eye muscles! In fact, many people close to me can attest to their continued healthy eye rolling abilities. I know she would have asked such good questions that I might never had gotten this far in this sharing, this conversation.

Oh, dearest reader... I will need to ask for your continued patience. In this current sharing, what I'm inviting you into is not an academic or an intellectual treatise on any particular type of bodywork or any of the sciences. Not even accurate to our anatomy and physiology. Not even really a day in the life of a cranial practitioner. This is somewhat intentional (actually, very intentional), this is an attempt to experience the *feeling* first, the *experience* first. This is a steeping of effort before the Jellyfish brain gets her tendrils into things, well, our brain likes her tendrils in everything (she's like that). YUP, PATIENCE! This is the part of an ongoing conversation that circulates, is meant to be felt, steeped, sensed, allowed to pause, to circulate all the delicious, facetted aspects and ingredients of our experience. Then to drop, to slide back into a few moments of Non-Doing as the Taoist would say. It's not, not doing, it's not using any mechanical engagement. In this non-doing, you soften yourself, just 10%, without collapsing. This allows your awareness to flood back into your fluids, flood back into your body and finally flood back into your Bones! While your awareness is steeping back into your beautiful 'coral reef' bones, you're then going to allow your attention, which is a different aspect, to become an odd sea creature that can move around and...

Oh well, getting ahead of myself. This is how I've learned to trust, especially Christie - she (as well as inferred others) keeps me somewhat on track! So dearest reader, hopefully your patience is close at hand, I will just drop us in, 10,000 words later...

## Let's Try Experiential Tea

So let's do this, let's make an experiential tea together, see if we can steep and nourish and feel our way into the layers of what's coming from this book, finding our way into our root beds. The layers of this conversation, between Christie and myself will hopefully, maybe, if we're lucky enough, will even make the Jellyfish brain squirm a little, maybe make her a little giggly, definitely a little bonkers.

Let's try...

*Alright, you're here, right now with this sharing, this book, held in your living hands. These hands of yours are beautifully tendrilled, rooted and full of coral reef bones, your wonderfully aquatic garden wrapped in a living, pliable membrane. Your exquisitely sensitive skinned hands. Meanwhile, simultaneously, your eyes, two delicious sea anemones, each held inside a bulb, each eye being held in a grouping of coral reef bones that make a bowl (especially when lying on your back) that hold them perfectly. Each bulb with its own sea anemone, they're both sisters really, both being tickled right this instance by the deer tracks, the symbols, the spilled words we've left on this page for you to soak up, add to your experiential tea. Please take a moment, take a pause, please spend some time feeling this. Do a few rounds of feeling your* own light-soaking bulbs, your beautiful eyes, maybe just close them, take some time, then come back to the tickle of these words spilled as deer tracks, then let's make it a small measure of music and play it a few times, let's make this experiential.

Let's practice this type of steeping, pausing, spending a few minutes so it can build up some potency, some chutzpa, (hoots-spah, thank you Vivian), this will be unique to you! Only you know when you are full, tired or bamboozled or??? When that feeling is sensed, you need to PAUSE. We're dropping YOU into OUR conversation and there's no rush. Please take time and feel your way through, absorbing this Tea. Only you know when a round is done, when a measure is enough, a cup of Tea has left you full and when (if) you've followed (read) through these deer tracks (the book) then you can come back through and wonder around.

PATIENCE PLEASE!

Now one more time, go slow, let this be absorbed into your sea anemone eyes and circulated through the tendrils, the actual roots that come off the back of the bulbs, in the bowls, in your face. This is very lovely to say out loud, so ready, out loud, sea anemones, in a bulb, in a *bowl, in your face! (Actually, try saying it a bunch of times quickly!)*

*Back to the feeling of those roots as they go back from the rear of your eyes, find a feeling of moving backwards through your head, pass the place where they share a bundle of roots. Keep wandering along these roots until you're almost to the back of the bowl of the back of your head. Each of these roots, the nerves, each of these tendrils are spilling their gathered (visual) tea into your visual cortex. By the way, it's not just one place, but two, there's two visual cortices, two sponges soaking up that wonderfully absorbed view of the deer tracks left as words, the alphabet soup of symbols gathered and steeped into a visual tea. Oh, dear reader, not just from tendrils of the sea anemones, in the bulbs, in the bowls, in your face, but from tendrils that come from all throughout your beautiful aquatic garden, your body!*

Now, just pause, go soak, put this down, go steep for a few rounds, please just steep, just sense, just add a little time, there's no need to rush, steeping and circulation need the ingredient of time, some patience and this is a good tea we're making!

*Welcome back! Now, let's go back into the garden patch of your hands and feel this book, this sharing. Begin to feel into this object, the space of these pages (unless of course you're using a different medium, if so, go get a favorite stone or something precious you can easily hold). Now let yourself soften, just 10% without collapsing. Let your attention begin to move, swim into the middle of the space this held object occupies, remember it's a funny little sea creature, your attention. Let your attention begin to move gently into this space, the quality of whatever it is that your holding, go slow, just steep there. Now gently bring/move your attention out of the precious object and back into the coral reef bones of your hands. Gently linger inside your hands. Then let yourself notice whatever you notice. Next, swim/move/feel your attention going out of, away from, the interior of your hand and into/towards the middle, the interior space of the precious object that your holding, gently linger/steep and now notice what you notice. Then slowly, gently, begin to go from one space then to the other space, slowly back and forth, taking a moment or many to linger and steep with whatever sensations YOU get! This is TO-and-FRO, from the belly of your Bones to the belly of your precious object! OK?!?!?! Now that you've gone back and forth, to-and-fro for several rounds and hopefully have a sense of the different qualities of each garden patch, each belly space, we're going to move/swim back to our coral reef bones in our hands and do one more round of back-and-forth. In this next cycle, this round, you'll do both, feel both areas at the same time and just feel, linger, steep: This is known as...Your Bones...Their Bones... Our Bones.*

Now rest, take a break, please go nourish yourself. Maybe a nap and then come back later (Jellyfish Brains hate the word 'later').

What did you notice? What did you feel? What did you sense? Now just revisit this. So, gently allowing the experiential ingredients to soak literally into the bones, roots, tendrils and fluids of your hands, a tea will begin to brew, an experiential tea that, when ready, will begin to circulate amongst your tissues, amongst your aquatic roots and towards your jellyfish brain. This steeping, this sharing, this endeavor takes time, drives the jellyfish brain bonkers, just toss her a gentle giggle, a little empathy for her impatience. She has a need to coordinate everything, there's an immediacy to this, she does not like waiting, her antithesis word is 'later'! So now, what about where your sitting? What's supporting your coral reef bones right now? What's coming to you? What's pushing into/onto those coral reef bones? Feel the quality of that contact, let it make a tea and let it absorb.

Where else do your coral reef bones have a contact? What kind of contact? The flavor, quality, sense, maybe sound or a felt color or maybe the most delicious feeling of "I don't know?!" Besides, there's always a push from the world. There's always a coral reef bone in contact with some-thing and between the coral reef bones and your contact with the world are all your marvelous roots, the vascular, lymphatic, fascial, muscle and of course comingled amongst them are the tendrils of your Jellyfish Brain. Their serpentine, aquatic, wonderful tendrils interweaving, dancing within your actual living aquatic garden, yes, called your body! Very alive!  So of course, just steep a bit, sense, feel, have a few rounds with this fluid, serpentine quality of your interior and the Jellyfish Brain that lives within there. Hopefully another pause, go nourish, walk, nap, rest, what are you noticing? Now go pour these sensations, these experiences into, towards something else, your next activity, your next round of singing and sauntering or prancing and dancing, maybe even just steeping again.  Thank you for your patience and time!

So, dearest reader, hopefully you're back with an established cup full of our beginning together and some patience!

I'm dropping you into my interior world, not my professional world of differentiating, unwinding and tending to a person's aquatic root beds, tendrils and tissues. That's just the gardening, the hands-on part. My gardens just happen to be 'people'. This is the Sharing, the endeavor to bring you into my privacy, the life-size space I occupy and the space where I self-nourish and orient myself, tend to myself. The space of our privacy is life-size, grows from how we nourish, how we tend to ourselves. What that takes is a unique set of ingredients that may be common and shared with others, or not, but the dance of it, the action of tending to oneself...the sensing, then gathering, then steeping of our literal and experiential ingredients. This then grows the person we're becoming. This is our privacy. We may share our tea that is brewed within our privacy, we may not. Mostly I feel it's a lot of both and it's different than secrecy. Secrecy is of form of retreat, coping, a way to protect. Secrecy takes constant effort even if it becomes a habit. Privacy is where we rest, there's no reaching, just steeping our tissues, sinews, tendrils and roots so they have their time to soften, integrate and begin to grow, available for sensing and responding to the next round, the next session, the next opera that you're/we're moving towards.

This is an important landscape to open up and begin to cultivate, to be able to feel what you need to nourish yourself, not just what goes in your mouth but your ears, eyes, hands and Soul. This sharing, this endeavor is dropping you into a form of my privacy. This is how I orient and tend to myself before handing this oriented, deeply felt, bone stock tea over to my practitioner bones, to my partnership bones, over to my friendship bones, over to the ??? bones, etc., etc. Oh, let's pause...

You'll have to extend your patience towards trust, that most assuredly, no matter the distance or relationship to time, I am doing this oriented, bone stock tea/soup making pause with you! Or damn close...

Maybe a recipe is in order?

> #1. Where are your bones? Careful, they're a bit feral!

> #2. Where do you feel the push of the world? There's always contact with a bone.

> #3. Have a giggle ready, your brain will want to do something, gently toss a giggle at her and circulate back to some bones, back to #1.

These three together are an orientation. A circulation of experience.

So, oh patient ones, this sharing, this endeavor comes out of an ongoing conversation. A layer of which has been ongoing for a miraculously long time. Then with Christie, may her heart continually be blessed, she had the patience to put this to print! Both of us have enjoyed and have been deeply worked by this conversation, this book. 10,000 blessings to our partners, as well as our supportive, run-ragged-as-they-were/are community. They all deserve a big thank you and, for those who would partake, a shot of high-end smoky Mescal! Well... just feel it...

So good luck my dearest reader and always, I'll ask for your continued patience.

"M"

P.S. Remember it's more poetry than... It's not so easy to write and speak what happens in silence, in quiet and within the murmur underneath the opera at hand!

# Chapter Three: *Interview #1*

**Michael**  Hello? Hello? Hello!

**Christie**  Yeah, you're doing fine. Well, I think I'll do a new question which is... sometimes now and then you say to a client, to me, that you were an advocate for the biology. So what does that mean? What would that mean for the practitioner and why do you say that to the client? Me?

**Michael**  Wow. Where do you start with this one? Um, advocacy. You're, you're making a commitment to be willing and able to tenaciously hold a space for some particular aspect. Right... so in my office, I'm an advocate for all the things that don't have a tongue. That's pretty much our whole biology, you know, and, and what's lovely about that is that it can sidestep but not exclude the psychology. So I get this luxury of using my time to advocate for things that don't have a tongue. It gets very funny for me (probably more in my mind). So I start always with a corner in which I advocate for the bones, because it's a wonderful statement that kind of stops part of the Jellyfish Brain, which then says, "What? No, you're my advocate." I'm like, "No, actually I'm not." It's a scope of practice issue, you know. I'm an advocate for the body. It's really the biology, and then ultimately for me it starts with bones, and it starts with the living aspect of bones. That's what I love about it.

There are many modalities that work with bones and tend to use them as handles. They use bones to get pressure off the nerves. That is still neural-dominant behavior. They're still neural-dominant advocates. (Ah, nerves are overrated!) So really, making that statement starts the use of the voice to start naming and saying, "I'm here on behalf of this layer of you. I do this all day long. This is all I do. I play and listen with bones." So for me, that world/layer is very alive. They have this wonderful quality of a quiet cello experience. The bones have a low-end bass note resonance, they're wonderfully mineral, they're really tubes and they're really coral reef-like in their matrix. They have these wonderful lattice matrixes that are very alive, grown, woven, from the forces put upon them and the lack of forces put upon them. They're very interactive in the gravitational field, both the pull of gravity but also an equal emanated force that comes from the planet. The planet kisses us into Her and there's an opposite and equal Glee that expresses from the planet. Our bones actually absorb that Glee, which is the quality of Her emanated forces.

So when the bones get to be the baseline, then the body starts looking and feeling and behaving differently (from my point of view), from the neural-dominant perspective, from our daily, i.e. "We're up in the world getting things done. The Jellyfish Brain has got the reins. She's going to get what she gets as she gets it." Which is fabulous. But in my office, no, no, no it's not fabulous because that behavior the Jellyfish Brain has of reaching and wanting to interact is, is everything for the Jellyfish Brain. Her senses are all designed for reaching. Her tendrils interlacing throughout the body are all designed to coordinate, to manage, to move and walk towards deliciousness and run away from that which is not delicious or is terrifying.

It turns out that a lot of the physiology doesn't give a... it doesn't have any (um, without being theatrical) it doesn't have any investment in that behavior. Bones in particular don't care. They only know the steps you take. They literally only know the steps you take. They're growing in response to those steps or the place you lie or the place you sit. That's THEIR experience. It's unattached to any concept model, any idea, any neural behavior whatsoever. In fact, the only thing the neurology can do, the only thing the Jellyfish Brain can do, is to come up with exercises to increase or decrease that force on the bones, depending on what the neural-dominant practitioner sees that matrix needing, but they're still doing it to make a healthy Jellyfish Brain, not necessarily on behalf of the bones.

**In the office, when I say 'advocate', it's my job to attempt to give voice for that which can't talk, or for that which cannot express itself and doesn't express itself neurally.** I get to be the sheep dog for that space, those layers, going, "No, Jellyfish, stop. Not because you're doing anything bad or wrong or, or maybe just the opposite. You might be doing everything right, but just pause for a moment." But asking a Jellyfish Brain to pause puts her into distress. It disorients the Jellyfish Brain. Well, then it becomes a Catch 22 humor because you get to reorient her to her actual coral reef bones. She's got these bones that literally float, take up space, in an aquatic environment. It's the craziest thing... so she has ballast and a keel within her wet environment, inside the skin, that her tendrils are co-mingled with and are co-mingled with the tissues that are around the bones, literally just like a coral reef has all this living stuff that happens around a healthy coral reef. Turns out the bones have similarity to the coral reef... a bunch of healthy stuff around them... and when the Jellyfish Brain pauses and begins to orient to her actual structure, she actually starts to get a different type of

39

information, a somatic or body layer of information from her fibrous and fluid layers.

The problem is, is that if she comes at it through neural dominance, she'll go to the cortical homunculus for her information, which is the chalkboard of all the pictures/ places of everything in her body, and she'll go, "Oh, oh no, no, no. That pelvic lamp needs to be over an inch." If it's not there, she panics, because she has a picture and a mapping of her orientation, which she takes as primary information, but is not actually primary. It is not the actual place of her hip or her leg. That tendency to look at the picture or map first is called habituation. This circulated habituated information says, "No, THIS is THAT experience." And, because the Jellyfish Brain is dominant, and because her job is to coordinate everything, she has to do it very quickly, and she does. The cortical homunculus is so much closer, and the chalkboards are so much prettier (except when there's been trauma, and then the drawing of your leg bones get slightly washed and becomes opaque). So, Jellyfish Brain uses all the information from the cortical homunculus first. This way of gathering information has now become habituated/autonomic. In that wash, she gets to do a bunch of strategies, and that habitual response is called coping.

Now the Jellyfish Brain has to do a batch of splinting and a batch of behavioral counterpoints around that wash that used to be a leg bone before it was run over by a truck or fell off a horse, as examples. Um, and she'll actually set up another construct, saying, "Yes, that happened, but look...", she cinches up the tissues, splints them, and now that's her picture of the leg. Years go by, something else happens. And she goes, "All right. OK, we'll add that in." So this cortical homunculus chalkboard series gets convoluted, until someone comes in and reeducates the Jellyfish Brain. Then we come into the office and, as that advocate for those other inner neighborhoods, literally in the body, I get to go in and say, "Well, this is how the garden *is*." I'm not attached to the story around it either, you know... sidestepping psychology. That's pretty significant. The person may or may not respond. Their response is secondary. Whatever happens outside of that contact is secondary, because I'm the advocate for that neighborhood, everything else is, yes, secondary. There is something beautifully orienting about that, and there's something powerful that happens when all of a sudden the body has an advocate to challenge the Jellyfish Brain and its view.

Now, on my end as a manual therapist, this whole process of differentiating the map from the actual somatic reality gets very interesting because Jellyfish Brains can get very grumpy and self-justifying, that's their leg lamp that just got moved on the office table and they want to put back in the middle of the table, and you're going, "Well actually the lamp/leg can move on it's own, or, hey! That's no lamp. That's your leg!" So that advocacy is really putting everything else in the body aside on behalf of the actual neighborhoods, their actual physiology/biology... their actual structure.

(Certainly sounds like actual Actualism) [Michael's pointing at the recorder as well, as Stan may actually listen to this. Stan is Christie's husband and teaches a practice called Actualism, now called ActualDesign].

**Christie** (Stan wanted to know whether it would be OK with you if he could listen.)

*Michael* (Stan, it's OK, but you can't take it personal, but I will take my shots when I can, but I expect to hear a recording back. Tangent Number 36...) I'm so in my version of Actualism. I use the word a lot now more than I thought I did in the past. (This is like my first recording in 30 years. ) Um, that actual information is vital, but you have to challenge a batch of habituated information to have the new information circulate through. As the advocate, I get to hold that gate or hold that space or hold that dynamic primary. For me, I get to laugh at the Jellyfish Brain, laugh at the neural net and let it be secondary, which is very counter to a neural net that's always considers itself primary. It has all the justification of the world to justify its behavior, and I don't want to mess with that.

However, in my office I get to advocate for another layer, and in my personal experience as well as my training, neural-dominant behavior is just that. It's only neural-dominant behavior. There are other dynamics and behaviors going on. They don't behave neurally. So then it gets very interesting to express to somebody in pain, while you're causing them pain to get them out of pain, that they get to even be more challenged and that they have some homework to do. So being the bones' advocate allows me this whole landscape in order to work with a person's garden, a person's dynamic. I have the lovely luxury of challenging the Jellyfish Brain, you know, using her own landscapes, her own dynamics to trick her, and to tease her, and to really make her absolutely bonkers, and I have modalities to do that. So she gets slightly displaced, slightly just put to the side, put into a non-dominant position that she never likes, and I know that, as does the client, from me prompting them.

So I have many ways of doing that. And then on the other hand, using some modalities as a form of trickery, I can keep her held distracted while I actually get some work done because otherwise she's going to get tendrils in there and try to help, you know she is, because it's her garden and she's very feisty about it. So it's a very interesting place to...!

Again, when someone comes in, I tell them that the advocacy in the office is for the physiology/biology. I used to say the structure, but people immediately go to buildings and cabinets and, you know, actual structures, and then they look... their Jellyfish Brain turns around on herself, puts up her mirror and starts to see herself as a bunch of structures. So I've learned over the years to change that to 'neighborhoods', and just say the word physiology and sometimes biology, and to start to use these other, um, analogies and metaphors to both challenge the Jellyfish Brain but also displace her a little bit, give her something to chew on, you know to teach and show her *HER* actual garden.

And what's funny from an advocate point of view is I can be so literal, and someone will still take it as a metaphor or symbology. You can really watch the neural net, the Jellyfish Brain, do all these things to musically counterpoint, organize, and to orient itself to its own ideas, language, and the cortical homunculus map. The Jellyfish Brain will go there first before she ever actually tries to find her actual leg bone. There's this whole elaborate thing that happens, it's funny and challenging as a therapist, but also sometimes terribly problematic, but that's the advocacy part. I get to really hold my line, saying all her experience can be true, and you, Jellyfish Brain, have this living garden, her living structure, and you can begin to change behavior to actually orient to your actual structure, the actual garden as opposed to your idea or concept of your structure, and it's going to drive you, Jellyfish Brain, nuts. So, we name all that up front and that's that first stage of advocacy, "Yeah, you're a Jellyfish Brain, it's true."

And then the Jellyfish Brain goes nuts for the rest of her life. You know, it's a dark humor thing, but it's kind of fun because then all of a sudden one day someone says, "Oh crap, my bones are...well they, they must be alive." They, they are like, "It's not what I thought." So then, all of a sudden, they understand the advocacy. If they come to the office for me as the practitioner, they're going to get a certain tenaciousness for pursuing and including their hairball... and I don't buy into their trip. I take their trip very seriously, but I don't buy into their version of their trip. I hear the neural-dominant perspective of it, and I'm curious about what their garden's perspective is in some of the history of that sharing, you know, and maybe some of the other layers' perspective as well.

**Christie**  So you started out with the bones I would assume because of many reasons...?

*Michael*  I start with the bones because that's the one thing that the Jellyfish Brain can't mess with. The Jellyfish Brain can't mess with them because bone growth is slow and steady. The nervous system is very quick and cantankerous and loves stimuli.

The bones don't have sensory nerves...well there are sensory nerves around the bone in the form of periosteum (which loves didgeridoos, African drumming, Harley Davidsons, low-rumbled drones) bones grow at a very slow rate. They only grow to the force put upon them. So they're always dealing with what comes to them, which is mostly outside the skin. (The baseline includes your body's weight and mass.)

And this is a hard... people get a little grocky about this, "Well, but there's bones that aren't touching something and they're growing?" And I'm like, "Yes, they're getting secondary and cursory information, but it's still coming through the body." There's a beautiful example of this. There's a wonderful skeleton in Ireland. It's called the fishwife. There was a woman who spent her whole life literally carrying fish from the shore into the village. She left a wonderful skeleton. So the woman is carrying the basket on her shoulder her whole life, same shoulder, same position every day for a whole life. Her scapula had grown into her ribs and her ribs have become one piece in response to the weight of the basket of heavy fish on her shoulder, walking every day for miles. And I forget the exact information, that was a rough paraphrasing, but it's a beautiful example, and it's really stuck with me, because "... bones grow to the force put upon them." This is called Wolff's law.

So to start with bones in the office gives a person something that they always have, and bones grow in time differently than neural tissue, than all the other tissues. The bones actually ballast, give reference to all the tissues in the body. It's a good place to start and bring someone back to. Also, bones don't care about concept models or ideas. They don't care. They don't organize that way. As a therapeutic process, it's a safe way to start to undermine people's ideas because everybody comes in the office with a different set of belief systems, you know, and their beautiful Jellyfish Brain is looking for accordance/discord, agreement/ disagreement there. She's looking for this range to counterpoint. She's usually capturing the counter to the countered counterpoint. So there's this whole thing happening in that dynamic, where it should, but it doesn't affect the bones unless it affects their walking to and from those concepts, right?

So it's a wonderful way to, to bring a person into my world in a kind of fun, it makes for an interesting way, but it also give me a corner that I can hold as a fulcrum, literally on the table, referencing a person's bones in a way that their body has to organize around the fulcrum that I'm providing with my hands. Fingertips literally. You're creating a teeter-totter, you know, and the tissues have to respond. All the tissues cannot not react. So if I can get that fulcrum to go from my contact into their own bones, if I can make sensation that can challenge the Jellyfish Brain in a way that says, "You know, all your ideas and concepts are awesome even if they are a mess they're functional. Then I don't want to mess with that."

So it gives me these wonderful circles/cycles to play with, to bring a person back to, well...what do their bones feel like? And that's what brings us to the most important question ever. Um, Number One, "Where's your bones?" Open-ended question. It's an invitation. And then I've added, over the years, this idea of them being feral because it seems like a lot of people understand what feral cats are. Nobody's come in and said, "What's a feral cat?" It's the humor, it's another layer of playfulness and I love the humors of all this, but it's like calling out to a feral cat. You actually can't reach for them. You can't reach for a feral animal. They'll look at you funny and run like hell, right? Unless you have a lot of food, then they still will run like hell and come back later for the food. You have to sit. You have to sit and slow down and meet that creature in its environment on its own terms.

Feral is such a beautiful word. Our bones grow to the force put upon them. There's nothing the Jellyfish Brain can do except change its interaction with that force, which it has 10,000 ways of doing (that includes Zumba by the way), which is lovely, 10,000 modalities that change that force. But it doesn't change the bone's behavior. It can only influence its density. The bones are still growing on their terms in their way, no matter what the Jellyfish Brain says... that's feral. They are going to do what they do as they do it, no matter what! The only thing that's going to stop them is the cessation of blood supply or certain bone diseases. And even then, you know... until that bone actually dies, and then horrible things happen to the rest of the body because in that bone is also bone marrow, making blood cells and blood serum, and it's a whole mess when the bone starts to not do its behavior, its job, its nature!

Then the Jellyfish Brain knows she's got some serious shit to deal with, but in the office, using bones as an orientation, we come back to this, this first statement. Of all the things in the world, I've become an advocate for these bones, The Bones. This is the first statement of having a person begin to orient to them because they're their bones. They've grown in time more slowly. The person has had several personalities through one set of bones. Maybe, maybe not, maybe... depends on the person. But it holds true. It always is true that the bones are there. They take up space and they move in time differently, and they have their own behavior. They're not neural-dominant...they aren't neural structures. So this is one of those moments that you see that the bones are alive, and they have their own nature and it's feral. They can't be forced to do anything unless you put in the time. If you're willing to take the next two years to change your relationship with your bones, you can change your bone matrix.

So it's gardening. So if you want to sit down with your feral bones and really get to know them and do something different - great - or if you want to force them down the alleyway to grow differently, you can do that too, but it will take the next nine months to orient differently... and your bones will be different - guaranteed. Then you have to follow it through for the following nine months to have the tissues completely change in relationship to the new matrix laid down in the previous nine months. Right? And this is also where people make a mistake because they don't get it that all the tissues are holding tension, which is putting a force on the bones in relationship to the outside tension coming in. So the bones first say, "OK!", and then the bones say, "They'll give up." Half the tissues are saying the same thing, "Nope, they'll never make it. They won't make it six weeks let alone nine months." So, all the tissues are in what's called 'coping'. That's the beauty of coping...Perseverance/Coping. Coping and habits hold, skills circulate.

All these tissues are sitting there just laughing, like "We're doing this... you can change your eating, you can change your walking habit, you can change all this. We're going to wait you out. We were here long before this new thing showed up, you know!" They're (the tissue and coping talking) saying, "Oh, by the way, we got this person through the first part of their life and puberty. The first three puberties, thank you very much." So, there's a lot of successful behaviors, a lot of coping, successful coping. It's a sacred thing, don't get me wrong. I will tease it though.

So, the bones are doing their thing. You've changed your behavior for nine months and then your bones go, "Oh, they're not kidding!" You have an internal dialogue change and then your bone matrix starts to lay down differently, but now you're in...nine months just to get through the first gate, the first new season of activity trying to change a fundamental... right?

You're in a season, a chunk of time. Now you're in the garden and now you have to stay with it because now the bones need that new information. You've now convinced everybody that you're gonna 'change'. So now all these other layers/facets, they're going, "Crap, we gotta change!" And then they all start scampering. Now they're all trying to figure out what the new neurological and biological baseline is. So it becomes jazz very quickly. Literally it turns into jazz. Your physiology is just jazz incarnate. So in that jazz, the new baseline is being laid down. You've kept with it for a few seasons, measures of music. So now everybody's going, "All right, we'll do it your way." So they change their behavior, and their harmonics. It takes a big chunk of time, but now you're in...

So now you're into the new song and the bones are going, "All right. All right!" They've been being convinced that there's this new force put upon them, this new literal tension. This new bass baseline. So now they're in, now they've grown a layer and they're going, "Oh, if we do the next thing, it's going to be a big deal." So, the next nine months is critical because you have to stay consistent. You have to stay in the new bass baseline because now everything's unraveling and letting go and falling apart into the layer that you've just cultivated. The bones are holding through, but now their matrixes are changing, now they're really laying down new matrixes. It's all getting established, and then when the new matrix takes over, there's this little 'clunk' and now there's a new pull line through the tendons, the new baseline is established.

Tendons take a long time to grow like the bones do. So, all of a sudden there's a new tension in the bone while the tendon, growing in relationship to that bone, is now able to change its matrix. Now that causes the muscle tissue to fire differently, grow differently, changing the behavior of all the nerve tissue that's interlaced with those fibrous structures. And then the vascular bed, because it's been stretched and moved and having to get new blood to new places, it's behavior changes. The lymph is taking out the trash and its behavior changes, so you get this beautiful change of the garden, but actually it takes a big chunk of time.

Now!!! You will need to have support, inside and out! You can't make those changes, because at about six weeks, parts of your physiology and psychology are going to go, "Fuck this... we've never had to do this before!", you know, and they can't make the psychological association that actually changes a lot. The neighbors have changed location, changed jobs. There have been all these wonderful changes that are actually pretty significant from a physiological point of view. And then we're in Taoism... "You can't change unless you move." You have to change your environment to change your environment. You have to have a change in the environment, to have a change in that environment. You have to change the forces put upon you to grow into a different person.

It's very hard to do if you're in the same place. It's very, very difficult, but you can do it if you put in the time, you know, roughly a couple of rounds of nine months, you know, a couple of birth cycles. Go figure!

So... the advocacy is there. It gives me a strong corner. This getting to know and handle and garden the bones has added to that layer of my experience. I have a strong advocacy in my job title, in what I do, and then there's my body of experience of actually going, "Holy crap, there's something to this. Oh, my goodness!" I mean that's great, but I have to handle bones in a certain way because I have to respect their feralness. I can't treat them as handles, right? I can't treat them as an excuse to pick on other tissues. So we spend a lot time in what seems to be 'holding/support/contact'. And, because I'm not creating a lot of stimuli, the nervous system isn't getting overstimulated. I'm not doing a lot of proprioceptive stimuli. I'm actually doing a lot of anchoring, a lot of making fulcrums with my hands and using lines of force, vectors to work with pressure. So, I've turned into a very complicated spider in many ways. I'm taking up the threads and the tensions in the body and working with the person's personal history of the hairballs in their body, but everything I'm doing is referencing to the matrix of their bones, to the placement of the bones and the relationship from one bone to the next bone, because one bone is entirely its own neighborhood with its own experience and its own expression. And then the neighborhood next to it may or may not be something completely different.

**Christie**  That different?

*Michael*  OMG, they can be really different. Those bones are literally alive and can be very different from one to the other one. When I'm slowing down and starting to find words that have a palpable expression that someone can feel instead of intellectually define, that's what I'm doing in the office. I'm using language and I'm using the things that we know and the sciences we know, and some of the fun stuff that we know, um, both to mirror back, educate someone but also to distract them, to actually give their Jellyfish Brain something to chew on or else it's going to get involved in what I'm doing. It's going to get antsy. It's going to get the shpilkes, for those of you who are Yiddish. Yes. Right. Ants in the pants. There is that place of acknowledging, handling someone and then training them to come back to their own bones and finding the palpatory responsiveness in their tissues to their attention. When someone asks, "Where's my bones? ", there's that pause. You actually have to do something there and then something responds. The bones actually respond. They cannot not react. Tissues are wonderfully responsive, even bones, but because their behaviors are so different, it gets very interesting. Then the Jellyfish Brain comes in really quickly, so we have to add in a question about where the bones are getting their information. There's a contact - sitting, lying down, standing. There is never not a contact with bones. (Yes, it's a double negative.) The world is always touching a bone a certain way, even in water. Water pressure itself is bone contact. Bones will grow to that, and even in outer space, bones will grow to that lack of pressure. They get brittle because it's not enough force for us. You have to actually create 'G'-force to give the bones enough of their gravitational information that they understand in the factors that they understand. So here on the planet earth, we don't have this problem. It's lovely and our bones are designed perfectly to be on this planet.

So in asking the first question of "Where's your bones?", then we have to bring in the second question, which is, "What's supporting the bones?" This gets very interesting because the person's psychology is so interesting. Some people - the idea of support - can feel that. Yeah, they reach out with their senses (those of you at home, try this, #1 - "Where's your bones?" – #2 "What's supporting your bones?"). For some people, the statement doesn't work, so you have to... If they're not really kinesthetic, they go "Who, what, support? Huh?" The Jellyfish Brain will go crazy and turn it into a psychological issue, "You mean I'm not supported? What do you mean? Well, I did have this issue with my father..." Another whole psychological hairball ensues, right? The psychological sock puppets go, "Oh, it's a delicious moment, we can feed!", and the poor practitioner's going, "Crap!"

So now the practitioner (me) has to come up with different statements. So, the statement is "What's the support for the bones? Where's the support? Or where is the contact, the feeling of contact or where's the push of the world?" So sometimes you have to educate the Jellyfish Brain that there's something coming to her, that there's a push coming, and the bones are absorbing that push. So, it's been interesting over the years because everybody's a little bit different. Some people really love 'the push of the world'. Their whole body goes, "Ah!", and softens, while other people go, "What?" And go into panic. Other people go the whole psychological thing, like, "What do you mean I'm not supportive?". And some people... just the touch of something is very nice. They can feel the touch of a sheet on the table or the pants on their skin, or you know, there's that place and they can find the feeling of their bone through that. So then, in that round, things start to get particular to the person...those first two things together, "Where's your bones?" and "Where's the support for bones or the push of the world?" Those things together are an orientation unto itself. I'm doing that when I'm working. Now I've got the person doing it with me, and some of the bones respond. Some don't. They're very alive. It's information for me as a practitioner.

I'll go and work with that. But for the person, you just let them know this, "This is very alive. You'll find some bones and others you won't. The bones are feral. You gotta sit there a while." This drives the Jellyfish Brain crazy, crazy, crazy! So then you have to acknowledge the Jellyfish Brain, that's question Number Three. #3 is to have a giggle ready, and that's why humor is so important. It's technically not a giggle = funny. It's a flutter. It's an "Ahhh/Ohhh!", because if you do the first two questions, if you try to orient to the bones, your Jellyfish Brain has to do a really bizarre thing. She has to soften her tendrils which is counter-intuitive to a neural tissue/Jellyfish brain. Neural tissues don't like softening. They like reaching and finding and touching, "I want more information... gimme more", you know, even if they have to make it up. That's a place we start to recognize the Jellyfish Brain as an organ, as a tissue, because she cannot not react. She literally cannot **not** react. Even if she doesn't react, that's called freeze response, which is a very specific kind of non-reaction reaction, right? It's freezing. And that takes a hell of a lot of effort. The person freezing will say, "I'm not having a reaction." You're looking at them going, okay, I have to send you down the hall (to a psychologist or a Somatic Experiencing practitioner). Ok, now figuratively I'm going back to work, "Let's go find some bones."

So, those three questions together are significant because in finding your bones and then orienting, you're actually starting to give your Jellyfish Brain real information. So we've now, as an advocate for the bones, we've now created a situation where the person can orient themselves. They can start to get actual information, which for a ton of conditions is very important. For some conditions, it is extremely difficult because the Jellyfish Brain will want to organize around ideas and concepts, and orientation to bones undermines all that. (And that's why I like it so much!) So that's why this kind of advocacy for the neighborhoods of living tissue that are not able to speak is so important.

**Christie** So it feels like you start with the bones. The bones are a primary entry place for you, and as a place to teach your clients to orient to... and when I think about my own bones or feel my own body, the bones are the other big part of this, you know, I mean, when you die, what's left? There's the skeleton, it's like it's you ...

**Michael** You dry up and have this wonderful combination of minerals.

**Christie** ... and when you're working, do you also advocate for and listen to, help support the other systems, too, that can't talk?

**Michael** ...and it brings us to the next layers, right? Here we've done this advocacy for the neighborhoods, as the bones are the central aspect of that neighborhood. From a musical standpoint, it is the central bass note of the tune of the song of yourself. It's a bass line, it's the bass drum rhythm, the bass rhythm is in the bones. So, for me as a practitioner, I'm having to practice what I preach. So, when I'm working, as I start to venture into other tissues, now I've got a bass line, baseline, to work with.

Then as I venture into the other systems and into the other tissues, I don't get disoriented! If the person on the table starts to get disoriented too much, I can also step back. I can have them step back, in their proprioceptive ability, and I can pause. I can do a functional pause, so at any moment I can go, "Whoa, wait, wait." I can back up... "Wait a minute. We were in this neighborhood of bones a moment ago and then we ended up in this big hairball, what the heck?" The person on the table can go, "Oh wait, oh, wait a minute." I can say, "Back Up. It's OK. You're starting to freak out in all the ways that that happens." A person can trip out on humors as well as on the scary stuff, but as you get in you can start to venture into someone's hairball, which is a literal statement.

**Christie**   Yeah well that is the next question...

*Michael*  ...that IS the next question!

**Christie**   What are hairballs?

*Michael*  (who makes a big noise) But you can't deal with hairballs and the question of hairballs if you don't have an orientation. If you don't know where you are on the map, you shouldn't be going there. You can get yourself into trouble.

So, we've got our ability to find something stable, within a body, within our ideas, too, so we have that. I have it as a practitioner, the person on the table has orientation. Now we can explore towards hairballs. A hairball is such a literal statement, from my point of view, from my experiential point of view. Here's how we're going to try and make it understandable.

When you go through an overwhelming event, you cannot not react. It's impossible. You can't do it unless you're on some really good psychotropics or medications that interfere with such reactions. And then it's still considered a response. It's just a non-response. You go numb, which is still a response. In venturing into and with a person, you've got a sense of their neighborhoods. While you're finding their bones, you're starting to get a sense of the roots between you and their bones, between their skin and their bones. There's this whole landscape there, and that landscape is grown, you are grown, it doesn't just happen, it grows.

Now we're back to those ideas of habituation and the way the Jellyfish Brain copes in her drive to manage and do a beautiful job of... getting to the next food source, her next experience, etc. Whether it's a delicious idea or delicious cup of tea or really good food, a fine friend, in that the tissues grow in response to a person's actual experience, and so if they were yelled at a lot and never touched, they will still have this set of tissues that have built up a response to being yelled at... an overwhelming stimuli.

The tissues will thicken. They will get concentrated and get dense like dense soil in response to the overwhelm, the force put upon them. Being that the person doing the yelling in this story...usually they'll be habituated, too, because it never just starts. It's never the first time, which is a crazy thing to think about. There's never actually a first time. It's this interweaving of experiences. So, say a little person is being yelled at by a big person. Chances are the big person would always yell from the same direction, the *same attitude*, and the little one's first response to the first overwhelm will then be a similar response to the second one. Even if it's from a different direction, a different attitude, they'll try to maneuver their bodies because they've come up with a successful response. Right? And that's important because people forget that the things that are driving them crazy today most likely were a lot of successes from previous experiences, previous seasons, previous bones! And we forget to consider that our response to trauma or overwhelm or overstimulation is actually successful. And those little habits can sometimes become little sock puppets that are self-justifiable and show up at all sorts of opportunities to help get a person through an overwhelming situation.

**Christie**  So, just because it might be helpful to explain 'sock puppets'... so back up just a little bit and say that again.

**Michael**  So, we've made contact. You felt your bones. You are starting to orient. From that perspective, you start to sense both what's working and what's not working. What's not working will have a hairball, because those tissues are not behaving like the other tissues who are able to respond. The success of the hairball sometimes can be benign. No big deal. If there is more of a responsiveness that neighborhood of hairballed overwhelmed craziness will sometimes take on a character, and as it gathers it's own experience, it gets more particular. Being that we have a feral part of our nature, in some cases a hairball will take on a personality.

In my office, we label them 'sock puppets', because they ARE sock puppets, because the person, when they're talking about their hairball, will always start drawing something with their hands (Michael's hand right now is flailing about) that's slowly turning into an actual character, a sock puppet. The client's voice gets activated and goes, "Holy Crap, there's this hairball. I've had this pain forever!" At some point the person will start drawing with their hands and acting out the feelings. Then it will take on a bit of character. Imagine Jim Henson sitting with Michael, trying to give a sock puppet an examination. His hand in a shape, the hand being the bones of the character being expressed.

**Christie** He's got buck teeth.

*Michael* Yes ...well, it's the whole, it's how Jim makes Kermit do those expressions, and you/he moves his fingers and hand to make the motion of words, drawing expressions which is puppetry. Thank you, Sesame Street - because it's true! There is a Sesame Street inside of you. And if you've had any trauma, chances are you have a trauma street named 'Sesame', and it won't open when you ask. So, you come to someone like me, who's whacked out of their gourd and watches the drawing and dance of a person trying to express...

**Christie** ( and... it will have the character of a sock puppet.)

*Michael* It will have its own character. And then chances are, and this gets very interesting, is that there'll be a counterpoint to it, right? So now, in response, their Jellyfish Brain's doing counterpoint to what was just drawn and danced without filters, without the Jellyfish Brain knowing, until it is being expressed "Hey, you shouldn't be over there being a sock puppet holding my hip like that and causing lots of pain in my butt!" The sock puppet responds with , "But it's what I'm doing, because I'm protecting the neighborhood in pain..

So that's, that's the dynamic. So, as you move into someone's tissues, you start to get the lay of their land. If they've been through anything, it'll be in their body and it'll be tissue that doesn't feel like other tissue. But this is what's cool. As a practitioner, not only do I have to practice stepping back and slowing down and including, but I get to put the people on the table into the same state.

Now at this point, I'm singing the song like I'm doing exactly right now without someone in my hands, which, you know, makes the sock puppets interesting. Usually, I have someone in my hands, so I'm sock puppeteering them (that's partly true). Um, or they're dropping into a deep state. Their state of consciousness is of no issue because I'm the advocate for the part of their body that doesn't care about their consciousness. It doesn't care about their Jellyfish Brain state. It's doing the same job whether the person is lying, or sleeping, or dancing, or in an altered state, or Zumba, (I don't know why Zumba today).

So, you've got this range and it doesn't, it, it... there's a corner that is tracked where they are consciously dropped out or needing a lullaby to keep them busy while I try to get some work done 'cause it's gardening on behalf of their bones, not their Jellyfish Brain. All this hands-on work is actually done to make more room for their Jellyfish Brain to dance more easily. Now that's a life statement!

So, the hairball is their *experiences* grown in the neighborhood of those experiences. Somewhere in their body that overwhelm is going to house itself... primarily, secondarily, cursorily.

**Christie**  So like the example of somebody yells at the little one...

*Michael*  ... somebody yells at the little one, it's consistent. It's never once... will never just be once, right? So, there's an adaptive thing. The person learns to turn away to avoid the individual giant yelling at him or her. So the little one protects and curls into a ball, and so the tissues will have that strategy. Well, any loud noises, the little one's gonna turn the same way because there's a successful response, a successful coping, a brilliant expression of our intelligence. So then it goes from coping to habituated, then habituated coping, and they've got this turn in their system, and then one day, they try to turn differently from the grain of their body that has grown one way to protect, and they break the grain.

So you'll hear this in people's responses, "I just leaned over to pick up a piece of paper and my back sprung." *Michael:* "How many pieces of paper do you pick up a day ma'am?" *Client:* "Oh, not many." *Michael:* "In your whole life?" *Client:* "Never." *Michael:* "Oh, but you should be able to do an action you've never actually done in your past?" *Client:* "Yeah, but I can bend over!" *Michael:* "Not to pick up a piece of paper, it goes against the grain." So, we're grained. We are gardens; we are grained. And those things happen, and the Jellyfish Brain tries to associate in the immediacy of its environment. She doesn't sit back there and go, "Oh right! I never pick up a paper like that. I haven't picked up a paper... I've had people pick up paper for me for the last 30 years. What was I thinking, why didn't I hire out?"

There's lots of... you know, this is metaphorically and poetically said with humor, but the truth of it is the truth. We have a certain grain, we have a certain pliability, and if we go against that grain, usually, while we're not paying attention, 'snap', in all the forms of 'snapness'. So, in that grain is a hairball. The system has set up a certain configuration, and that configuration will be dense on one part and slightly atrophied on the other part, because those tissues aren't doing the same job as the other tissues. So, they make this configuration that's conducive to a certain type of pliability.

Well, when you're touching somebody, it's very inconvenient. They think they have it all down and their Jellyfish Brain thinks it's all OK and it should all be homeostasis and there's all these concepts as a practitioner that everything should be in homeostasis. However, because you've got this reference of the bone, and then, as you move out into these other tissues, you get these shapes and configurations that are like soil, and you have roots within that tissue. You have a vascular root and the lymphatic root and the neural root bed, and their root beds co-mingled with muscles, tissues, organs, viscera, etc. You've got this wonderful aquatic landscape that has a behavior and a shape to it that gets very, very interesting tactilely, and because I can always slow down and back up into that, I can always reference a bone.

So, I go back and forth, and in doing that I start to train the tissue to re-coordinate and re-reference itself within its actual environment, within its actual means, exploring its options. A hairball... there're no options. It can only do the behavior it's always done, and everybody's different there.

**Christie** Because the hairball is the location of the habituated?

*Michael* That's right.

**Christie** And so the Jellyfish Brain...

*Michael* So that whole neighborhood has been doing the work that the hairball should have been doing, but now has turned a bit feral.

**Christie** ... so the Jellyfish Brain, somewhere unconsciously or whatever, neurologically, is all keyed in there too. I mean it's like this is, this is how we do it.

*Michael* This is how we do it. That's right.

**Christie** But then I'm still back here with 'root beds', I want you to explain 'root beds' more in a minute with hairballs.

*Michael* ... very similar, you know, a highly adaptive root bed becomes a hairball.

**Christie** So what is a 'root bed'?

**Michael**   So we have these bones, we have these coral reefs/bones. Off and around these coral reefs grow tissues, literally, literally grow tissues, tendons mostly. So you've got these structures starting to happen. Within those structures, you've got these root beds. So your vascular system, your blood system is its own root bed. It's a complete system unto itself.

**Christie**   OK, so you're saying the root bed is the, is the basis of a particular net?

**Michael**   Yes. (Oh, you're going to let me talk about nets!) Three nets... fibrous net, includes all muscles, bones, tendon and fascia connective tissue, depends on who you're talking to. The fibrous net is our actual structures, and then you have the neural net, which is your Jellyfish Brain and all her tendrils. She's a complete system. She's her own system. She has her own way of doing things. She's her own thing. And then lastly, we have what's called the hormonal net and this is where the anatomists got a little too general.

The hormonal net is all fluid bodies. So, the hormonal net will include lymphatic fluid, as well as the vascular blood. Blood is considered a connective tissue in some regards until the tissue's been severed, because it's a complete root bed, but those tissues are hollow roots with fluid flowing in them, right? They're our drip system for our garden. So, blood, lymphatics....um, the wonderful fluid of the lymph.

The lymph's a complete system matched to the vascular system, but a little more ancient in a way that the vascular system has a pump, it's the dancers of the heart, that keeps the pressure and keeps a movement happening within that system. The lymphatic system does not have a pump. Movement is the pump, our whole movement is dancing the lymph, and what's cool about the vessels of the lymphatic is that there're all these one-way heart valves. So, lymphatics can only move one way in the body. It moves along the body.

Then you have the endocrine system which are the actual hormones. You also can include the cerebral spinal fluid in the hormonal net. So, the thing that holds the spinal cord and the Jellyfish Brain, that nourishes, cleanses and feeds her, is considered the hormonal net, whereas the neural tissue itself is considered the neural net. These three nets cover everything that we are, but each net does not talk directly to the next net. They have what's called emissaries. So, from the neural net to the hormonal net is an emissary. There's a different emissary that goes from the hormonal net back to the neural net.

**Christie**  What are these emissaries like?

**Michael**   Emissaries are the interaction of how one net
translates the information coming from the other net.
It gets way too complicated for my pea brain, but the
neurophysiologists out there... they love this stuff.
They love it. So same thing between the hormonal net
and the fibrous net, and the fibrous net and the neural
net. Each net has two emissaries... one going, one
coming from the other net; three nets, two emissaries
go between each net.

**Christie**   And all the nets are relating to each other?

**Michael**   They're always interacting. We can't say that they're
related. You can say that they interact. They aren't
actually related.

**Christie**   The neural interacts with the fibrous and the
hormonal net.

**Michael**   That's right. That's right. And the emissaries are
different, going and coming. It gets complex really
quickly.

**Christie**   So is that what you're calling the root bed?

**Michael**   Yes! Anything inside the skin.

**Christie**   Yeah but each one of them has their own signature/
behavior...!?

**Michael**   Their own song, their own behavior, and they don't do
what the other two do. That's why they're 'net'.
They're complete unto themselves.

**Christie**   But they're a root?

**Michael** Yes, they also have this behavior of root.

**Christie** What does that mean?

**Michael** The root is just like plants in the ground. They are their own structure, their own behavior, their own communication and their own needs, their own expression. Each one is independent of the other. Thich Nhat Hahn would say that they're interdependent with each other. Independent of each other. They each have their own feral nature, which cannot be coerced, but they're also interdependent with each other. One can't exist without the other if the tissue doesn't get pizza and beer. The Jellyfish Brain can't go to a movie.

**Christie** I'm having a hard time keeping track of all this!

**Michael** You're doing great! So, a hairball is trauma that has happened in a neighborhood, and all the tissues have responded to that trauma, each in their own way. They make a new configuration because what's beautiful about what we is, is that we're highly adaptive. In fact, one might say we're completely adaptive, so due to the input put upon us, our body will grow. We're always growing our body, so it still thinks it's growing in response to that little one being yelled at, in some respects, because there's lots of noise in the world. Until that's interrupted and unwound and reconfigured, then those responses are

74

going to be the same because that instrument has been made to do that action, to respond. . .so a hairball is that created instrument of response inside your actual body, inside your root beds.

**Christie**  Hairball?

**Michael**  Well, it's the whole... it's a hairball because that's how it feels. (I'm sorry, folks, those of you at home.) It's such a literal hairball because the three nets have changed their configuration in response to the trauma put upon them, to take the new load, which is always overwhelming. They've created something to work with that load, and in doing that, they've protected something, so they've encapsulated something, but they've made a new structure to keep out the overwhelm and redirect the load around the hairball.

**Christie**  All three root beds are involved in that?

**Michael**  All three.

**Christie**  Where does emotion come in?

**Michael**  All over the place! (I know those of you at home wanted to hear that.) Emotion, you know, is that wonderful place between psychology and biology.

**Christie**  So it just seems like my association with hairballs is trouble. You know... trouble.

**Michael**  Overwhelm, overwhelm is always... well there's happy overwhelm, but it still ends up causing some havoc.

75

**Christie**   Yeah, and often there's the emotional... if you mess with a hairball, it seems like emotions get released or...

**Michael**   Because the body's on alert. You've got this neural net that's now vigilant. There's a vigilance. It gets so spectacular and complicated. When there's a hairball, the tissues have changed their configuration, they've made a safe area, they've changed their shape and their behavior. And then that in turn, and oftentimes in the same moments, changes the configuration of the matrix of the tissues in the response to the overwhelm, and there's something being protected, right? Whatever that something is (the thing we all argue about.) So in that, it creates a density.

**Christie**   So it's kind of like a burl?

**Michael**   It can become, in some cases, an actual burl, but oftentimes it can become like a cyst. It encapsulates. So, what happens is that now all those guys are doing their individual dances, now having become their own neighborhood within the neighborhood, and now they're invested. They're protecting something, and they're giving time for that something to regrow. They're protecting the baby. They're protecting what was overwhelmed, right? Well, this gets very interesting. So, we're on the inside of the skin. We're in the actual neighborhoods that make the actual person (actually)(I'm going to get that in there again. Hi Stan. We love you. It's true.).

An interesting thing happens in the neural net, in that when it gets entangled that way (and that's what you're talking about), it gets sensitive at location, but then there's a numbness around that part of the protection, but it is also part of the change of shape and the density of that protection. So, you've got a layered situation in that it shuts down part of the proprioception and starts hypersensitivity around it. Then, we get off the skin of the body and we start out into the environment. There starts to become a vigilance in the field of the human being (add in a neural net, generated by electricity, thrown in a big batch of water and blood, and you have a field, physics). The vigilance is the part of the hypersensitivity out in your field, outside your skin, which tracks for anything coming near the patch of the neighborhood being protected. It has to try to interrupt and catch whatever's coming close in the environment before it gets to the actual hairball.

This hypersensitivity, the vigilance of that, is anywhere from a couple inches to a couple miles (sort of exaggerating by the way), but at least a few hundred feet off your skin. So, a part of your peripheral nervous system and proprioception is now tracking the environment in a hyper hyper-sensitized way to protect the cyst of what got injured in the overwhelm, no matter what the overwhelm was, whether it was yelling or trampled by elephants, right? The tissue will behave the same in its response to that overwhelm. It'll encapsulate/protect. Now if you're lucky, you get trampled by elephants, and that makes a hell of a lot more sense than someone yelling at you in your early development. Right? But both are very hard to find because the tissue behavior's the same. It's self-protective, it's feral, it thinks everybody else should go away.

Meanwhile, that tissue has changed its shape, changed its job, has started to adapt, and come up with adaptive strategies, which now the Jellyfish Brain thinks is way cool because she gets more things to coordinate, and she gets very invested in that coordination.

Meanwhile, all the jobs that were being done by those hairball tissues are now encapsulating and protecting. Now their former jobs are being done by other neighborhoods. So, this gets interesting. Couple of years go by and nothing changes. It all becomes normal. The Jellyfish Brain says, "OK, great." It's got this blur on the cortical homunculus chalkboard (the picture the brain has of her garden), but meanwhile she's added other life experiences around the blur, and it becomes fine... it's a really fine coping, brilliant adaptation, new strategies to coordinate.

Then, one day the tissues that have been doing the job of the hairball start to get really tired. Their job was to get away from the incident. Their sole job was to persevere, protect, and get away from the initial overwhelming incident, no matter how many moments or years that may be. The tissue doesn't quantify time. Only the Jellyfish Brain quantifies time...sometimes she does it better than other times (many layers and types of time).

So, years go by and you're very tired and you pick up a piece of paper and the cyst breaks, something breaks, because you've gone against the grain of the adaptation in the entire system. But you've also got these tissues that have been doing double duty, their jobs and the hairball tissues' original jobs. The tissues are very tired and they're like, "We've got to be safe by now". So perhaps the person takes up an exercise program and starts getting really strong, and then all of a sudden, they break down because they're challenging that old strategy. That hairball starts to get challenged, and/or part of the psyche says, "You know, we used to be able to..." but a hairball always gets run into. There's always a hairball, and sooner or later there's gotta be something done about the hairball.

Some people, they've got simple hairballs, so they take up becoming a marathon runner and you know, they spend a couple of years growing new bones, new tissues and their hairball lets go, and all of a sudden they have a little bit more freedom and they say to others, "Well, if you just exercised!" Right? Now other people have hairballs that, you know, they've spent all their lives just trying to learn about, before all of a sudden, they realize they have a condition, and they go, "Oh right. I just need support. I got to quit hitting this hairball, making it worse." You know, it's a full spectrum, and everyone's body gets very unique, very quickly... but a hairball is that entire response of the neighborhood to trauma, to overwhelm and trauma.

In this case, in this conversation, trauma is any overwhelming situation to the tissue. Marion Woodman would say, "Trauma is any arrested action." So if you were in the middle of any action and it got interrupted, that would be traumatic. She was brilliant and a Canadian psychologist.

So back to the bones. Yes, we always get to go back to... come back to the bones, even in our tangents, in our orientations.

**Christie**  It's good to come back to the bones, and orient... and then there's a...

*Michael*  Then we're reaching out from the bones because that's our actual reference. If we come from outside in, we're going to hit that hairball and all hell is going to break loose.

**Christie**  But if you come from...

*Michael*  If we come from the bones and start our way out, then that hairball and all our other references always have a place to come back to.

**Christie**  So that's how you begin to work on the hairball.

*Michael*  That's right. We actually set up orientation because at some point we start to train the neighborhoods and start talking to everything around the hairball, so that the hairball has some place to begin to explore out from because the hairball also will have a developmental aspect to it. A hairball is in its own developmental sequence. Everything else is in its own developmental sequence. At some point they'll get very grumpy with each other because they're discordant. Yeah, and we're back to the jazz (it's always a safe place to go).

By the way, in that discord as you start to go towards a hairball, it's good to set up a place for the person psychologically and biologically to reference because, as that hairball starts to explore its options, starts to unwind a bit, it's going to do like what the Jellyfish Brain did at the beginning of this conversation... it's going to be disoriented. The Jellyfish Brain, in having habits to deal with the hairball, now is really going to be disoriented because she's going to want the hairball back to what it was and the hairball's gonna want to go back to what it was. All the tissues are saying, "Come on. We don't want you to go back to what you were doing because we want to go back to what we were before all this mess, hello!", and so there's a lot of disorientation.

The bones are the only thing that can give a reference in those moments because everything else is moving way too fast and is disorienting, all their behaviors are so different from bone behavior in that bones actually give the reference within the system, within  that neighborhood. Most people are trying to get it from another system dealing with yet another system. Here we're saying, "Actually you've got something in the neighborhood of your distress that can help you. Besides, if not, then let's go to the next neighborhood that you can 'feel', so that those tissues are getting the information, and the input, and encouragement and the exercise of starting to explore by reaching back into their environment", because, as they do that, they're going to have to start their cycle over within their own development.

**Christie** So... and this is all basically through felt sense through the body?

*Michael* Yeah. I think it's, it's all the senses, but most of it's tactile. Most of it's felt sense consciousness... that's right... it's bringing it back to that actual factual information within palpation.

**Christie** Yeah, so it's like coming back to where the tissues are, age wise or whatever...

*Michael* ... whatever that was, whatever that hairball went through...

**Christie** ... from inside, from... and then you're, as a practitioner, facilitating the client being able to actually feel.

*Michael* ...to actually more than feel, to actually facilitate, in a way, if I'm lucky. What I'm shooting for is the ability to have a client walk out of the office with some ability to self-facilitate, because ultimately that's where it's going to work, because they're going to have to go back and forth and retrain themselves not to just recognize coping, but to challenge the habits in a safe way and start to feel those tissues in a non-neural-dominant way. The neural always moves too big, too fast for the physiology, and then the physiology gets protective of itself and frustrated, which is its right to do as a tissue, as an organ. That's their right to do as a neighborhood of tissues, but then here we're back to the advocacy. How do we train a person to advocate for their own bones and tissues, to explore within the habitual habits? Oh My Goodness!

**Christie**  Well, so when you say it like that, that's a big job.

*Michael*  Yeah. There's just gardening from here on out, ma'am.

**Christie**  It's like, what do you do? You're, you're...?

*Michael*  The advocacy of it is that I get to step back into the pure gardening of those root systems, literally. I'm literally unwinding those tissues and exploring options within their range, which doesn't look like anything terrestrial.

**Christie**  Through touch, right?

*Michael*  Through tactile contact and verbal content. So personally, what I like about my work is that ultimately, it's non-verbal work. It's literal manual labor gardening. I'm literally unwinding and referencing bones, and unwinding the tissues in relationship to those bones, on their terms, in their range. And that's a lovely thing that can keep me busy all day long.

**Christie**  And you do that.

*Michael*  And I do that. Period. And also with my hands.

**Christie**  With your hands.

**Michael**  ...like with my hands, physically. It's manual labor, and I have to find a way to deal with the neural tissue, and hence the psychology, because the mind and the neural tissue are so involved in each other. (Why he likes his job.) So there has to be a way for me to verbally interact with the neural tissue, both to sometimes acknowledge what's happening, to name it well, to be able to walk the person back and forth because they're gonna freak out. I'm going to get involved in their entanglement, literally. And then also to give them some skills so they can do some of what I'm doing. They can't do it precisely because it just, it's impossible. Their hands can't reach these root beds.

There's a lot of people on the planet. There's enough of us to help each other. Really. I think that's why there's so many people because there's so much happening. Um, so it's manual labor first. The verbal stuff has to be there, too, because at some point the Jellyfish Brain just... she can't take it anymore. She wants... she wants what she wants, how she wants it. She wants to understand it, she wants to control. She really wants to put the lamp/leg back and you've got to convince her not to put the lamp/leg back because that's the injury. That's the trauma. Yeah, but she's so used to... she's so invested. What's curious is that she's invested, whether it's been a couple of days or a lifetime. You've got to have the verbal agility to deal with that, but what I enjoy about it is that I get to practice what I preach. I can always pause, "OK, where's the bones for me as a practitioner? Where are my bones? Let me orient." Well, the limbic system is a very curious thing in the Jellyfish Brain in that, in proximity, she's doing a great job of being an always-on cellular phone. She's the original cell phone, the limbic system!

One end of the limbic spectrum is scanning for saber tooth tigers. Still in our day and age, feral cats scare the shit out of us. They can grab shit and they got claws, and their claws are the perfect length to touch bone. Oh goodness! And that makes them horrific and turns them into a saber tooth tiger. That's just way too big... that's one end of the limbic spectrum. And then it goes to burglars, surprisingly enough. So, saber tooth tigers and burglars have some things in common. They're both just troublesome and opportunistic. Then, at the other end of the spectrum are love songs.

**Christie** Love songs, any of them?

*Michael* Oh sure. A hummingbird can come bug us and we don't get frightened. But let us say a saber tooth tiger purrs and gets happy... and it still makes us wet our pants a little bit. So in proximity, which means anything eight to 12 feet (unless you've been very abused and then it's miles) in that proximity what the limbic system is scanning for is tiger, burglar, love song. Our limbic system is just brilliant at scanning the environment.

Then I pause and find my own bones, because I've gotten so into tackling the hairball, that I forget.... I'm salivating, my sheep dog has got his teeth bared. I'm going after the wolf. I'm tackling the hairball...

I have to pause. If I find my own bones, it also trains the person to pause, to find their own bones. They cannot not react. They cannot not respond. There's this wonderful thing of having to also model what I'm doing and...also leave room for my own hairballs, because a person's hairball may or may not ever change, but the environment around that hairball can! And... that's the gardening part of it. Everything's growing, right? Some hairballs are horrifically large, some of them are ancestrally large, you know, some of them are stupid post-it notes that throw everything off kilter and really make a mess of a person's afternoon.

In some people, I've seen stubbed toes literally ruin a few months. You know the right thing at the right time in all the wrong ways. So, you know, and I've seen other people...the shock from getting hit by a car, they can get up, walk away. No one checks them for concussion, no one checks for any other bruising, any other jarring to the system. They go six months, and they start to fall apart because the shock in their system touched their adrenals and gave them such an activated cocktail that they can get through anything, and they literally get through anything, and then at six to nine months the body is far enough away from the event, it starts to go, "Oh thank goodness!" It has enough other stimuli, right? Its body of experience is displacing the previous body of experience, and they start to fall apart, and they're going, "What the hell?", because their Jellyfish Brain can only associate immediately. It's just looking for, you know, it's going, "This isn't the love song. It's not a saber tooth tiger!" It's all mixed together, and then. all of a sudden. you start to ferret out the story and the client is going, "Oh my God, something really big happened...oh shit, I was hit by a car!" How could someone forget being hit by a car? It happens. So that hairball, it's really fantastic. Our adaptability, our root beds are all so alive and responsive and, given the right circumstances, even in overwhelm, they can adapt, change shape, change jobs in a heartbeat. *Literally* in a heartbeat. And then the Jellyfish Brain goes, "All right!", and she coordinates all those new configurations because she loves it, and she can do it, even to her own detriment, and that's her nature.

**Christie**  Ok, another question. No. Well, it's a related question. I think that we're going to probably revisit hairballs again and again...

*Michael*  Most certainly.

**Christie**  When you talked to me the first time when we were at the coffee shop, you said something about (I don't know whether it's Upledger and Milne), I don't know how the training of the Craniosacral practitioners tends to be oriented towards the release...?

*Michael*  I think all trainings are neural-dominant because, neurally, the neural net wants release. Ultimately both physically and through certain psychotropics, the neural system... she's a jellyfish, she wants to be released. She wants the freedom to swim, how she wants to swim, however the swimming can happen. That's her whole nature. So, our trainings are geared towards release, and I'm not sure that should be the main intent.

**Christie**  That's what it seemed like you were saying. So, if you could explain that a little bit relative to what you've just talked about. So, you know, if... how would...?

**Michael** If I could do THAT, I could probably go to school and get a doctorate, for goodness' sakes. I should've never gotten out of the classroom. Yes, if I could DO that!

**Christie** Well, you just... you just started... look right here. You said... This is kind of the way in which you work with hairballs. I mean we just skimmed a little surface here, but going back and...

**Michael** Hairballs are really important. They're sacred. Coping is sacred. So, this idea of release... what happens is that a practitioner will be working with a dynamic hairball, whatever term they use, right. They're working with the trauma; they're working with this situation in a person. And their intent is, in my experience most of the time, they're advocating for the Jellyfish Brain. They're advocating for a release from the current situation. The tension of the situation drives towards release. And the tension of our hairballs, um, forces us to get experiences. The drive is for release! Neural dominance wants release.

**Christie** Are you saying release or relief?

**Michael** It's hard to tell the difference, I think, from a neural standpoint. Um - the dilemma is, is that there's not enough emphasis on taking the time for integration...what's happening in the other parts of the root beds. If something gets to let go, can it integrate? So, at the let-go, at the *release*, there is a wonderful change of the environment which neurologically, neurochemically, involves a bunch of endorphins and some very, very happy cocktails being made (physiologically speaking of course). There is a moment of relief of the tension on the tendrils of the Jellyfish Brain, on the strands of neural tissue where the pressure has been changed.

It's awesome. And everybody's happy, and you get high from it. The dilemma is that it may not be integratable. So, all this focus has been on that neighborhood. It hasn't been in prepping and making sure the other neighborhoods can change jobs with the release, with the opening up of the trauma area, and whether or not that person can follow through and help integrate that release. And that's been one of the dilemmas I've found. Um, there's, there's so much emphasis on this, you know, figuring out what the problem is, working at it, etc., etc. I mean, we all have this. I mean all the industries have this. Well, there's the hairball, the person screaming. You have to get to the first baby's screaming *before* you can get to the other ones.

And so, when you're advocating for the bones or going into the cranial system, going into these root beds, and starting slow and getting to know all the tissues as they are, then it starts to set up a situation, kind of like circling the dragon. You're kind of getting to know the landscape. You're starting to prep the ground. So, when the hairball starts to disturb, because you're going to go after it, sooner or later, no matter what your discipline is, you're gonna go after it, because it's a delicious thing in there. It's in a wrapper. You're gonna unwrap it. We have tendrils. We are gonna get involved!

So, what I'm noting, and partly why I think I stopped teaching as well, is that there's so much emphasis on coming up with the modality to break the hairball, for the release or the relief, that we forget to prep the soil. We forget to prep the personality. We forget to prep the situation. We forget to make sure ...do they have someone they can talk to? Do they have someone at home? Do they have some way to follow this through because, it's going to be a high for a little while, but they're going to have these habituated parts of the Jellyfish Brain that are going to put the 'lamp/leg' back. Believe it or not, and this is just the funniest thing, that it's going to go hunting for the pain. It's going to go hunting for the tension.

**Christie** Absolutely.

*Michael* So if you can't train a person to pause, and be able to pause as a practitioner, the other things get to go at the same rate they've been going for billions of years.

They don't get slowed down. They don't meet tension with tension. They don't go, "Oh...the tension field needs to be here. This situation's been here awhile. Let's start to prep. Let's start to see how other things are going to adapt when 'this' releases, when this wonderful relief happens. Can the body handle the high of it, not just the low of it?" That's something I see is really lacking in a lot of therapies.

**Christie** Well, it seems like in...

*Michael* ... not to counterpoint or diminish those therapies in any way at all. It's just something I'm noticing as a practitioner.

**Christie** Right. Well, it's something that hopefully is a contribution that you're making to verbalize that or to say that.

*Michael* To name my experience.

**Christie** Yes... to name your experience and just to name what you see and that's what the truth is of what you see.

*Michael* That's right.

**Christie** Well, but also what you're advocating is if the practitioner... well I don't know what you're advocating really...

*Michael* I'm advocating for bones. If we can get the practitioner and the person to slow down and orient, they now have options to use skills to deal with whatever trauma happened. And, and this is a wonderful statement from aikido, "Everyone falls." Everyone falls and it turns out they fall a lot. Maybe not as often as others, but you are going to fall, so how do you fall? You know, it's an art. It's a martial art, it's something you have to put time into, so in that vein, my advocacy is if we can pause, do a functional pause that puts us at this gate where the person can orient to their actual bones, not to a concept. It takes a layer of the high out of it, but it doesn't change the high. It's the hardest thing for me to talk about. It doesn't change everything, but it reorients everything and so that would be my advocacy. That would be my little 'preach', my little thing like, "Whoa. If you take a moment... don't just take a moment. Orient that moment. Find your actual information, which is not in your concept. It's in your *actual* garden with her bones. You have to train the Jellyfish Brain to do that because she's different than her structures."

**Christie** Right.

*Michael* The Jellyfish Brain is neural-dominant. It's a dominant force to be reckoned with. It's got a dynamic to it, and in its function, it precedes other functions (or tries to). She will be dominant. She will coordinate all the nets. She'll coordinate anything within a five-mile radius if her Napoleonism is strong enough, and in some cases, continents, in some cases it's just 10 feet, but it's proximal. If we can challenge that, what happens is that then the Jellyfish Brain learns how to behave differently, and she actually learns that she can soften a wee bit. She gets more actual information. She doesn't have to jump to concepts to make up the difference because she's not getting that information from her cellular structures. She's getting her information from ideas, from external stimuli instead of orienting that external stimuli to her internal root beds and the tissues that are actually getting that information. Not all those tissues are neural, so it creates a different kind of catch 22. It creates something that's a little, um, more palpable and a little bit more actual, which is true.

Christie   So what happens when you teach this?

Michael   I don't teach it anymore. I just try to... I just try to coerce and entice.

Christie   But why did you stop teaching?

Michael   There's a whole esthetician's layer that came into the industry and this is the hardest thing for me to talk about cause I both think it's sacred and so important, and it's the biggest pain in my ass ever. So, I had been teaching for 15 years, a long time, in a local massage school. Simultaneously, I had been assisting and co-teaching with the staff at the Milne Institute for 10 years.

I started my bodywork massage adventure legally in 1986. It was a really a glorious time because I was exposed to many devoted practitioners such as Marion Rosen of Rosen work, John Barnes, the myofascial guy, Lenore Jones, who is probably one of the best, most delicious cantankerous women on the planet, an anatomist and a Trager practitioner, who made anatomy one of the most living things ever. I was very fortunate to study with a couple of people who were involved deeply with Randolph Stone's Polarity Process, Rolf Institute, Milne Institute, Esalen-style massage, Shiatsu, etc. Wonderfully diverse! It was such a wonderful historical time when, when thinking and trying to relate and experience with tissues and physiology and psychology and spirituality... all that was really fresh. And those devoted practitioners were really wrestling with integrating all of these things.

Today, 30+ years later, by the way, it's changed. There are 10,000 books on all this. There's all this literature. There's so much YouTube. Everybody can put their opinion out. I can have this conversation with you and have all my opinions, um, but I find a lot of opinions are based on other opinions, based on opinions, based on some hands-on work. I stopped teaching because it started to invade the classroom. I wanted people to feel the behavior of vascular opposed to lymphatics, feel the behavior of bones, feel the responsiveness, feel the behavior of the Jellyfish Brain, and really learn how to engage in those conversations, tactilely speaking, and they are conversations, not... do this and that happens, as in some kind of formulas.

I've also spent nine years in several PT clinics, so I know what it is to be clinical and there's a place for that. I'm a complete advocate for a medical model with people because it's still a living form of shamanism. You've got highly trained people willing to meet people in their most distressed states on their behalf. So, they're advocating for the health of that traumatized person. Their training is to meet strangers and then help them. That's shamanism. It's the most beautiful thing, but we forget, and we get entangled in our dialogues about what is 'this' and what is 'that'. Well, that was happening in the classroom for me personally. We were getting people in who just wanted a couple of tricks that would cover all conditions and then they wanted to get out there to the spa and make a lot of money, and that was just stressful for me and stressful in my development as a practitioner.

What used to be easy to encourage students to engage with a living process, like, "Oh my God, bones are ALIVE. Let's feel them! That's it, that's it!. OK, pause.", became more difficult. Instead, people started getting very grumpy. They got really upset because they wanted the tricks. They want the data, "What's going to get me work, so I can make money. What's going to get me a dozen clients because I can say and sing what I need to do to get work." Um, and then the buzzwords... what used to be whole concept models for me, and encouragements to engage in the process with someone, were now buzz words and quick fix modalities, and that was hard. That was hard. It's still difficult.

And then I started, the last couple of times I taught, which wasn't that long ago, really, 2006, um, I realized I was getting aggressive in the classroom. I wanted them to be in a place they weren't. Whew! I was the wrong advocate for them. My experiential body wouldn't let me go back to the song and dance of the beginners. I was screaming, "The bones are alive!" And they're all going, "But how do you get the blood from the finger to the elbow?" And I was like,

"Argh!"... my eyes would roll back, and I would start to be frustrated.

In addition, there's an esthetician spa layer there now, so anyone can go and get contact at a spa. This is where it gets to be a problem to talk about because I, I love that all that's there. In fact, I think it's essential for the community to be met by a layer of the community. Right? Meeting people where they're at. Well, most people aren't ready for contact and different types of process. They just want to be soothed. They, in fact, some of them, don't even want to be touched. They just want to be able to tell their friends they went to the spa and got a massage.

Now that can be very frustrating from a certain perspective, but it's an essential layer in a person's development. It's essential that the community has a place anyone in the community can go. If they come to my office, they're not only going to get touched, they're going to get gardened. They're not only going to get gardened, they're going to get a little challenged. Not only that, eventually I'm going to piss off their Jellyfish Brain, and it's all for her benefit, because I'm an advocate for her bones. I'm advocating and so I'm willing to drive the Jellyfish Brain nuts. (If you've got a problem with driving the Jellyfish Brain nuts, you've got to get a psychotherapist or go to my wife, Jodi, who's an advocate for the Jellyfish Brain as a Somatic Experiencing Practitioner.) And so, um, that was one of the things that drove me out of the classrooms...and as I started to unhook from teaching and some other lifestyles, I started to thrive more in my office. I found that I really like gardening people one on one, and that kind of advocacy freed my Jellyfish Brain up and freed up my skills.

I don't consider problem-solving the main event in the office. I consider gardening and advocacy the main event. We may or may not get what we wanted done, but always get something gardened! It may or may not be able to be talked about. It can always be talked about. There are these wonderful things that can happen because I get to fall back on the physical engagement of it, and then language gets to come out of that physical engagement. So, if nothing else happens, we're going to be able to make more room for the hairball, be able to train a Jellyfish Brain to pause and do the same, you know, despite all the habits and all the pressures that want that thing to return back to what it was or get away from the tension. And, we have to understand that that's sacred as well. That's called perseverance. That's coping, and without coping and longing, we can't get the bodies of experience needed for that hairball to actually let go into, because it's not going to let go into nothing. That's being 'high', which has its place, but not the main objective in my office.

**Christie**  So, so what impact has your initiation into the lineage had on that movement away from teaching?

*Michael*  What time is it?!? Let's, let's, let's discuss this question! What impact does the lineage, which infers a tradition, which we haven't talked about yet, have on all this?

**Christie**  Yeah - the movement away from teaching and into the office to do what you're doing?

*Michael*  Because in the classroom, at another level, which we have not talked about, I was hunting people.

**Christie**  You were hunting?

*Michael*  ... hunting them because I was advocating for their soul, was advocating for their bones. I wanted them to learn, even if they didn't want to.

**Christie**  Yeah

*Michael*  That's not the agreement in the classroom!

**Christie**  No. That's true.

*Michael*  Ah, you know, in the classroom as a teacher, you're the advocate for expressing the information of said truth, in the classroom and out in the community. When in the classroom, you have to... just like being a therapist... your face, the agreement is that your face

101

gets to be put on the other person's material. However, there can be different levels of this. There is the role of instructor, which is a person that just expresses information. There's no emotional contact whatsoever. In fact, most times people don't care about the instructor personally, but the instructor has information. They want 'instructor'. That's the role, that's the archetype. And then there's 'Teacher', a smaller percentage in said classroom, um, and for clientele, for that matter. A small percentage 'get' you. So you're not only passing on the information, you're also modeling the information in a way that they really understand. They're getting an understanding, not just the concept. 'Teacher'. Then a smaller percentage falls under 'Mentor', and 'Mentor' is a complete resonance. It wouldn't matter what you said. The person gets it, and they get it in a way that's both verbal and completely non-verbal, you know. You're passing more than information along and you're doing more than modeling. You're resonating with them as a soul.

On that note, under that...the lineage piece. People of the high Andes around the city of Cusco, the Q'ero, hold an indigenous lineage, an unbroken line of information, a cultural experience of earth medicine, a line of technology that has been handed down and passed on. So, I'm a lucky Anglo person who, who got nabbed by a tradition and has earned the rights and privileges of said tradition through initiations and doing classes and studies and practice. I've earned my 'Mesa', my bundle. So that's just a quick thumbnail overview. So, from that indigenous place, it's about engaging with the things that will grow. If it grows the corn, ya gonna do it. If it's not growing the corn, you're gonna get rid of it.

So, I come back into the classroom with a little more chutzpa under my belt, trying to practice this lineage, and I'm going after their soul. I'm really going, "We're going to get somewhere. I don't care who you are. You're on my turf. We're going somewhere." That's not the right set of agreements for a classroom. That is not the right contract. I don't have the right to do that unless the people are coming formally for that layer of work.

And indigenous earth medicine training is tricky because it's experiential, and then we throw and grow the words the best we can, you know. In that tradition... symbology and energetics and laughter... whatever it takes is used to get the gardening done for the day, you know, and this resonated with me because early in my training it was about meeting someone where they're at.

**Christie**   Early in your training?

**Michael**   ...in my training as a body worker at the practitioner level of things. The encouragement was, "How do you do that? How do you meet someone where they're at?" That's the first gate. That's the advocacy. You can't advocate for them, if you can't find them, if you can't meet them. How do you meet someone where they're at, despite other sock puppets? So that in line with this lineage view, you know, 'what can grow corn' practicality gives me more chutzpah, gives me more encouragement. It gives me the pliability to change my skills in a moment if I need to, if that's what it's going to take to meet the person. Ultimately again then there's the advocacy. I'm an advocate for their bones. How am I going to meet that? You know, there's all this encouragement to meet the situation where it's at, even an interview like this. You know, I can have my trepidation and my vulnerability and all my emotions and feelings around it, but there are these other layers now that have been watered and tended to. So I go, "OK, well, let's see. I can grab my 'I don't know'. I can be in my developmental 'I don't know', and let's see how I respond. I don't know how I'm going to respond...I've never done this before. Oh, my Goodness!"

So, in that way, an indigenous lineage, especially when it's cross cultural, gives a way to engage a mythic layer that opens a quality of interaction and the encouragement to dance. The encouragement to meet a living space and quality with a living space and quality. It's a little bit more encouragement. For example, this conversation is a living exchange. Sitting here together is a living exchange. Being on this property (land) is a living exchange. How easy it was to get here today...sitting here with you is very comfortable. This land is very comfortable, very nourishing. You know, all those things interact in a living way...from an indigenous point of view they are important! So, for me as a practitioner, it encourages me to not only name and go to the edge of my scope of practice, but also to be able to name the layered pieces for the person as I'm working in their other root beds that aren't neural. I also get to feel for and include the eco-psychology, not only the place where we are in the community at the time of the session, but the place in the community at the time of their trauma... important different ingredients of their and our experience.

If I were a psychologist, I would bring their layers of experience up into the storyboard. I would bring it into the psychodrama and wanna ferret out that hairballed experience, bring that up and get that moving and dance with it. If I were Jungian, I would want to start to bring in their dreams around that experience and how their experience is transferred through time, and archetypally how we open that up more, so this person can self-facilitate and really get engaged there. Other therapists would try to help find relief and release for the client from the torment of that longstanding hairball. For me, I just have to acknowledge it. I get to feel it, find my empathy for it and, named or unnamed in the act of doing that, I start to model to them the ability to pause and have empathy and to just bring space to this experience. We just take time to let the senses actually feel that, to the best of their ability. While everybody else wants to solve the problem and try to release it, I'm wanting to slow down and actually feel their hairball, their experience, to get to know it first, to see if feeling it is even possible, you know.

Oftentimes, at that edge of the psychology into the environmental eco-psychology, the community's gotta be able to hold that, too. The person is not going to shift if their community can't meet them as well, even if that person has to then, through the tension of that discovery, move to a different community to find the resources to continue to work on their hairball and to build a new layer of their garden, their base of support.

So, I find that the lineage is really the larger communal aspects of ourselves. I'm taking that larger communal aspect of earth medicine, an indigenous lineage and it's concept models and experience, saying, "OK, how do we bring that to this individual?" I personally have the luxury not to have to use rattles or drums or songs. The beautiful challenge, the pressure and encouragement to uphold the tenants of that lineage, deeply informs and continuously nourishes me!

When I'm handling someone, their skin is the drumhead, you know... they have their songs already in them. Their soul is already alive in its dance and in its development. I have to find it. I have to meet it there. I have to try to meet them. Add a little bit of movement, and the whole body is all sorts of different kinds of rattles. For people who do different types of Earth medicine, they'll have an array of rattles because different rattles cut through the energetics or cut through space in different ways. Different drums elicit different aspects. If you're working with trauma, you are not going to use an elk hide, which can be love medicine. That would really not be very good. There's all those little understandings and experiences.

So in working with the person, I get to be informed
by that lineage and bring that added support and that
added encouragement from my own experiential
body, and go, "What is here?" Pause/Orient, "What
else is here?" That becomes a much more alive
question, "What else is here? What do we have to do
to help this system open up its root beds so this
person can grow and nourish?" Because, ultimately,
it's about self-nourishment.

(Yeah, you just threw in that question of "How's the
lineage inform...?"... Holy crap!!)

**Christie**   Yes...holy crap!

# Chapter Four: *Interview #2*

**Christie** Ok, number two.

So the first question is... you use the word 'gardening'....

**Michael** Oh yeah.

**Christie** ...as in gardening the body and stuff. So, the whole question is, um, why that word and why is it important and, and how would you garden a 'patch' of body or a...?

**Michael** ...a 'patch' of body... as if we were walking along and found this leg. It was just a 'patch' of a leg, and we tried to bring it to him, see what he would do with it...

**Christie** so...

**Michael** "Why" questions..."why" questions should be avoided at all cost. "What", "where", "when" and "how" questions are wonderful. "Why" questions tend to spin the psyche outwards.

**Christie** I know.

**Michael** "What" about gardening... literally, for me, there is a wonderful thing that happens in a therapeutic context, which we don't have to spend any time with, but I just want to name it. There is a counter transference and a transference piece, especially in proximity. There is no getting around it. There's going to be this wonderful dance and then underneath that a wonderful archetypal dance, and underneath that et cetera, et cetera, et cetera. So for me to work with the transference process over the years, in my brain, I've just assigned the whole process all as 'gardening'. One... the phrase, 'gardening' allows me to change my modality tools on the spot. If something's not working, I go get something else. You know, it's so akin to my shop, "This isn't working so I gotta get another tool!", you know, so it has that effect. I think from the years of teaching and handling bodies, having had to teach many different modalities and respond to so many different people, it turns out the biology doesn't care. It doesn't care about the concepts or the ideas behind the modalities. It only understands the contact. So if I'm enjoying handling a tool, a modality, whatever that might be, the body tends to be responsive. It's responsive more from a gardening responsiveness of walking outside and tending, you know, than just a psychological responsiveness. And since my modalities are more on the physical end of things, attending the physical, it falls nicely into that gardening. So that's the idea in my mind. And then it turns out that the way the systems are layered are so literally 'roots' ... like there're times I can be in our actual garden at home and messing with a plant and handling its roots. The corollary to human body is so similar and so direct. I think too, I had the wonderful opportunity to be part of a cadaver class. I think that did something for me viscerally...the experience of seeing the nerve roots are actually roots, right? I saw that the vascular root bed, the capillary root bed is literally a root bed.

**Christie**  So what do you mean by 'bed'... 'a root bed'?

*Michael*  So if we go out right now and pull up any of your plants, the space that the roots take up is called a root bed. It's the bed the roots are lying in.

**Christie**  So it's a much bigger, usually a much bigger space.

*Michael*  Yes, it's whatever root space that plant's roots take up. Um, and in our bodies it's the same thing. Each system has a complete root bed. So last time we talked, we called those 'nets', from an intellectual and a concept model. The word 'net' allows us to be able to engage it in a somewhat sensible conversation. Technically they are nets, in kind of a way, but more technically they're actually root beds. They're actually complete root systems and they take up space...they co-mingle either directly or indirectly, which is pretty fantastic. When you're handling someone's body, at least when you start to slow down and have to start differentiating tissues, roots, nets, layers... it's really lovely to consider that you're working with root beds. So, when you're working in a 'patch' of person, that 'patch' as a literal cross section would be comprised of

111

these different root beds/layers that co-mingle, and I think for me it makes it engageable, you know. In my anatomy training with different anatomy teachers (and I've had some really wonderful ones as well as dull ones, but mostly really wonderful ones, luckily) ….even there, there's still such a neural-dominant view. That view is very important for academics and our own understanding, but practitioners can come at it in such a mechanical way, "Yeah, yeah. It's like this then this and that, and that's where that corresponds with that." And um, that's all just fine because it makes the Jellyfish Brain very happy. And then if the Jellyfish Brain has its anatomy cue card ready, all those other Jellyfish Brains salivate like crazy, you know, they go, "I can get my cue cards on all my anatomy and go…. Where?" (wonderful really)… "Oh there 'it' is!"

So, bringing it back into root beds and thinking about those root beds commingling, for me, it gives it a better visceral engagement. Like I can be handling a 'patch' of person and be able to go in and be pretty exact about what's in my hands, then very easily get to the next neighborhood, the next place the roots are extending through…

**Christie**  And be pretty exact about what's in your hands?

**Michael** ... the actual anatomy. I can go in and track the anatomy, but because I'm treating it like a plant, I'm treating it with that kind of respect, like, "Well there's a root bed in there. I don't want to be just mucking about." Right? So, it's causing me to slow down a little bit and start to bring in that layer of respect and that understanding that there're layers of root beds in any 'patch' of person. It's a comingled layer of root beds wrapped around that bone in there, that coral reef bone in there. It gives me a sense of their landscape, and it gives my mind a different way to engage 'their' landscape. I'm not going at it as an intellectual anatomist, going, "That's *that*...and that's *that*.", I'm coming at it as a gardener, going, "OK, now we want to see how this ground soil is doing. Is it too compact? Is it too loose? Is it too airy? Is it too damp? Is it too.... what's the quality?" So, all of a sudden, I'm working in qualities like, "Well, what is that garden? What is this 'patch' of person? What is their quality? How are their root beds in that quality of soil, in that quality of matrix of the person at that patch?" And then, because it's a root bed, I get immediate feedback like, "I'm just on a 'patch'. So what's happening in the next 'patch', without moving or doing anything? Well, how does this 'patch' relate to that 'patch'?", you know, and as I'm moving through somebody, that information is allowed to steep and add up on its own. Yes, the person comes into the office with whatever, you know, "Why is this, why did this do this, why is that?" Right? And then we defer/deflect them away from "why" as quickly as humanly possible without hurting their psyche, so they don't spin out. "Why's" are spin out questions.

That gardening piece allows me then to keep a sense, at some point, of the totality of a particular root bed. So I'm working on an area and there's constriction, a little hairball, so I know that the lymphatic root bed's going to be a little bit grumpy, and the vascular system is going to be a wee bit tense because it's having to work harder to get blood through to all the tissues and cells, and I know the tissue is working a little bit harder, and then I can take my attention and move it down a particular root bed, so I can get very specific and very general at the same time and work between those qualities. The 'gardening' allows me to have a sense of the whole 'patch' of person as opposed to a piece of 'a patch' of a person. It allows me to keep that sense of their totality because it's a complete environment. It's a complete root bed. It's 'root beds in a bag', you know, that can move around on their own, unlike plants. It's a way to keep and give myself a framework that sidesteps the intellectual prowess of anatomy. It also keeps me from getting bogged down by the terminology and allows me then not only to sidestep the specific intellectual aspect of anatomy, but then also the psychology pieces. It allows me to sidestep those, too, because then, from a gardening point of view, the story's just a song within a song, within that garden. This is just how things relate, and the songs come out of how these things are relating, even if they walk in the office in the middle of their operatic aria, singing, "Oh my God, this is really fucked up! Oh, it wasn't like this before. I don't know if it'll ever get better!" It's the beauty of every good opera. Good opera will have a good aria. That's the formula. So it is with our lives. Every season better have a little heartache, or you're in trouble.

So the gardening allows me to do that, allows me to be adaptive with my tools, with the modalities that are available. It also allows me to leave room for the person to squirm and scratch and fuss and discharge and have all the responses they have, you know, because problem-solving becomes a secondary function. Investigation becomes a primary function, and the gardening allows me to do that because I can't do anything until I investigate, because it may or may not be true. Their 'birdsong story', you know, could have been in the same aria they've been singing for 20 years. I don't know.

I've met those songs, and then I have to go, "It's gardening. " I can sidestep that so I don't get pulled into that transference, countertransference, back and forth, the chase that happens or the counterpoint that happens. I can leave room going, "Oh, there's a place for that. There's a layer in the garden that needs to be there. Great." So, then another invitation... it becomes an invitation to investigate and then be responsive, you know, on both sides. It also allows me to run that garden ragged because I may decide that I need to do a lot more than I have the ability with my hands to do, so I'll prompt them to do something.

I'll prompt them to go find a bone or move their attention, because I'm paying attention to their garden and how they move their attention around. All these things become ways to gather information. To value 'gardening' gives me that construct to gather information and it's hard to get satiated from that place. You know, there's always stuff to be tended in a garden, whether it's healthy or not. So, it turns out human beings aren't any different. There's always something to tend to, healthy or not. And sometimes it's better to go tend the healthier stuff then to wrestle with the hairball. But if you get caught in some of the other concepts, you're going to be antler-locking and wrestling with a very highly intelligent hairball that may be even helping them out of the wound, and those hairballs are highly successful and very cantankerous. And hairballs will always wait. You know, you can engage in a wrestling match with a person for the time that you have them, and they go away, "Well I got wrestled!" and I go away, "Oh I got wrestled!" But nothing got *done*. There was just a lot of wrestling. So, another couple of weeks go by and the high of the wrestling carries them through another cycle, a little season. There's a place for that, but it's not really interesting. It doesn't do the advocating on the garden's behalf, you know. I'm there to tend that garden, so I do everything I can to get information and get my hands in there so I can begin to differentiate those root beds.

**Christie**   So. So, when you are getting in there, you're using your hands and your kinesthetic sense to feel into what you feel there?

*Michael*   Yes, I try. I am attempting to use my root beds,

**Christie**   Your root beds?

*Michael*   ... my root beds in a responsive way to their root beds. This gets interesting because I could go full-bore kinesthetic, grab my rototiller and get a bunch of stuff done. That doesn't seem to be a dilemma for me. You know, I've got a gorilla-nature that way. I will get my mitts in there. There's no, I have no fear of a body that way. I've handled enough crazy bodies that there's, there's nothing that really trips me out unless I get in there and, all of a sudden. I'm tripped out... my response to 'their hairball'. So, as I'm making contact, I have to be available to be contacted. I have to leave room like... we've talked about before... there is a jazz conversation happening, and so I need to leave my vascular bed available to sense their vascular bed, to be responsive because they're resonant, like creatures. I have to let my lymphatic bed be responsive to their lymphatic bed... they're similar creatures. I have to let my bones orient me, so my bones can tell me where their bones are and vice versa. Um, what I like about that is that it also allows a person's body on the table to track me, which I think is terribly important. There's a nonverbal responsiveness brought into that language of contact, and you know, there are times I'm like, next thing I know I'm holding a chisel going after somebody. In a funny way, I want them to know I have a chisel, and I'm going after them in that way, right? It's one of those things like, "I've got to chisel. I'm going after you. We're going to get this done, you know." In that place, I have to hold and make such a fulcrum in my response that there is no doubt of what I'm doing. I'm going after this piece. It can't run. It can't hide. There's no place for it to go, and things are going to get a little squirmy. So that contact when I go in to do something, as I'm doing that, I'm letting the rest of my systems be responsive to the rest of their systems. It is really gardening meets gardening, in a way, because some of the information is from contact.

The other layers of information are from my own systems, and how they respond to a person, and that gets more... um, I think more difficult for language, more difficult for a casual conversation, because all those layers of conversation can't be had at once without talking about jazz or without going... well... unless you really understand what Miles Davis did, the conversations are moot. They aren't going to fall on anything sensible. If you don't understand that there's a cacophony of crazy shit going on and there're going to be moments when you can do a coherent summary statement, musically or kinesthetically. If you don't understand that these things are happening in rounds, in measures of music, in cycles, in circulation patterns, then you're apt to chase the idea that the person came in feeding you with, or your own idea of going, "Whoa, that's not what I see!", and going after that, and in a funny way I get to play with that because I'm still going to do that round of engaging.

Also, I'm going in to get information. I'm going in to check the quality of that 'patch' of person, but, but it's lyrical in the responses. Yes, my hands are picking up how the soil is, the density of the tissue, the responsiveness of the tissue, the kinesthetic qualities of that landscape, but those qualities are, are also imbued with the feelings, the colors, the flavors, um, the energetics of the space. And for me, I'm translating them into that gardening like, "Well, how is this garden?", you know, so I'm going back to being very generalized, and then I get to come back in and get more specific, "Oh this root bed's doing this, but that root bed over here is doing that, and ...wait a minute, how is this... ", you know? All of a sudden, I'm involved in a much larger conversation, but it's so close to jazz. It's so close to an aquatic musical place. Of course, I'd like to say 'it' is an aquatic, musical, living landscape!

So, you're coming in being really strong with tissues that may be really frightened and they're singing a frightened song, which is why everything else is bracing, and then the garden is coping. So that garden doesn't want to disturb that hairball because inside the hairball is a very panicked, protected, and tangled trauma, right? There're all the ranges of that coping response from it really being so pissy that it will kill you if you touch it, to distractive behavior where you go after something and everything else responds to draw your attention away from the actual hairball (peewit bird behavior).          So in that responsiveness, I get to be strong in holding the space clear, but like Miles Davis, I'm coming into somebody else's conversation, to somebody else's music. You know, he had to handle other musicians and create moods to express musical dialogue, right? When you enter into somebody's body, those different root beds have their own songs. They have their own experiences. They're not always in concordance, but they're always working it out, and then we have to bring in the statement of homeostasis, a strong idea, by the way. And I get a lot of flak for that. I get into great arguments around this. Um.. homeostasis is a nice idea. It's the drive for things to be in balance or the drive for concordance. OK, so we might say that Miles Davis was a master at bringing homeostasis to a song. He could take the craziest interactions and then do a summary statement that made it come back around into a cohesive piece and tie it together.

So in body work, those circulation patterns, those rounds, those waves are really important. But I have to leave my systems soft to be responsive to that. So, I've got to know where my waves are, where my patterns are, my placing is, because I'll be using those to be available to somebody else's dynamics. That interaction gives me lots of information and then there's contact, and then I come in kinesthetically. There's kind of a whole walking into the garden metaphor where you're getting all this beautiful information, and then you get to substantiate that in a way with contact.

**Christie** Yeah.

*Michael* And then there's work to do! By then, you've already been working. You've already been in conversation and your different senses are available to be influenced, to have that information in conversation. And in turn, you model and affect the person on the table, the person in proximity. You're affecting their systems as well. You're letting their system stay responsive, even as you're starting to decide how to corner them or not.

**Christie** 'corner'... Is that what you said?

*Michael* "I've got a chisel! ...don't know how this chisel got here... yep, something's going on... all of a sudden, my hand made a chisel, it made that chisel shape, gotta get working... you're not going to like it!", or the converse, "You really want to be chiseled and run over by a truck. But I'm only gonna work on this one area like that. So the rest of you will be terribly frustrated with me." All those things happen, and more. So yeah, the contact piece is terribly important. But there are so many layers to that before you've actually made physical contact, before the kinesthetic. The kinesthetic covers such a broad range that it includes proximity, right? So, you've got contact and you got your root beds, checking each other out in a way, being responsive to proximity. And then you've got the nervous system's beautiful ability to do the same tracking using the other senses. You've got a limbic system that's taking all this delicious information, deciding whether you are a saber tooth tiger, or burglar, or love song, or a friend, you know. It's adjusting to that. There're all these parts of us that use aspects of contact that have to do with the quality of space around us. And oftentimes (about to get myself in trouble again... here it comes!), oftentimes people relegate those layers to energetics.

**Christie**  You rarely use that word...

*Michael*  I avoid the word as often as possible. Um, because I think many things get lost in the use of energetics, and many things get transcribed into the ideas of energetics, that may or may not be true. Some of them are just kinesthetic aspects of our systems checking each other out, doing what they do to track in proximity to another, and it's not just the facial sensors and proprioception that does that, you know. Turns out all the root beds understand their environment, and it turns out our wonderful cellular phone limbic system can track a great deal of space. It can cover a city block if it needs to, you know. It's, It's quite... if someone's really, really wounded, they'll shut part of the body down to create enough umph to reach a city block. They'll be able to reach a span that's really phenomenal. And then we get into some trickier aspects of the psyche where the imagination is actually quite mobile. Add a little imagination into a little proprioception and a little panic, in a wonderful limbic system looking for a love song or really, really deeply afraid of saber tooth tigers (still/currently), they'll reach really far. The system's, the garden's ability to protect her root beds is phenomenal!

**Christie**  ... so... but that's not energetics?

*Michael*  From my point of view, that may include some energetics, but that hasn't gotten into energetics yet.

**Christie**  OK

*Michael*  Those senses are still using the palpable kinesthetic aspects of the root beds, depending on which root bed, you know, but they can scan, too. It's not just the limbic system that scans. It's not just the proprioception that senses. You know, we've got this wonderful overlay of our senses, wonderful overlay of root beds, and then we have this very interesting set of sinews that can also resonate, be responsive to the qualities happening around them in space. And I think that includes energetics, but I think there's a grosser anatomical layer to it. All too often people put into that definition 'energetics' because their psyche wants the freedom to roam and do whatever it wants to do as it wants to do it. You know, throw in energetics, and all of a sudden, a person doesn't have a sense of their own bones, where they're sitting, what's happening in their biology, their psyche and their wonderful imagination. All those wonderful things get a little taste and go off on a journey. I hesitate to use energetics because I think the magic of the root beds is much more palpable, and much more delicious. And... I love the idea of a lot of the energetics, but I find people's dialogues with energetics, um, tend to span closer into imagination and concepts and ideas and, and some loose ideas about how frequencies play with each other, and the electronics of that. We get so tricky, cause then you fall into the quantum physics group, which are also supporting the esoteric dynamics. Then you can get off on these wild, wonderful, very palpable things and they feed many parts of us. Meanwhile, our biology and our actual root beds are going, "When you're done playing and making those cocktails...Hey, how can we participate?" All that gives you and your coping an associated satisfying experience. But your biology still doesn't know how to digest that experience, doesn't know how to integrate it. So, a lot of ideas I think are good coping constructs, but they do very little for the actual garden, in my experience, of course.

**Christie** That makes sense to me...I mean what you've described is much more magical in a certain sense to me at the moment.

**Michael** And that's my problem as well. I find because everybody, including myself, goes into a therapeutic context, we have all these things that want to be met and this produces an interesting range of vocabulary, right? I find the actual biology so much more magical than any of the energetic concepts.

**Christie** That's what I've been learning from you in just this last period of time that you've been talking about this... like, wow!

**Michael** It's so much more magical. And yet, I also see some of the biology being co-opted by the energetic models. So I think the quantum physicists in their sight, their little helpers across the conceptual boards, are really lovely. But the biology, it's not, um...the energeticists still co-opt the biology. They still want to have energy and spirit be first, and biology be second. They still are coming at it from a neural-dominant perspective. It's difficult. I have a corner set up for those difficulties in my psyche, in my office, but I get to disregard them because I get to garden, right? I get to go to work, you know. I don't have to deal with a lot of things that psychologists, etc., have to deal with. But for my actual work of choice...

**Christie** It just seems like in what you're describing about the root beds and the contact in a reciprocal way... it's very alive and very rich and primary.

**Michael** Yeah, very primary and very primitive. Deliciously so. Um, and from those places, then a person's dreams make even more sense. And then their psychology, for me, makes even more sense. You know, I actually have a place I can take it now instead of a neural place that I have to transcribe it to.

**Christie** Take it for yourself or take it with...?

**Michael** Both, because there's other layers of information. It's like, "Oh, there's their story. There's their ideas, there's their concepts, there's their view of what they add it up to. OK, if they've never handled or included the body before, if they can't feel that connection, the person will fill in the difference with previous ideas, concepts, and previous experiences. So I can take that into consideration and then go explore. If it's true, it'll be true.

**Christie**  In the body...

*Michael*  In the body, right. If not, then I have to find out where (because it's never black and white. Oh! My Goodness!)... where the roots of their story fit into the roots of their body, and how that is specific and then how it's generalized, and then where does it feed their coping and longing, and what are they actually working on? Are they in a place they can begin to displace their concept models and go, "Oh my God, my body, oh my God, Oh my God!" Because people have that experience of waking up to their body, or... does everything have to be re-transcribed back into their neural way of coping, right, and as I learn from their reactions, sometimes we can't go there yet. They don't have enough potency (Thank you, somatics!). They don't have enough potency built up in their system to have it be contained, to be held, to be integrated. They don't... a person has to have a lot of chutzpah... gotta have a certain potency in their root beds to contain their experience, and then do stuff with that. It's so... the garden's body is so beautifully alive. But I think we're just getting to the beginnings of a body of human experience that's literally a body of human experience that's not so transcribed into whatever concept is convenient at the time or whatever socially agreed-upon concepts are OK. Um, all those layers are terribly, terribly, terribly important. And um, I don't have a way to talk about both things at once, the coping construct and what happens then in a person's private life compared to their social life compared to their society. You know, those are different root beds as well. And I respect those as well. But I'm an advocate for a person's biology, so I find their biology much more magical than even the concepts of biology because I don't have to worry about the concepts of physiology and biology. I mean that's... the doctors have to deal with that piece, and they do all right, you know. Every once in a while, you get someone coming in and saying, "Oh, my doctor finally figured it out." But usually there's a bunch of conversation between the person and the doctor as well. I find that in interacting with their biology directly in helping differentiate those root beds, literally spending that kind of time with a person's body tends to start to displace their fantasy and coping and starts to set up a more sober dialogue. And I find that sober dialogue more magical than any of the concepts.

**Christie**   So a sober dialogue internally?

**Michael** Internally, yeah... and then there's 10,000 things, because then you've created a delicious moment. Then everything comes in for a feeding frenzy.

**Christie** Well, that was another question, which is what is soup stock?

**Michael** So, the root beds make a delicious soup stock. When you slow down and start to differentiate and pay attention to root beds and give them a certain type of gardening respect, even though you might be getting ready to grab the rotor tiller.

**Christie** By 'you', you're talking about the practitioner...?

**Michael** That's right. When the practitioner is slowing down and starting to have conversations with the other person's body, whatever living garden they're working on...when they're slowing down, it starts to change the quality of interaction in those tissues. And then there's 10,000 energetic schools going "Yes! See, he does agree, no he doesn't. Yes, he does, no, he does both at the same time." So, when you slow down, the quality of that space changes. You start to respect and start to handle those tissues differently because you're discerning what tissues you're working with. You're actually going in and having those funny little dialogues, "Where are you? What are you? Where are you? How are you? You did what? When?", um, so you're having those dialogues and then the tissue starts to soften because you're spending more time with it, and that's pure physiology at that point, you know. You're starting to change the collagen qualities of the tissue because you're adding heat and the heat's a byproduct of a good conversation (Is that all you're going to hear? He's talking energetics while saying he's not.). It's true. That's what makes it funny.

So, you've slowed down and you've started to differentiate some tissues. You're actually getting to know that 'patch' of person in their garden and so in doing that, the quality of space changes. So you start to go from a very activated adrenal driven experience, a heightened activated experience..."Oh my God! Oh my God!", which includes all aspects of pain which make you go, "Oh... Oh my God!", which includes all aspects of bliss, "Oh my God! Oh my God!" You've got a whole spectrum there, but the quality of space - because the practitioner is handling that and taking time to acknowledge and explore the root beds of the 'patch' of person - that quality of space changes. Well so... it drops out of that activation. It may still include activation, but now activation isn't being fed. You aren't feeding fire with fire, so they say. You're starting to slow it down. You're starting to add time into it. You're starting to literally spend time in the activity at hand (Everything is so literal what I'm saying right now). You're starting to spend that quality time, and that changes the quality of space, changes the quality of tissue and it starts to literally heat it up as a secondary process. (In my mind, I'm having this great argument with some energetic schools of thought who do all this magnificent maneuvering in order to create heat and create the ultimate human ultrasound, which is all it is. Thank you very much. We'll argue about those later.)

∞

*(Side note: ultrasound was developed by some very interesting people, a lazy doctor who figured out that he just had to hold people for a while to figure out what the hell was going on with them. It created a heat in his hands. The heat changed the quality of the tissue. He went out and got drunk with his friends. One of them happened to understand radios and how to use crystals and develop specific frequencies and he said, "Hey, you know, if you run current through a little bit of crystal at the specific frequency, it'll heat up specific tissue at a specific level, at a very precise place and, ta da, ultrasound!" Amazing modality and an amazing tool when properly used! So there!)*

∞

So, human hands do the same thing, but we're letting that be a secondary process. We're letting all those circulation patterns be secondary to the intention of, of kind of seeing/feeling what the roots are doing, to keep coming back to being their advocate... like, OK, all that stuff is happening, but

132

that can be secondary. "What's, what's, what's..." (you're always asking "what's"), so that questioning changes the quality of space. Then, suddenly, there's an inclusivity, kinesthetically, in that 'patch' of a person, and you start getting a tea. You start getting something that's thicker, more substantial, um, very inclusive, and then something really interesting happens in that, as you move through the session in this way, the tea gets thicker, and it turns into a soup stock.

So, we have all these fluids in the body. So that's where the soup stock analogy comes in. It's like you're, you're actually making a soup stock that is going to benefit all the tissues. You're disregarding the adrenal rush. You're disregarding adding fire to their experience or amping up their experience (and there're times for that, and that becomes a specific therapeutic context). But overall you're creating this quality of space that the tissues and the root beds are being acknowledged primarily, and you're letting the neural-dominant views, concept models and agendas move into a secondary place... knowing that they won't like it because those parts of us have self-justifying capabilities. They'll get grumpy because you aren't feeding them directly, you're choosing to make their environment more cohesive and more stable, and ultimately, you're just gathering information. You're just being a responsive gardener and tending to things as you're asking questions.

So, there's a little bit more simultaneous responsive jazz to it. You attend to the quality of spaces as they change, drop out of activation and out of a neural-dominant daily habit. As this, this conversation, continues, and you and the tissues drop into the feel of this conversation, the feel of contact, the feel of the tissues' actual environment. Adding more time to that strengthens all of that and displaces the neural dominance even more. All of a sudden, the Jellyfish Brain gets a little comfortable and it goes 'flippa' (we don't know what that is actually), but that's actually what happens for the brain... 'flippa'... and the brain becomes an organ, one of many, and it becomes a root bed, one of many. It's no longer dominant, right? For most people, this is deep sleep. So as that quality drops in, what's cool is that the practitioner's paying such attention to the tissues that the tissues give way to that. Usually, it's the person's brain paying all the attention and maneuvering and coordinating, but now the practitioner's brain and body responses, responsibility, responsiveness is taking over some of the primary responses of the person on the table.

So, there's, um, that field of being tended, which any good therapy will do, and there's a high from being tended, especially tended well and honestly. That creates this soup stock that ends up continuing to feed the person even after they stand up and their Jellyfish Brain grabs the steering wheel of their body bus and drives it onto the next location, going, "I don't know what the hell that man just did, but something happened!" Soup stock. Soup stock is a very inclusive quality of space in which all the tissues have been tended in a way and had that attention. And so it creates a thicker, more nourishing environment. And that stays with the person. That ends up becoming the nourishment that their drive to go have somebody handle them is doing. That drive to self-nourish is remarkable in the 10,000 ways that that happens, you know.

**Christie**  So does the soup stock itself heal? You know if somebody comes in with a...

**Michael**  *(Note to self, she used the 'H' word...should have drawn up contracts ...we're allowed to cuss, but we're not allowed to use certain words. Let it be noted that 'healing' is one of the weasel words.)* Again, I don't know anybody that goes into their garden and works all day and comes back and says, "My garden is healed." I've never heard the word 'healing' used in gardening except for the person's personal experience of tending that garden was felt as 'healing'. Did anything get nourished in that interaction? Something did.

I've had a problem with the word 'healing' my whole life, you know. Yes. Things grow. Is that healing? Oh, I hope so. Um, I've seen a lot of things happen that people said were healed and they weren't. You know, it's just, it gets to be problematic. It's a problematic word. It's a coping. I think that the idea of healing and the longing for healing is essential, sacred, it's essential. What actually happens, I think, is a lot more magical. And sometimes, um, those processes can take a person a lifetime, you know, the drive to correct something, the drive to meet oneself in a certain way, you know, is amazingly rich. Um, and along the way a bunch of stuff happens, but from my point of view, I see it more as, um, a tended garden than a formulaic, "Do this, this and this and then this thing is done."

You know, I've seen hairballs become manageable. They aren't healed in any sense of the word. And yet the person has changed their relationship to themselves completely in order to tend themselves. And I'm not sure the word 'healing' can be used in that context. And I'm not sure the person in that position would use the word 'healing' in that context. They would say they changed, not that they were 'healed', right, so the idea of change, I think it's much more apt than the word 'healing'.

**Christie** So then the words 'soup stock'?

*Michael* Soup stock is ripe. Everything gets fed in the way that the particular things like to be fed, or at least held in a way that they *can* be fed, and then things grow, and things grow to that experience. So, all of a sudden, the person who goes, "Oh my God!", goes into a contrast and goes, "This feels really nourishing. All this other crap does not. What the hell were my previous selves thinking?" I think the soup stock sets the environment for things to be fed, you know, and then the differentiating of tissues creates a space so that life can be circulated. And then, the opportunity for those tissues to have a more nourishing engagement happens, whatever it is to that tissues' thing, because it's so diverse in one's body, but it gets a little delicious inside the 'patch' after a while.

**Christie** And then there's the... and then there's a counter to that too. I mean it's kind of like, well not a counter to that, but it's just...

*Michael* Well, the hairballs are also being fed, right? Cancer is also being equally fed. The illness is also being fed. So be it. Then this, this is where I get myself in really big trouble with a capital T, um, (which ends up in some musical that I can't recall at the moment). This gets to be troublesome, I think. Because, from my point of view, it's about tending the garden. I'm not looking to resolve their cancer. It's not in my scope of practice. It's not my place to do that. I have to be mindful because certain cancers, if they're fed too much, will proliferate in a body...and that's true.

And for the record, cancers are just cells that have been switched on and created little incestuous pockets of trailer courts, where they are incestuous and they create the same cells over and over again, and then we have all the things we do to counterbalance that, to try to interrupt that experience. So, cancers are just happy cells that don't know that they're incestuous by repeating the same process over and over again. They just don't know. They're hungry beasts, and they go crazy. It gets to be interesting because at the same time you're trying to feed and create an environment where the other tissues can have the opportunity to come in and say, "Ah, no, no, you crazy cells don't!", they might have an opportunity to form a cyst around the cancer and, maybe, even drive it into a benign state, which would be lovely. And it's difficult because, um, we're so alive, that there are all these things that find us really delicious. Right? I think it's tricky from a practitioner's point of view, my point of view. I want to get a person calm so they can sense what they can sense and be able to be informed directly.

**Christie**   Yeah.

*Michael*   And um, I have to fall back to that aspect of gardening, going, "Oh, that part of the garden's like crap. That's a little bit too much bramble bush for me." So, we'll tend to the other parts of the garden body, knowing that it will indirectly affect that 'patch' of bramble bush in the person, you know. So, there's lots of... it gets very specific to the person. There's lots of strategies. It gets tricky. It gets tricky. That's where the gardening piece gets really tricky, you know, because by nourishing an aspect of them, everything's gonna get fed, so if that's a more nourishing moment, then the stuff that's troublesome is also going to get nourished. I'm in the position of acknowledging that counterpoint and those dynamics at the same time, going, "Well, but we need to get them nourished and calmed down enough to be able to start discerning by looking at the behaviors, and then taking other nourishing actions to have an understanding of what directions they need to go.", you know?

**Christie**   Yeah. I just know from my own experience, just that arriving at the point of being in a soup stock or the soup stock being me or however you want to talk about that, then there's a part of me that starts to vacate, you know, I mean, part of me that has trouble accepting nourishment or receiving nourishment. It, it becomes a practice to keep bringing my attention back and actually being able to receive it. So that's also what I meant when I brought that up. It's just that the deliciousness of the nourishment sets off the counter to not being able to accept that. And then that's great because then I can see that and work with it and encourage myself to come back and keep receiving.

**Michael**   Beautifully said... and that's the point, you know, that's what I think it is to try and meet someone where they're at and tend that/them, so that experience becomes a dominant experience and eventually that becomes the, "Oh, let's feed this part of us first. Then we can see what else." But there's, I mean there's really um incredibly complex developmental issues and physiological issues there. It gets to be very complex rather quickly. But getting a person to that very point is crucial. You know, that's part of tending the garden which is to set it up to where that person can begin to self-facilitate. So the next time they come and need someone like me or someone like you or someone like anybody, they have a little bit better sense of themselves, therefore maybe a better sense of what needs to be tended that day. And if they don't, then it's on the practitioner, and if they do then it's still on the practitioner. But now... they're involved at a different place/space. There's a relationship and circulation between the two people that, that is of benefit, you know, is more nourishing and it doesn't stop you from trying to counterpoint the hairballs. You start to actually include and work around them. At some point you realize you have to cultivate a space to meet and understand that hairball, you know, that you can't go in and demolish and chemo the hairball, although that may be needed (those of you who aren't counterpointists), because that may be needed. Then, in that place it's interesting because then those people start to put better people around them while they go through those more difficult experiences, because those are hard experiences. And then it gets more interesting because then a person learns to self-nourish and learns to ask for help, realizing they don't have to do things alone. They have to do a layer of work themselves; but, then they're also in a larger garden and they have some maneuverability. Then,

141

they start to set things up for their support, and suddenly they're looking at things like gardens as well, and they're starting to go, "'I'm growing a human being. Oh my God!" And they realize that the previous human beings were grown by the previous human beings they were...and those were grown by the previous little, teeny tiny human beings. And there gets to be a sober home gardening perspective of their lifeline. It's not a psychological intervention, so to say, although that's lovely. Any intervention is just lovely. Um, they start to get that 'self'. They start to have a different sense of their roots and how they grow and where they actually came from. Then they are able to look at the next six months, the next year and start to go, "Oh, I want to grow That human being!" Then they get practical. They go like, "Can it be done? Well, then, what are the next couple of steps I need to do that?"

You know, you start behaving differently and, all of a sudden, you're tending a soup stock instead of managing a bunch of hairballs, knowing that your hairballs are a part of... you know... it's a matzah soup. (Those of you who aren't Jewish, look it up. Simple soup, the big hairball dumpling mind...it's really delicious!)

**Christie**  What I want to do next is go back to one of the things that got lost in the first recording we did, which is intuition, insight, imagination... because you, you've also today mentioned imagination a couple times when the issue of energetics came up. You talked about imagination, and in the first meeting that we did that we lost the recording of, I asked you what the importance of intuition, insight, imagination is in the practice of what you do, and um, you know, what is their place and how do they arise and is there a difference between intuition, insight, imagination? Are they all kind of part of the same thing?

**Michael**  I think they are (Better just take that or you'll just keep asking that).

**Christie**  What part do they all play in this whole practice and how do you use them? How do you foster them all in yourself, and how would you help the client or person access their own if they want that?

**Michael**  Um, they don't have a choice.  So, when you orient, right...

**Christie**  When who does what?

**Michael**  Anybody, from my point of view. In the garden of the 'patch of person' there is orientation that precedes orienting, and that's "Where's your bones?" Out of that wonderful question, there're responses, right? And, usually, some part of you will go 'blup' because all of a sudden, you'll go, "My bones?", and it becomes very alive and you'll go and try to find your bones in a myriad of ways. So, the Jellyfish Brain gets very excited and confused and disoriented all the same time. The second part of that orientating to bones, which is my trip, um, is, "What's supporting my bones or where is the contact or where's the push of the world?" There is a force coming to you, and it's pushing against your bones, and your bones are absorbing that force and laying down their matrixes in response to that dynamic. Wolff's law - "Bones grow to the force put upon them." Adjunct, the force is not internally generated. It's an emanated force that's a response to gravity. Gravity is the big planet giving you a big kiss and sucking you down into her. And there's an equal and opposite reaction of Glee or an emanated force. And the bones grow to that emanated force opposite of the pull of gravity. So those two things together start to reorient tissue.

**Christie**  Which two things?

*Michael*  "Where's the bones? Where's the support of my bones?" And so, you're feeling for your bones and then you're sensing for the contact pushing against said bones, and then you're immediately into a very interesting thing, because, between the world and the bones lies the tendrils of your Jellyfish Brain, and

144

those tendrils feel a tickle because they're being asked to feel and the brain wants to do something. Well, number three is to have a giggle ready because your Jellyfish Brain's going to want to do something and you're not going to do anything, because you're taking yourself out of the stimulated nerve dominant, neural-dominant Jellyfish Brain driving the big old body bus in that dominant place, and you're dropping her back into her aquatic water environment, which is your Jellyfish Brain's actual environment. It's actually purely aquatic, the semi sea water of craniosacral fluid. She floats in it. Her little brain, her little brain stem and her wonderful spinal cord, and reaching out of the Jellyfish Brain's wet suit fabric called the dura, the wet suit of the Jellyfish Brain, are all these tendrils that are your nerves. So, when you sense that, between the world and your bones are literally nerve fibers/tendrils. So, if Jellyfish Brain gets tickled, she's going to want to do stuff, because her job is to coordinate everything.

So, she's going to want to put the lamp back. She wants things the way she remembers they were when she was in a previous groovy place. She's going to want to do this thing and wiggle and fuss, and you're gonna meet her with a giggle, #3.

You're going to meet her saying, "Oh honey, honey, we're not gonna. We're not gonna do that. We're gonna go feel our bones and we're going to make some tea. We're going to take a few minutes and we're just going to sense for our bones, but we're gonna sense for the contact and bones and you're not going to do anything. You're just going to steep." It's the antithesis of what the Jellyfish Brain wants to do. It's so not her tendency. In causing her to pause, you actually disorient the Jellyfish Brain, so she scrambles. It may sound like a nice idea. I know a lot of concepts self-justify by using ideas to trick the Jellyfish Brain. I'm doing the same thing with mild trickery and humor, except we're actually orienting her to her actual environment. Brings us back to 'actually'. That actual information is very lovely, but you're having to disregard a bunch of other stimuli. You're actually telling your neural-dominant external world sensing to piss off for a few minutes, "Oh piss off. I'm making tea out of my own bones." So that's, um, that's exquisite. There's something that shifts and moves in that process. So those three things together are one round of circulated rest, or one felt round of sensing, one measure of music, or one little season. A couple of rounds and you start to have enough experience to steep, to make an experiential tea.

**Christie**  Which three things?

**Michael**  Number One – *Where's your bones?* Number Two –
*Where's the support or push of the world?* Number
Three – *Have a giggle ready*, your Jellyfish Brain's
gonna wanna do something with it. If you do those
first two things, the third thing that *has to be there* is
little giggle for your Jellyfish Brain because she's going
to want to do stuff and she's not allowed, which starts
the cycle all over again, because then the Jellyfish
Brain goes, "Oh my God, we're not doing anything?!"
Nope!

We're going to go back in and find our
bones...Number One – Where's the bones? Number
Two – Where's the contact for bones? Number Three
– "Oh honey... nope, not this round either", and again.
We do another round. So that next round of activity
(actually three or four rounds by now), there's no
mechanical involvement. It's a non-doing (the Taoists
love this, by the way), it's not a not doing, double
negative, it's a non-doing. You aren't mechanically
engaged and, in fact, you're disengaging your Jellyfish
Brain into a non-dominant position, which is her
antithesis place, unless she's in deep sleep or in deep
mediation or on psychotropics. Then she's really
happy, but psychotropics give her a counterpoint,

going, "Oh, I'm on psychotropics. This is great. I'm still in control, though sort of..."

Here in 'this' orienting, you're putting her out of control and you're disorienting her, so you have to have a tenderness ready for that. You have to have something like, "Oh honey, I know...", and a little giggle to meet her neural-dominant response to reorienting to her own bones. Do this orientation for a little while, and all of a sudden you realize when you're neural-dominant, you have a certain shape. You have a certain quality of space, and then when you slide into your bones (you guys can't see this at home, but Christie's sitting across from me now and just went 'bloop'... some part of her attention slides in and over her body).

Now this is important because I'm actually answering her original question. That sliding... the quality of what happens, the substance that goes 'bloop', is the quality of your imagination. It's an actual substance. It's not an esoteric concept. That motion, that movement, that non-mechanical visceral ability to change shape, to move, is the quality of shape that is actually *you*. It is not only energetic. It's not only your imagination. It's substantive, and yet it's unseen. So, it gets coerced, co-opted, nabbed by all these other concepts that want to feed themselves, at one's expense usually.

So, imagination is terribly, terribly important because the mind uses the substance of imagination to do stuff. When it's relegated only to the mind and the neural dominance, then it's kind of opaque and kind of 'out in the field', and some people use it to leave the body sense and go visit other planets, other places. Some people use it when reading books and have their imaginings landscaped beautifully with their minds, which may or may not be internal, because for some folks, it's internal. For some folks, it's not an internal. They open a book and the whole room changes. Some could argue that some people open up a book and the whole world changes, you know, and that's true. It's the substance of imagination that does that. In my work, that's important because when I'm prompting someone, when I'm getting the feel for their garden, their root beds, I will prompt them to find a root bed, to find a bone or a toe or liver or kidney.

That substance that is imagination has such a coherent, cohesive quality, and every person without exception (for the 30+ years I've toyed with this) has this, so I know it's a substance. Um, something responds, moves, and the person's shape changes in response to the prompting. I always prompt towards a bone or an actual location because it's actual information we can use and it's delicious, and it's real (OMG). And then 10,000 concepts show up to feed on such a delicious moment! So that dynamic is part of the imagination.

And then there're tangents that the imagination can take in all these forms and do amazing things, but the viscera, the body, the biology, and the physiology respond to that as a substance, as much as they respond to blood, as much as they respond to proprioceptive information. And you can train somebody to track that. As they learn to sense themselves, they're feeling for the slide of imagination over their bones, right? And then there's lots of things you can do with it which gets very specific. You can teach the periosteum, the wrapping around all bones, which is nervy, like fingertips. You can teach someone to sense and rest the imagination back to the bones, so they're contained. Then, they are actually occupying the life-size space that they *actually* occupy. Then these other parts of them can respond to that intuiting, as well as integrating their awareness and attention.

So, intuition is an interesting thing because it's based on our body of experience. Our imagination is not like a limb, it's an aspect of us that has substance that can go do stuff. For most people, it's mixed in with their mind and just dissipates. It ends up just floating around all the time. In this work, we learn to help someone orient to their own bones, and then start to use their imagination differently, so then when other stuff happens - the change of shape or the change of quality of space – it gives them more information. They aren't hunting or reaching. They're not doing anything first, but they're getting all this wonderful information. As that information is steeped with their awareness, attention and imagination, and their viscera and body parts, and their 'patches' are informed by that delicious tea that they soaked in for a few minutes, then something interesting happens. An aspect of the mind starts to take it out of that mythic feeling. It becomes shaped. It starts to flow into symbols, into shapes, into senses, and then by this time the Jellyfish Brain and the mind can't take it anymore, and they start drawing stuff, and we would say that information gathered in this way would be intuition. It's based on your intelligence, but you're steeping in information without doing anything. Your intuition steeps into informed intelligence.

And then it just can't stop, and you're off and running. Right? The next thing that will incur is an action. Very few people can just sit with their imagination, with their steeping tea sensation. They'll want to go do stuff with it.

The discernment, for me, is that imagination is a quality of space. It's a substance that is part of our biology, is part of our psyche. Then intuition is informed intelligence. As that information gathers, it's going to build potency and it's going to flow into intelligence and start to organize thoughts and become information. So, intuition is informed sensation, informed senses, you know. Your intelligence and your intellect are going to mesh with the sensation and form something, and that forming is intuition, you know, and some people have a beautiful landscape there. There are other people...it's opaque and they very rarely visit that part of the garden. So they think other people are magical. Those other people aren't. They just spend a lot of time in that part of their garden. I've spent a lot of time in literal gardens that just happen to be people. All this has a literal end of the spectrum for me.

Christie   Well so, last time I slid in the lineage, and you said...
Michael   Oh, I carefully ran the hell out of the house!
Christie   You carefully gave it a name, and you were a little upset with me that I slid it in.

**Michael**  I was... things were thrown... the tapes were turned off... and havoc ensued. But that was just with our imagination.

**Christie**  You were very graceful, I thought. I was surprised. I was willing to just say lineage and just leave it at that, and you went in, filled in these names...

**Michael**  I did. I wanted our viewers at home who are listening on the radio to have a sense. Just can't throw in the word 'lineage', although lineage is another root bed. But lineage gets into a very intimate aspect of the social root bed. Lineages are interesting things, especially for people (that would be me) who pooh-poohed them the first three quarters of their life and took great pride in ridiculing and sarcastically running them ragged, and then having to turn around and say, "Shit! There's something to this."

So, 'lineage' is an unbroken line of communication, an unbroken song of collected experiences from a culture's perspective, from the body of a culture. There are lineages all over the planet. Usually, a lineage will infer some indigenous seed to them. There're some indigenous root beds that have cultivated a technology, a type of earth medicine, a way of seeing, a view that's unbroken. It's handed from person to person. And it usually incorporates some sense of ritual and some sense of having to go through some initiatory process to, um, earn the right to handle that technology from an indigenous point of view. There are lots of living lineages on the planet, and the livingness seems to be important because a lot of people create and amalgamate stuff, reweave stuff and do stuff. And there's a lot of stuff... (the phone rings) (M)... so wonderfully interrupted, but a beautiful example of a lineage and the thread in society and how we're plugged in through it all, because those are also important root beds.

This lineage was, and is, an example of a great root bed. And um, and for some people, the 'call' to a particular path is very similar to that phone call we just heard. They have a resonance to an idea, to a concept and they get the 'call', which is their intuition getting substantial. And then, all of a sudden, their imagination starts to want that. It starts to drool. It starts to get substantive. And they go, "I got to follow that." For some people, that immersion is necessary. For other people, they stumble into it. I would be considered one of those people that stumbled and was nabbed by it, by a lineage, a living tendril from a long-established social garden. I won't get too dramatic here, but it's... it can be a very dramatic, "Pause!"

[Insert dramatic pause here!]

I was fortunate to be in the right place at the right time and studying with one of my teachers, not understanding  I was going into an initiatory process (probably another book!). That tradition is from the Q'ero, the high Andes Peruvian people of South America. They have several unbroken earth-medicine lineages. And um, I was lucky enough to be part of that. That culture is beautiful because they are very symbolically oriented. They'll use whatever item is within grabbing reach and will take their imagination and take their intuition and mix them together and imbue that object with a symbolic reference to something else. And it will be true, it is true!. "Indigenousy" doesn't belong to any one thing or peoples. It's the... there's no verb... 'to Be'. Go figure! (Thank you, Martin Prechtel!) And they use that so they can access that mythic layer that can't 'be' said or shaped, to find a way to feed what in the moment needs to be fed, and for them, nothing gets in the way of that. It can look sloppy and silly and graceful and sacred, and usually should have a little bit of humor to it from that culture's point of view. The Q'ero are wonderful in that way. So as an Anglo, I got to have the good fortune of spending years in that training process, so I have earned the rights in that lineage. I've been initiated. For me, that's a very private corner. It takes us into a whole different type of dialogue.

But privacy is what nourishes me. It may not be what nourishes you. What nourishes another person may not be what nourishes me. Part of your privacy is what you use to self-nourish. For me, that tradition nourishes a corner of my soul. And it so happens I have the luxury of having a practice that allows me to hold the tenants of that tradition and still practice in an Anglo way, um, and work with people to have this gardening perspective of, "How do I meet a person where they're at?" This lineage is another way for me to have an added view and an added set of resources, a way to feed my imagination, a way to create a larger landscape for my intuition to scramble and dance upon. And so, in my responses to another human being, I have these options. I spend a lot of time there privately, a lot of time in those layers, that part of my 'garden', long before I leave my nest, my home and go out into the world.

Then, when I get to the office, I spend my time preparing my office because my office is not my private space. It's a communal space. It's a space for the community. I'm its gatekeeper. I'm the tender of that symbology, the living symbology of an office to be available to another person's experience. And so, I get

to handle their bodies, I'm handling their skin. I'm
handling the skin of a living drum. I'm using movement
and I'm exploring their root beds. The rattle and
substance and song, and expression of that garden,
gets to come through and be handled and I get to tend
to that. That all falls within that lineage's point of view
about tending the soul, about tending a person,
tending the connection to the community.

So for me it gives me great strength, but also it
gives me resources that can take my usual views,
habits of working, and turns them upside down, cuz I
come in with agendas and the people come in with
agendas and there's a real office full of agendas, or we
come over to Christie's house, and we have these
agendas in these questions and then we're seeing and
sensing what we can do.

So, the lineage is one corner, the cranial work is
another corner, um, other aspects of my life are other
corners. And then I have a corner that's a big, "I don't
know!", developmentally speaking, which is the most
fantastic corner ever. I can use these different aspects
as perspective and places to be responsive to
somebody else's experience, somebody else's body.

**Christie**  My experience is that if I ask about the lineage and
what you have taught me, about the layers i.e. the
literal, the symbolic, the mythic and the spirit... those

layers, I don't even know what you call them, layers of existence, layers of reality, layers of experience..?

**Michael**  You could say that they are levels of engagement.

**Christie**  ...levels of engagement..

**Michael**  would be an easy, would be much easier.

**Christie**  So does that come from that lineage?

**Michael**  It comes from that lineage, in particular. It comes, I think, from other things as well, but what I like specifically with the South Americans... they, especially the Inca, were/are really good at consolidating their world, and that's all the Inca did over 150+ years. Not very long, but they took all these different communities, these 'patches' of people, the legs of the culture, and they wanted to make a cohesive circulatory system between these 'patches' of people. Not unlike inside of a body. You can have great discord in one part of the body, which has learned how to do one thing, has its own language. Another hairball of the body has it's own different language, and this shoulder over here was hit by dad when you were two so that has its own interpretation and fear of the world. And then mother yelled at you through your left ear. And so that has its own thing. So, a human's body has 'patches' of existence. In South America it was true, the Inca, their beauty was going, "Wait a minute. Let's just reorient here for a moment. It may take the time it takes, but we're going to do it." And they wanted to make a cohesive connection between the 'peoples', the 'patches', of those communities. They didn't want this disparate, this village counterpointing that village, to have a sense of self. They were like, "Wait, we're all a big body and we're all stretched out long, but we're connected. So, let's get connected." It was really lovely. They went in and consolidated, made cohesion, a circulated common song!

What was beautiful is that they didn't go in and destroy. They went in and sat, and they prayed, and they talked to the elders of each village and the youngsters, and they had a lot of conversation. They met and palpated it, each village, to bring out, um, the symbols and the qualities of their beliefs that were still working, that were still feeding, that were still practically useful. And they went from place to place to do that. After they did a huge span of a lower continent and they're like, "OK, we can do this." So they laid down 'the roads', the Inca Trail. They laid down the wonderful venous supply of South America, the Inca Trail, which are a capillary bed and the arteries of that culture. They set up runners. They set up a circulatory system of communication so that there could be cohesion, and they rebuilt temples.

They found the temples, the centers, that were still very alive, and if it wasn't alive, it was broken down and reused in the areas that were still alive. The ancestors of those individual 'patches' were acknowledged and deeply, deeply respected, but only if they fed. If they were bastards, they were broken down, which has a sense of justice to it, which I really appreciate, as a practitioner, as an Anglo, as a human, as a living creature!

I personally really appreciated that, because in therapy you're doing something very similar. You're looking at these lineages of a person's experience, these segments of time, these seasons in one's life, and the stories and things that happened within those individual seasons, and the things that went from season to season, and you're trying to pull out the things that are nourishing and will still continue to nourish, while disregarding, and sometimes breaking down, the things that aren't nourishing, the things that are literally just holding on for no practical reason, holding on and managing their 'patch' out of habit.

The Inca were masters at attempting to destroy habit and replacing it with nourishment and giving a cohesive language so that a villager could go to another village and interact. It's really quite beautiful and done in a relatively short period of time...that kind of reorienting to the bones of the culture. In that respect, it's very encouraging to me as a practitioner, to be cross-culturally pollinated, informed but still maintaining my Anglo-ness, realizing, "That's another culture." And I have deep respect for the difference of that.

That same respect of differences then gets mirrored back in my practice. Person comes in, they may look one way, but their behavior and what happens on the table may be completely different. And that has been in my face time and time again, you know? Yes, some of us are our cultural lineages for sure but, surprisingly enough, it's usually cross-cultural and, maybe, even half the time there's another living aspect to a person that's non-culturally based, which I find fascinating, you know? Or they might be deeply informed by some whole other concept. These things that feed a person get to be quite complex and quite fascinating and need to have a high level of respect. A certain hairball may be odd, but if it nourishes and feeds this person, I may tease it, mind you, to tease it out, but I won't go there unless I already have a sense of respect for it. If I have a sense of respect for the process, and my little sheep dog or Jaguar gets triggered, I'm going on the hunt, you know, and we're

going to get some work done. It has that kind of
tenacity, but it's a tenacity on behalf of the person, on
behalf of their garden. That's where the advocacy of
gardening or advocacy of being there on behalf of the
parts of the person that can't speak, comes in handy.
There's definitely a layer of the work that's informed
by another lineage or by a tradition that belongs to
another culture. Respectfully said, of course.

# Chapter Five: *Interview #3*

**Christie**  There are a bunch of questions that came up from last time. So last time you talked about the lineage being a cornerstone and then you said Craniosacral was another and then you had several others. Just wondered what about Craniosacral...what tools or what context or how does it result in it being a cornerstone for you? That's the question.

**Michael**  Nice question. The cornerstone is, is um, William Garner Sutherland himself, the grandfather and founder of cranial osteopathy. Really it's osteopathic in its intent.

**Christie**  Which means what?

**Michael**  Osteopathy was founded and developed by Andrew Taylor Still, M.D. D.O., in the late 1800's. He was a doctor in the Civil War who came out of it not wanting just to chop people up, but to get involved in their physiology, their biology, um, from a sacred point of view, from a deeply devotional point of view, an active prayer point of view. So that created Osteopathy. William Garner Sutherland became an osteopath, a D.O (Doctor of Osteopathy). I like his story because he started out very interested in newsprints and newspaper writing and wanted to be a writer. At some point he liked the whole mechanism of the printing

press process, which in those days were these long

conveyor belts, you know, and the types were set, and

they were layered, and there was a precision that

needed to happen for a newspaper to happen, for

information to be circulated. There had to be these

processes in place to have that happen, which at the

time was very magical. Writing is still magic, in all

traditions.

So, William Sutherland had this background from

an early age. He got to work on printing press lines,

and he got so fascinated with it and so good at doing a

print press line, he could figure out where the

machines needed to be adjusted in the line to keep

the layered process happening, because if you were

off at all, the end--product was shifted to "Unreadable

print." Oh yeah. So, everything was layered on top of

everything to make it come together clearly. A little

shift in that process and the information doesn't end

up clean, crisp and legible. He already had this

mechanically deep experience, and also then

understanding a bigger picture, like being able to look

at the whole line. These things were very, very long

and involved and intricate. He had to be able to go

find what needed to be adjusted. This was long before

he knew about osteopathy. And then through his

circumstances, he needed some help with his health and ended up with an osteopath, got touched by it, and decided he was going to go off to osteopathy school. And he did that... He got the call!

Every day at school he walked down a hall by this cabinet of bones. In the cabinet there was a model, which was a disarticulated skull. The cranial bones were exactly in place but blown out a little bit, so there's a little space between every bone. It's a very precise model but you could see between all the bones. This captured his attention during his education. He didn't know why.

One day he was standing staring at this disarticulated skull and this little thought came to his head. He was looking at the temporal bones, which are where the ears are on the head, and they are squamid like a seashell. "And they are beveled like gills of a fish for respiration... For the respiratory mechanism." That was the statement in his mind, "Beveled, like the gills of fish for respiration, for the respiratory mechanism." So they float on each other, you know... and something happened. He went on with his education, but it haunted him. He thought about it all the time because, even in those days, it was considered at some point that all the bones of the head fuse. In fact today, a lot of educated people still have this idea of fused joints for the head. They think it's a solid thing. Um, technically that's not true. Even though it's been proven not true, there are still a lot of people who hold onto that 'solid' view. They're not interested in how a small joint moves. They like the big joints.

So here Sutherland is, back in the early 1900's at this point, you know, having this thing haunt him and he starts to privately, in his 'privacy' to deeply investigate. And the curiosity doesn't completely leave him. He goes on with his practice... he's working with people as an osteopath, and so he's going on with his life. He's acquired a couple of skulls, and he starts to disarticulate them, using a little pen knife, and really noticing and really working with the joints and really learning to pry them apart to see if they're actually joints. He's so taken... but he has to prove it to himself, because osteopathy is still a scientific study. The osteopaths don't go for a lot of um, let's say flippant ideas, you know. You have to prove your mark. It's still a science. He was like, "I don't know if this is true or not, but I can't stop thinking about this." So he started experimenting with skulls and disarticulating them himself and putting them back together, and really seeing this respiratory mechanism that happens in the dura in the cranial system. The dura is the surrounding of the brain and spinal cord from head to tail, literally. And that dura is a thumbnail thickness, and if you cut a thumbnail and soak it in water overnight, it has mobility, but it doesn't have elasticity. So there's this amazingly strong fabric, and it holds its own seawater. Craniosacral fluid is its own substance and it's very akin to sea water. It both nourishes and holds and cleanses the brain and gets manufactured in the brain as well. It's also a manufactured fluid. It's its own *unique* thing. The fluid has such consistency that hydraulically the brain can't hit the sides of the skull. The spinal cord doesn't touch the side of the membrane. It's actually held in fluid. You can do an experiment with an apple and a closed jar full of water. If you shake the jar, you actually can't get the apple to touch the glass because fluid has a certain viscosity to it, and a certain hydraulic pressure to it. That's a whole different science. It's very fascinating. The physics of it is just fascinating.

Well, here he (Sutherland) is in the early 1900's, working with these ideas and also having a practice working with people who are coming in who were injured and diseased and going through all their things because he is considered a doctor. He starts to do little experiments on himself. He creates this helmet out of leather by which he starts inhibiting specific bones of the head. His wife proceeds to express her concern, and also sees the changes that happen, which he logs. So, he's doing all this, and he does this for 30 years before he ever starts to write about this in the journals of osteopathy. After 30 years going, "No, there's something to this. This cranial mechanism is a respiratory action. It has movement, it has flow, it has pulse, and the bones move in response to the circulation patterns of cranial sacred fluid as an indicator of health to the cranial system, to the neural system as a primary system."

That fascinates me as well. Not to the extent that I want to become an osteopath, but to the part of me that got introduced to the cranial work early in my bodywork education, you know. Within the first six months of my massage training, I was introduced to Rolfing and Rosen work, Polarity, Shiatsu, regular massage and, ultimately, cranial work. I had these different exposures, and I liked the science of cranial. I liked the physiology and the biology of it, of cranial work, all of it. For me, all of a sudden, anatomy and physiology were just like 'wah', like my brain kicked on. I was in my early twenties, so I was ripe, really ripe, and Sutherland's story personally really spoke to me because here's someone who had a practical background. He didn't have a trust fund (no offense intended), he didn't go from college right into medicine, you know, he had a previous life. I know there's something about that really touched me and really spurred my own interest.

So I got involved with the Milne institute, which trains Craniosacral practitioners, and I started assisting and I was allowed to co-teach. One day, I heard Hugh Milne of the Milne Institute say that he would have liked to have seen a potential teacher have a practice for five years before they became an instructor. He was starting to notice this parroting happening in the institute. It was a very young institute at the time. When I was there it was before he wrote his books and before, you know... he was still putting together his institute. I was really in the right place at the right time. I've been fortunate to be in many things at that kind of transitional time where things are a little wacky. I like it, I get nourished by it, I need it!

So the cranial work, it really got me. Later, come to find out, I started having memories of my own head injuries and spinal injuries and I was actually in a great deal of pain that I didn't know about because I had coped with it since birth. Everything just kind of added on another layer. But I was thick and numb and strong and shut down and could lift a house but couldn't put it anywhere. I had no mobility, no elasticity, but a tremendous amount of strength. I was a very strong gorilla as a young man. I could grab my kneecaps up until my mid-twenties, so I was actually a gorilla. Then I had a growth spurt, thank goodness!

So, the cranial work, I just loved it. I just took to it. It made sense to me. And while I was in the massage school, I also started teaching, and so I was handling bodies every day in a private practice. I was handling them as a teacher in the classroom. I was teaching a little bit of everything, from Shiatsu to Polarity to just standard certification classes and assisting in the Milne Institute, assisting other teachers in other classes. I was um, what do they call that? A classroom addict! I had to be in everything all the time. I couldn't get enough. I ended up working in the office for a small massage school. I was just fortunate, and meanwhile I was in all the cranial classes I could get into as a student and assistant. I was assisting all the teachers who would let me. And, and I just, that was my whole world.

While that was happening, I met my mentor who was a Rolfing movement practitioner and teacher, Vivian Jaye, who was one of the main people for the Rolf Institute's movement work because, for her, she was born with a malformed hip, and so every time the

Rolfers tried to make her do a straight line, they took away her function. She didn't function in straight lines, so she had to get involved in the movement part of the Rolfing program, um, in order to teach the Rolfers that function doesn't mean straight lines. Ida Rolf was very structural, but she was structural because she needed to express this new information, this new aspect of biology. Ida Rolf was a biologist. She was very intense and very clear with her information, and she had to keep it clear. She held her whole world together, you know.

So Vivian came in saying, "Wait a minute, you can't set someone into dysfunction for the sake of the structure. You have to help the structure integrate into a new function and that has to be done through movement." So, Vivian ended up doing a lot of her Rolfing within movement, not driving her elbow down someone's thigh. So that, that was significant to me.

I was in a class and she came in and worked with our little group early on. A woman was going on about how the music had to be right, and the scene had to be right, and atmosphere had be right. It had to be healing, and she was going on and on, as new people with a new concept do, and I could see this little Jewish woman, Vivian, sharp as a knife in those days, get more and more agitated.

Vivien finally shot this woman down and said, "No, this work should be done in a bus depot." And the little street kid in me woke up, and said, "You're fuck'n right!" This is within the first couple months of my training. I was digging the love, light and happiness, let's heal and experiment with the body sort of thing. It was really cool in my early twenties, but Vivian's statement and her tenaciousness and her intensity were so real for me, so alive, that it spoke to me, too. So, I'm having this great other experience. I'm getting exposed to cranial work and Polarity, Shiatsu, movement, etc. etc. Meanwhile, there's this feisty Jewish movement worker going, "Wait a minute, you know, don't get off course. You have to meet a person where they're at, and if you're in a bus depot you should be able to do all this work. Everything you think you can do, you should be able to do... at anytime, anywhere, any place."

Within a month I was working at a PT office on top of everything because she was right. I was in this industry that was counterculture and being fed by the counter-to-the-counter counterculture, and doing their wonderful acid aerobics, which is awfully cool. Don't get me wrong. I think it's very good and beautiful. But the practical street kid in me, um, which is maybe another corner we could talk about, um, woke up and was like, I can't, I can't go counter point to the medical community because they're just as devoted to their practices, and everybody argues with each other. So that can't be a justification, you know, for counterpoint – duh!

So, then I was in this PT office where I'm working on really injured people, serious situations. I'm working with highly educated people, including an amazing, also cantankerous, physical therapist. (Thank you. Claire!) She came in one day and said, "You're doing beautiful, lovely work, but it's an expensive aspirin. You have to get in and work with and through the pain of these people. You have to get the job done. This tissue will not heal itself, will not do what it needs to do, if the scar tissue and these other situations aren't opened up." Oh, oh shit, I have a job, and I'm not there to be liked or be nice or any of that thing, (not that I wasn't), but that also woke up something.

So, I had these two dynamics and this access to people off the street who don't care about your belief system, who don't care who you are, who don't want to be in a PT office in the first place, ninety percent of the time, who are really angry that their life has been interrupted by their trauma, and you're touching their trauma, causing them more trauma to get them out of trauma. Your face is now on their material, and you've also updated their material. They either love ya' or they hate ya', and you have to get the same job done despite their affect, their attitude, despite their expression. Holy crap! Then, I go from there back to the massage school. Everybody's like, yeah, "Let's heal each other." Oh my God, it's juicy! "Oh, we can heal, and not hurt them. Oh, oh..." Yeah. In 57 different modalities! And then Vivian, "Hey, if you're in a bus depot..." Then the cranial community going, "Okay, but there's this other layer to the mechanism, to the interior. Yes, you guys are doing stuff with the body, but it's overstimulating. You aren't listening to this cranial layer."

Holy Crap... so I'm, I'm getting wacky, but I'm finding that in the PT office, it's the cranial work that's being very effective. A little rototilling to get to the cranial work, which sets up my lifestyle right there, early on. I didn't know it at the time, but I don't mind rototilling. I'm not afraid of a body, especially after being in the PT office because I'm, I'm working on all these crazy situations, and I'm having to *really* work, because I'm the hands of the therapist, you know? I'm the one doing that manual labor, which I love, because I am a worker bee, and then I'm also in this cranial work saying, "You know, there's this other layer that yes, you can do all this other work, but you've got to take a moment to listen to the actual distress, to actually listen and palpate the actual trauma, to actually be open to feel their psychotic corner, you know," and ...

**Christie** Psychotic and psychotic corner?

**Michael** Okay, so here we come and bring in Marion Woodman, who's the goddess of Jungian psychology, in my view, next to Dr. Clarissa Pinkola Estes, the other goddess of psychology. When something is traumatized, everything's affected. We can break it down and differentiate it and put it in its layers and figure out its working mechanisms from the Jungian to the physiological, you know, from the entangled, actual root beds of the physiology of the fiber on out to what happened in their life story, in their soul around that disgruntled hairball's fibers, right? It's across the whole spread. When something has been set in a person's system and psyche for a while, it creates this little bit of psychosis, this little bit of embedded attention, protecting attention, protecting a neighborhood of tissue who's in distress or perceived distress or overwhelm.

**Christie** So why do you call it psychosis?

**Michael** Um, because it's crazy and it doesn't fit into everything else that's going on around it, right? It's a, it's a psychotic situation. It's so self-protective. It will harm everything to self-protect, you know, and it doesn't have a global consciousness, right? It is literally a scared, frightened feral cat, cornered, with claws and teeth, and it can't do anything else but use claws and teeth. We have these corners, these, um, there's better words for it, but I, I like calling it, 'the psychotic corner'. Um, and other cranial work, like in Upledger, they view it as 'a cyst', they call it an 'energy cyst', which has a whole other inference. I like pursuing Woodman's. I like her phrasing, "Trauma is any arrested movement."

But it's that idea that an area that's so self-protective, is *really* self-protective, and it has to be understood and met, and it has to be met where it's at, not where we want it to be or where the rest of the body/mind wants it to be. Hence the word 'psychosis' or 'psychotic corner'. Because the overall person wants to get on with their life. "Get back to who they were, to do what they want to do when they want to do it, how they want to do it." And there's a corner of them that isn't doing that. 10,000 therapies later (Thank you, ancestors for your diligence).

In the office, at the Physical Therapy office especially, I'm getting these people and many of them can't speak English, so I'm contacting the last place they want contact. But the first place that needs to be worked on. Right? So, I'm getting this... begruntled human being. And then in the cranial work I'm giving this encouragement to come in slowly because you don't know what this material is. They can come in and say 'car crash' or 'abuse' in the relationship or the myriad of things in between, but you may not know...the underlying story may not be knowable, and you have to be sensitive to that. Marion Woodman is saying any trauma is an arrested movement. That's her statement. It's the most beautiful, eloquent grandmotherly thing to say really, "Trauma is any arrested movement, any movement that's not allowed to continue to its own fruition." The interruption of that starts trauma, starts all the physiological and psychological processes in response to protect something that's now out of sync with everything else. Oh, my Goodness!!!

And at the time, I'm just a kid. My brain is not even developed... age 28 to 32 is brain development's last stage before you're an adult, by the way (crazy people). I'm 24, 25 at this point. Holy Crap! So those two contrasts really spoke to me. I'm finding in all the things that I'm learning that it turns out that this layer of cranial work, this layer of going, "Wait a minute, there's a (cranial) system and the idea that the different parts of the biology really do communicate with each other, and that you can get involved in that circulated communicative process, and that you can meet that where it's at or even attempt to do that, is actually necessary." It was just blowing my mind. And trying to do it at a PT office, in a birdcage, while people are coming in and out all the time, can make you a bit crazy. Then to try to look at all these other modalities that I've been learning and using and working in my private practice, in the classroom, while being respectful to those ideas and concepts, then bringing in this other layer, in my own understanding was... it was beautiful... I was fortunate!

It was all a great challenge, but now you know, by this time, my Shiatsu is changing, and my Polarity is changing, and just general tissue work is changing because I'm looking at all these as part of a whole. Even though all these different concepts are saying they are part of a whole and look at the body holistically, um, they're still driving their intent into the tissue, right? Right! They aren't approaching the body slowly.

This is interesting because then there's these other modalities like Rosen work that sit and wait. Use the same idea from a completely different viewpoint. So cranial work can be very slow and you're really listening and you're waiting and really interacting with the whole community at the level of the little tissues. Rosen work is just coming right to the edge and hanging out there and waiting for the physiology to come to you. That was Marion (yes, another Marion) Rosen's brilliant discovery. Like, wait a minute, the body *cannot not react*. A living organism *cannot not react*, and Reich (Dr. Wilhelm Reich, MD, Psychoanalyst) discovered this as well, and mapped out its reactions at a cellular level (Thank you, Mr. Reich). So, Rosen just hung out and discovered, by really paying attention, that the body actually went through the processes that it needed to go through. She had her own grandmotherly, "Oh honey, I'm right here for you!", kind of attention. She was discovering that she'd go after something and it would just, it would scurry. It would go feral, but if she hung out, the feral cat would come to her because contact is a type of food. The biology can't not react, so if you give it something it can react to, and hang out there long enough, it will work through the things that it has to work through in order to establish that contact. But if you go after it, it turns feral. Hmm. Brilliant!

And then when you're done with that, you have to move. She loved movement. Movement was a part of it but not during session work. Process and establishing a healthier interaction through the tissues, through the systems, first, and then expression second. Experience first, and then the expression and exploration of that experience second. You had to move, you couldn't just have hands on the table and then say, "Oh, I had my release, and off you go!", and have your story. No way... after working with that, you had to move. It had to integrate.

So now we're back to the Rolfing thing. You have to move to integrate. Then we're back to the cranial thing. If it can't move, it can't integrate.

Oh, my Goodness! So cranial work, for me, gives me the umbrella to hold all these different practices and modalities and gives me a viewpoint. When I look at someone, there's this literal jellyfish in a Ziploc bag. There's this cranium and brain stem and wonderful cord, spinal cord, in its own container, in a human being. That's their primary system. Everything outside of that system is secondary, is a different system. All the other physiology is there to support the dance of the brain, brain stem, spinal cord and tendrils. It's a whole jellyfish, oh, my Goodness!, When the Jellyfish Brain can dance, everyone, everything, inside and out gets fed... back and forth, to and fro.

And then you start watching people move from that place and it's a whole different thing. It's not about this muscle doing that, that muscle doing this. We have to strengthen that. We have to correct this. We have the rototill that. We have to get that in balance with this. It's not, it's not formulaic anymore, but it doesn't discount the formulas you need to do the work on those neighborhoods, in order to support the expression of that person's Jellyfish Brain, you know, to express that aquatic nature of exploring one environment into another.

You know, our internal environment is aquatic. Our external environment is terrestrial. But air isn't that much different than water (So I learned in science class, and I watched it this morning as the fog came in and dripped all over me, you know? I'm going, "I'm praying for sun. Lighten this shit up or I'm going to drown in fog. I may be a Jellyfish, but I'm not a fish. Jelly inside, but I'm not a fish. What a kerfuffle!"). Cranial work is the other corner that allows me to palpate and meet someone where they're at, whether I touch them or not. It gives me an encouragement to, if I have the luxury of time and I'm outside the office I can slow down and you know, track someone if I need to.

But if they pay me, I have to put on my therapeutic goggles and go to work. So, I might rototill someone for a long time to get everything prepared for a layer of cranial work, because I believe in integration. I'm an integrationist. You can't just go do a little piece of cranial work, get a person really high because it will get the physiology very high. They will have an altered experience because you're meeting the psyche in a place most people don't get met. You're contacting them at a layer that very rarely ever gets touched but has always yearned for that. So, there is an altered state that happens, and this is what's funny... every good therapy, no matter what the modality, if one person meets another person, there's a high to it. There's an altered state that happens.

**Christie**  Well, what about cranial work?...can that be left 'secondary'?

**Michael**  What I like about it is that it can be left 'secondary', right? It can be left as part of the processes of the physiology coming to a healthier baseline, you know. I don't use homeostasis because I'm not so sure about it. Even after 30+ years, I'm not so sure about that. But I know that there is an interaction in the neighborhood of cells and psyche that likes to integrate, and some of them can get there, some of them can't. Some of the tangled hairballs and the trauma a person goes through can be horrendous. There is no homeostasis, there is no drive. It's not capable, you know?      So, you have to introduce and develop and grow a healthy baseline so that

process can find itself. That's the mistake I think a lot

of the new agers and a lot of the health people make

when they throw in the homeostasis thing, "The

system will drive towards homeostasis." Well, Mr.

William Reich discovered it doesn't drive itself. It

drives itself to coherence, and its ability to create a

coherent, manageable, coordinated system is

phenomenal, is so highly adaptive, but it's not

homeostatic.

**Christie**  Define homeostatic.

*Michael*  The drive for balance. It's an idea that's very

perpetuated in the health industry, especially the

alternative health industry. "If we just provide this and

this, then that'll happen."

**Christie**  Oh, I see.

*Michael*  It's a, it's a nice, gentle, but still formulaic expression,

and it actually keeps you from interacting sometimes

and intervening, right? Which some of the other

health professionals have in spades. They are willing

to intervene 'on behalf'. That's right. That's their

advocacy. Now we're back to that. Yeah. So cranial

work allows me to have my bone advocacy, to look at

the bones as living coral reefs that give ballast to the

aquatic system that ultimately the Jellyfish Brain gets

to coordinate because her job is to coordinate and

explore. All her senses are designed for that. So how do you help her get there?

**Christie** So it's interesting to me because, um, there's what we talked about last time... advocacy for the biology and, you know, you made a very strong argument or were strong that you are speaking for the tissues that don't have a tongue or they can't speak.

*Michael* That's right.

**Christie** And then today you just said, and then there's the brain and nervous system as the primary system. Yeah. What I'm getting is that there's... I don't know if there's homeostasis, but one can't really do its job without the other.

*Michael* Yes.

**Christie** Because many therapies, psychological as well as even physical ones, gear towards the neural...

*Michael* Yes.

**Christie** ...as primary, because it is primary in many, many ways...

*Michael* In many ways, in many perspectives, it has to be considered primary.

**Christie** ... but it can't do its job if the other is not able.

*Michael* That's right. Yeah, what a quagmire, right? Yeah. So those things probably have to come into balance. Oh, my Goodness!

**Christie** Want me to state...?

184

**Michael**  I'm usurping my own idealism with my own idealism
and counter pointing my counter to the counter to
counter the experiential counterpoint. And that's true.
It's very hard to put into words.

**Christie**  But it makes sense.

**Michael**  It makes sense. My job, what I've fallen into, is that
the cranial work gives me the advocacy to do
whatever I can do to help the Jellyfish Brain be
expressive, to help the Jellyfish Brain integrate and to
unwind. Beautiful word, unwinding. Literally unwind
the hairball that surrounds the psychotic corner...

**Christie**  Okay.

**Michael**  ... you know... which is preventing the expression. Um,
it, it's um,

**Christie**  The movement?

**Michael**  This is what's really interesting. I don't know about
preventing. It's definitely inhibiting. Right? It's
definitely caused a responsive and adaptive thing to
happen in the biological environment. It's definitely
doing its job to do that. What's tricky is that corner,
those hairballs, those entanglements can also be the
very thing holding the person together. Right? Right!
This gets tricky. You have a, you have all the different
therapies that are going in wanting to heal and solve
that current dilemma, but they're moving too fast.
They aren't slowing it down saying, "Wait a minute.

There has to be a lot of other things in place so that when that hairball lets go, there's some *There*, there."

So, now you've got all the people saying, "Develop your core!", right? Or the psychological people saying, "You'd better know your story!" Um, and that's all true, but I think it's a matter of pacing, of slowing it down and saying, "Wait a minute... yes, I want this person to feel better. This person really wants to feel better, but let's step back a little bit."

I have to be careful because I'm not a psychotherapist, but I have to acknowledge the person's story, and that's where that bone or body advocacy comes in. The story is right there in their body. I can go and look at them and say, "Well, if we unravel this, which is all of our wants, if our desire at the moment is to release the pressure and tension in the person's field, and now in my field, because they're in proximity and they're paying me to help them. If I go after that, there may not be things in place to help support them." Right - Wait just a minute. There's a lot going on there. Not only do they need to have the physiological and biological support for something to let go into, but they better have some people in their community there because they will have to maybe have some help in that support. In that integration there also has to be a community and a language and all these other things in place to catch them as well.

You might change their psychotic corner. They might resolve that issue, but now they're in counterpoint to their family and friends that are part of their psychotic corner. They're part of their managing... They've all (inside and out) developed these intricate, intricate relationships, as intricate as any physiology. These intricate relationships that are dependent on the song that they sing daily, and all the cross-woven, inter-related relationship lines are also dependent on this person's particular feel/color/song at the moment, which took their whole life up until that moment to develop and weave. You've just changed that feel/color/song. Now their friends are going to the person, "Who are you?" And they're trying to make them be the same person they were six weeks ago.

And their family goes, "Wait a minute!", and "We don't know what's happened in our family!" Right? But all of a sudden, the family's going, "What are, what are you talking about? What do you mean you remembered that or that or that. What are you talking about?"

In solving the physiological problem in their 'patch' of a leg (for lack of a better place), you know, um, you've now set up a discord in their life that they're going to have to be able to address. And that doesn't go well a lot of times. So, if you go slow enough, then you ask the questions of the person, "Do they have these other support systems? Do they have this other thing?" At that point, if those things aren't in place, then you just make nice, you do something small, you do something integrable, and, and you start talking to the person about their physiology.

So, the cranial work gives me a place to keep stepping back up into because I'm advocating ultimately, yes, for this person's Jellyfish Brain and full function and clarity in their expression, but I got to tend to the garden of their body so their Jellyfish Brain can have that ease of mobility - but it's not so simple. There's a lot, there's a lot of gardening, and that's why I like the term gardening. That's why the cranial work is a huge corner for me, why I'm so thankful to Sutherland, and why I keep coming back to his personal story - because it gives me a way to slow down and go, okay. That was his experience and look what happened. He actually gave me my field of work! There're a lot of different cranial views, you know, that we've kind of discussed, which I'm very grateful for, but none of them have put the time in that

|            |                                                                 |
|------------|-----------------------------------------------------------------|
|            | Sutherland did. 30+ years of uncovering, reorienting, and then sharing and training... |
| **Christie** | 30+ years is a lot! |
| *Michael*  | ... is a heck of a thing to do his own work and say to the anatomists and the medical field at the time, "Wait a minute. You're doing all this medical intervention, but some of these issues you're missing. You're mobilizing a person in all the different ways that we do, including surgeries, in order to help a person, but we're leaving out the most important piece, the brain... not only the brain as a neurological organ but the brain as a landscape and environment and entire layer of movement and motion, you know?! The brain's function is entirely dependent on the movement of her joints and it's not her big body joints. It turns out she has all these cranial joints. She has her own oceanic experience that needs to be in function and moving so that she can be nourished, so that she can be cleansed, so that she can be clear to have her neural functions moving the way that they should." And that's pretty, I don't know... it still completely speaks to me and gives me more encouragement to be the advocate for that environment, you know? Not to go after her directly, but to be the advocate for her - the garden, her environment, so she has that opportunity. Then to |

point out all the other support she may need and make sure that that opportunity is nourished and integrated, not just in her own biology but in her own inner eco-psychology, her own place, her own inner community. And that gets off on a lot of other tangents at that particular juncture for me.

**Christie** Yeah. Well, I just kind of got hung up there for a minute around the question of the 'high', you know. In a certain sense what I'm hearing you say is that it's relatively easy, if you know what you're doing, to bring people into an altered state, particularly through the cranial work, because of its rarity and because it's primary.

*Michael* Yes

**Christie** ...but what I'm also hearing you say, is that there are all these other considerations of what the right timing is and if you go for the 'high', it's kind of like sugar or kind of like...

*Michael* It may not, for me, it may not even be about that. It may not be integrable.

**Christie** Yeah, okay.

*Michael* It may be an expensive aspirin.

**Christie** Yeah.

*Michael* And then there's the PT statement, right? Early on in my career it's like these little statements that, "It should be done in a bus depot.", and "That's expensive aspirin!", really hit home from, you know, a person like me who grew up trailer trash and, you know, a little desperate in my own development, and those statements also spur engagement for me, "Oh, well, if this is an expensive aspirin, how do I not be an expensive aspirin, right? How can I come back to advocating for function?" Yeah. And integration. Yeah. Oh, this should be able to be done in the bus depot, I should be able to do cranial work in a PT office. I shouldn't have to wait to try and repeat the expanded state of the classroom when a charismatic teacher is teaching.

Hugh Milne has charisma, you know, he commands the space. Also, the most amazing storyteller and the most amazing Jellyfish Brain. People really enjoyed his stories and enjoyed his charisma. But he's also probably one of the most intelligent men I've met. His command of anatomy, physiology in a practical use...formidable. He just has that kind of intellect. And he has such a varied background that he can command the esoteric as well as the physiological, you know... his, his anatomical stuff. What I loved about his cranial teaching is that one quarter of it was completely dedicated to anatomy.

You know, anatomy was so important to understand. It wasn't just about being able to do the hold and have the release, you know, that's not what it was about. It was about really understanding how these things interacted, and to understand there was a psychotic corner, to understand that this living thing had a living story, and sometimes the wounding was so far in the story, that the story had to be contacted at the same time as a physiologic, that those two things could be contacted, and that you can see those things, in some way, and that you had to slow down and go into an expanded state to see/feel/sense that, to be respectful of the person's experience. Oh Yeah. And then his students try to do that individually. Then there's the PT Office, you know. Half the people were not English speakers. That was a wonderful challenge. Wonderful. Wonderful. Yeah, nine years' worth.

**Christie** So then now I'm kind of wanting to go over to this other subject a little bit to see how... to explore a little what you've talked to me about with the lineage teaching and practice... What you would call 'levels of engagement'?

*Michael* Yeah.

**Christie** So how do those... I don't know if you want to speak a little bit more, you know, just to lay some groundwork as to what that means, but how does that relate to what Hugh was talking about?

**Michael**  So Hugh's great because he really saw this need to encourage a person to see what they saw, and to slow down and soften so they could take a larger look at someone and be responsive to that 'seeing', so that 'seeing' was that 'heart of listening', which is his slogan. There is a heart to listening. There's a heart to seeing. There's an empathy that happens. For Hugh (and I avoid this word, but it needs to be used at times) there is an indigenous understanding, a shamanic engagement, and so shamanism oversimplified is the practical use of anything on behalf of another human being, you know, which in my world also includes the medical model, any devoted practice... this seeing another human being and trying to meet them and help them with their intervention is this shamanic approach.

In indigenous shamanism, the shaman has all their different skills, to see the person with their story, with their environment and to use all the practical, sensible but also mythic and storytelling, um, technologies at hand in order to help a person get a larger glimpse of what they're in, and deliver that, however they can. And that has a full spectrum from medicine people that don't speak and only do action to those who do elaborate song and dance and operas in order to mirror back to a person what they see in them to help

193

that person get an accurate mirror. And sometimes that has to be extremely elaborate because the complexity of what's happened to that person is so intense.

So, Mr. Milne brings all that in, right up front, in the first class, you know. There is a shamanic seeing to this. It is a shamanic practice to use our other sight, to use our other heart, all our senses, and to use our inner abilities to include them in this process of meeting another person in their distress, and he has his format to do that.

That was the introduction for me around using my whole set of senses. And then you get into the wonderful complexity that happens in a classroom with all these people, suddenly going, "Oh, what is my view? Oh, my goodness, I *see* these things?!?!" Some people see colors, some people see a person's history. There's some of us who don't see, as in 'seeing', but are kinesthetic, so we feel it like a spider feels a web. We may feel the hairball, we may feel the entanglement, and we may feel the twist, you know? So, there's all these different ways of 'seeing', of experiencing another person. It was really eye-opening to be encouraged to use our intuition, our instinct, to use all of our abilities to respond and to gather information about another human being in order to enter into their space with them.

So that spurred that. And then I had the opportunity of becoming part of a shamanic lineage, an indigenous medicine lineage. The views of that lineage got more intricate, like the layers of cranial work are very intricate, you know. The views of the lineage, of breaking it down into these different viewpoints, were very similar to some of what Hugh was saying as well, except that Hugh was having to touch into those as one of the supportive modalities of doing cranial work, you know? Ultimately, it's really getting your hands on the person and contacting those areas of stress, those areas of trauma.

So the two corners of Craniosacral and Shamanism (for me, 'The Lineage') sit next to each other and talk very much to each other...those layers of engagement, levels of engagement, um, uh, views, discernments, those different worlds fit with the cranial work in a way that you have this literal view, this literal level of engagement of you are going to touch their cranial bones, you are going to touch their body, you are going to handle that hairball. We're going to go and touch that psychotic corner. But there's the symbol of that. So underneath, the literal is fed from the symbolic, like this person's corner or hairball feels like,

"Oh my goodness, someone yelled at you!", or "Oh my goodness, it feels like you were trampled by horses!", or "Oh my goodness, it feels like you're being haunted!", or "Oh my goodness...!", right?

'This' is like 'that'. So that is a symbolic level of engagement; you're being encouraged to bring that in as well. "What's the quality that you're sensing? What's it like?" So, you're starting to open that up and expand your state a little bit more, and then underneath that symbolic, all of a sudden the story drops away, the symbols drop away, and there's this dance of movement that might feel like a plant struggling to reach itself out of mud or an old carcass withered out in a dry desert, Right? But you get underneath the symbolic statement of the feeling, and you get into the dance of that, the dryness of that, the quality of that.

The symbolic drops into the mythic. There's a quality and a dance to the space of what's around and in the landscape of that hairball, what's been incorporated into this person, and it's not something you can touch. It's not something you can forcibly see with your actual eyes, but if you soften your whole body, you are sensing that, and you can contact that in many different ways. You've gone to your mythic layer, now available to be responsive in reciprocity.

You're allowing yourself to be affected by this person's experience and staying sober enough to stay affected. So that's another layer of information, it's another layer of engagement.

And then, once in a while, you're involved in those three layers simultaneously, or picking one at a time, depending on where you're at. Then there's something else that happens. Then there's a very difficult layer for words. You know, something shifts in that time. Something shifted in that dance. Something else circulates, which includes all those other layers, and that can be called energetic or can be called spiritual or can be called spirit. Or there's 10,000 words, but it's the place where something disappears for a little while and comes back different, and often times that layer gets confused or associated or embedded with a mythic or a symbolic or a literal view. And so, what I liked about the indigenous lineage is they said, "No, no, no, those are different layers of *engagement*."

These all feed each other, but this spirit, this other thing that we all have and argue about, this energetic layer, can't be forced. It can't be contacted; it can't be touched. It has to be steeped in. It informs these other layers, but it's not a one-way street. These other layers also do their dance, inform, and drop back into this larger context. That larger context is known by the, "I was gone for the last 20 minutes. I don't know where I was, but I wasn't sleeping." There's this discernment point: I don't know where 'I' was, but 'I' wasn't sleeping!

But, in cranial work, it gets touched or related in the waves that happen when you're working on a person's cranial root bed. There are circulation patterns that are very large. William Garner Sutherland ultimately called the largest wave "the breath of life", which a lineage would say is spirit, you know? Sutherland wasn't religious. He didn't assume that it was spirit or God, but what he noticed is that there's a large breath that happens when everything else comes to a still point, then something else moves through. Well, it also moves through in deep sleep. People fall into it all the time, they disappear for a while, and they come back with an experience, you know, so Sutherland called it "the breath of life". A lineage would maybe call it spirit or energetics.

But in bodywork, energetics is so loosely used, you know, and often times misused. Although, in the *Polarity Process*, Randolph Stone used energetics very well. He actually tried to follow the responsive part of the organism's process, as did Wilhelm Reich of Reichian therapy. You know, there is this living electricity, a dynamic, a responsive organic quality that Mr. Reich named Orgone energy. There is this biological energy field, and it circulates, and it has its own behavior, and Reich was great, but that got lost in the shuffle... as many wonderful things do. People are oftentimes in the high of it, and when something is released in the high of it, they call that a success or healing. That may or may not be true, right? It has to be proven over time, over seasons.

What I like about these two things, cranial and earth medicine/indigenous work, is that they encourage the process to be slowed down and for you to pay attention to those discernment layers. When you're engaged with somebody, what layer are you engaged in? Are they expressing their story with their hands, and/or just expressing the story in the literal expression of their words. In that literal expression of their experience, the body doesn't move. They might end up saying, "Well, it's like..." and then you're getting it... there's the symbolic. Their body hasn't moved yet but something's trying to. They are trying to hold themselves still across from you and express their story, and then, all of a sudden, the hands will come into play, and the person will start drawing the experience for you. Now they're moving from the literal to the symbolic. The next layer starts to be revealed when the body starts to join in with the hands. This movement becomes a dance. Now the mythic layer of engagement adds itself in. Mythic can only be danced! So, now they're still trying to draw the story for you, and they don't really understand that they are now dancing their experience for you. They're just expressing, just telling you the story... they're so intent in the 'literal' that they're (literally) missing this whole dance.

Then every once in a while, the whole room moves and dances. Now the person is just trying to share their story and now you're receiving them...their opera, their dance, and the beautiful awkward expression of the layers of engagement.

So, in that way, the cranial work gives me the encouragement to stay in their story and see where the dance of their Jellyfish Brain is getting hung up, and where I can help facilitate an easier dance. But the indigenous is saying, "Wait a minute, be available to this larger story, to their larger opera. Whether or not they can express or share it is separate issue. What layer are they expressing... but don't discount the other layers. They're also being expressed, even if they're not being expressed. If they're in freeze response, that's a lot of information. If they can literally only deliver their experience in their pain to you at the time, the other layers are still expressing." Hmm.

There's a lot of information there. So both systems, the cranial work and the earth medicine/indigenous work, want the practitioner to be available to the full story, as an act of respect, and to be available to be affected by the story/opera of the person, the experiential body of the other person, you know, which is not housed in a moment in time, yet available in that moment of time ('both-and')... So, there's an expanded state that happens pretty immediately with this full experience!

**Christie**  Is the expanded state in the practitioner?

*Michael*  This is where it gets tricky. Ah, yes, it's in the practitioner, but it's also in the person sharing, also in the 'field'. Whew, because they're being.... someone's trying to hear them and all the things that are not being said, and they're trying to be heard in a way that their whole body is being allowed to be heard. I hear your story that your lips are saying, but I also feel the story your sinews are saying. I also feel the story's impact in your bones.

**Christie**  Right.

*Michael*  I also feel the impact on your life.

**Christie**  Right.

**Michael** We will try to do what we can, as the day will allow and permit, because it's gardening, so you try to meet them where it's possible, no matter the modality! You can see that if you take this chunk and shift it around too much, this person will not get up and walk out. They will get up and tumble. They will be too high, they will be too... in a weird way... (this is going to be weird thing to say) they might be too relieved. They may not be able to integrate the experience. I've watched this dynamic over and over again in both traditions, in the cranial as well as the indigenous, where people have this great emoted gestalt, this great healing, but it doesn't integrate. The healing becomes an imposition, an expensive aspirin (which sometimes is the medicine). Confusing huh?...right.

Now the physiology is really having to cinch down to protect itself from the drive of the high. Now the drive of the high has created so much relief and view and delicious, wonderful chemical cocktails that the person really is dancing around because they aren't feeling their pain, right? They aren't on a psychotropic, but there is a psychotropic that was produced by their own body. It creates an adrenal cocktail with lots of cortisol and wonderful chemicals that seem to say, "Life is much better now, thank you!"

Now, their system is really in trouble because of that low back disc pain they can't feel, because the rest of their system is too relieved. So, they leave your office, they think you're great, you think they're great, everything's great, and the next day they get up feeling really great, but the disc hasn't changed. Then they go do something they haven't done for five years, and their disc blows and they're in the hospital and they're having surgery.

That happens. I've seen it happen. You know, I've actually had my own experience with it personally. That's something both the cranial work and the indigenous work, um, recognize. They both have a way of saying, "Wait, let's slow down a little bit. You know, wait a minute." A lot of other modalities, types of education, and situations don't always slow the process down. I feel like I've been very, very fortunate having the people around me who have encouraged and supported me, and it still hasn't necessarily stopped my stumbling, but it's given me the cornerstones to now have a lot of fortitude to go, "Wait a minute, what is MY experience?" If I'm going to hold the reins of this other person while they're in my tending, while they're in my care, then it has to be on my terms.

The client isn't always right. The customer isn't always right, and what am I advocating for? You know, if I'm trying to meet them to help them with their health, then who am I advocating for? What aspect of their health am I really saying 'Yes' to? I have to be available to be a part of being affected by this other person. I can't be a neutral body and just the set of skills that I use to get them through the day. I have the opportunity to slow down, but to then also meet a person in their own opera, and that creates a high. It creates an expanded state because I'm expanding my state to include more of them. Whether or not I take action on that is separate issue.

What I love about traditions of a lineage, Craniosacral education, and my experience as a body worker, is that I get to take these levels of engagement and say these are also levels of tissue. They're these different tissues. They don't always correlate. They don't always come to concordance. There isn't always a healing, but there's always gardening and there's always helping support a functional next step, you know, and that's a great challenge.

**Christie** Well also just in your talking about Craniosacral and the lineage, and how you've worked with me, you often talk about seasons, and with the Craniosacral, I often hear you talk about circulation patterns...so you have a high... so what! I mean in the sense that...

**Michael**  It's a separate issue...

**Christie**  ...and so what happens after the high?

**Michael**  That's right.

**Christie**  And then there is a next step. I mean I think that is one of the most basic lessons that I keep learning from both you and Jodi (*Michael*'s wife, a Somatic Experience Practitioner) is that my own personality or conditioning has been to aim for this high, as if somehow the world is going to fall apart then, or, you know, Prince or Princess Charming is going to come and take me home to live happily ever after stuff. It's like in the child part of me there is no sense of life going on. Actually, when you've reached the high then there are lows and then there are in-betweens and then it just keeps going. And that whole education about slowing down and the seasonal work of things and the actual tempo of a body and how long it takes for bones to heal has taught me that the healing process is actually seasonal. It's actually circulatory. And it keeps going, until it doesn't.

**Michael**  And then it's a moot point.

**Christie**  Yeah. Right.

**Michael**   And then it's left to others, you know. And then technically your experience is still going on because you've affected others.

**Christie**   That is true.

**Michael**   You know there is a, a larger thing. (Thank you, Sutherland, Reich, Milne, Q'ero, a few Marions and Ms. Clarissa Pinkola Estes, beloved Vivian Jaye, Martin Prechtel, Martin Shaw, etc.)(so much for not naming) (and, of course, my beloved Jodi!) (anyone/everyone else!).

**Christie**   Next question...can you actually feel the matrix of your bones?

**Michael**   Yes.

**Christie**   So how do you...?

**Michael**   No words... I have no words for that. It was a very short question. It is a very short answer.

**Christie**   Yeah.

**Michael**   Um, because the... yeah, how would I put that into words? That's something I can only encourage someone else to try. And it's very...it's very nonverbal. It's um, it's a quality of space. All of a sudden, they (the bones) go from being very externally oriented to having a sense of mass. But that mass is not muscularly oriented. It doesn't move in the way that the tissues of our body move. It doesn't stimulate in the way that the proprioception stimulates. There is a quality of mass that um, our brains want to be solid. But the matrix of bone isn't solid.

**Christie** Right.

*Michael* You know, it has bone marrow, so there's a bit of heat to it.

**Christie** Does the bone marrow go through in a tube or is the bone marrow...?

*Michael* It depends on the bone. It's um, enmeshed.

**Christie** Okay.

*Michael* But it's usually at the center of the tootsie pop. It just has a different quality, and when I touch into that quality, it shifts my field as well, because now I'm including... I'm including that. My system starts to reorganize and reorient to that sensation, to that sensitivity, and I know through other practices how to hold/rest myself there in a way. And it's, it's difficult because I'm both holding myself there, but I'm not. I'm both resting there, but I'm not. And when I use terms like 'steeping', it's so much closer to that, that type of activity, in that it's an active activity that I have to participate in because the minute I stop, I clock out into a different layer, right? I can't stop... there's no possibility of just holding/resting my attention there, unless I'm holding/resting my attention there, so it's alive in that way. It's very alive, but not in the way that the other layers are.

**Christie** Well so what about different bones in different places?

*Michael* And there's the challenge. When I've gotten myself into that state, I'd like to go play tag, you know. Some bones will respond/participate... some bones will not. To do that, I have to practice all this crazy stuff that I preach, right? I have to treat 'em with the respect of a feral cat. I can go into that environment and say, "Hey, where are you guys?", in the quirky ways that I do that. And I usually make it a wee bit silly, so I stay engaged, because our system tends to like a bit of silly because it keeps it more engaged. The humors of that allow... I guess the word 'residing' would be a way to sit with it.

I can start to move and get more focused and pay attention to a specific neighborhood, and then try to get to know that neighborhood. Sometimes the neighborhood's responsive... sometimes it's not. And sometimes I end up somewhere else and I have to backtrack. And that's where the whole orientation thing comes from. It's like, oh, this is so alive, we're so alive!  And it creates such a delicious moment that all our other facets want to show up to participate in that delicious moment, which includes all the sock puppets, all the hairballs, all our delicious bits, all our very excitable bits. Everything wants a little taste of that. So, it gets really alive and slippery. It's like trying to hold a salmon, and then we get symbolic. (There're my own levels of engagements now. That was the literal trying to express my experience.)

And now I, I drop into symbolic... it is like a bear trying to hold a salmon. Sometimes you can hold it for a few seconds, sometimes you can eat it and you know each other intimately. And other times, just no way in hell there's... it's just not going to happen. And I think the livingness, the slipperiness of that is, for me, encouraging. But I watch how other people get discouraged.

I've been at it a long time, so I get very encouraged by that aliveness. It's like, oh crap, there's something to all this stuff, so it's humbling. And now because I, because I spend so much time there, not only with my own but with other people's, that I can't imagine doing anything else. In fact, I can't do anything else until I get that layer satiated, you know? If I can orient, I actually don't want to do all this other stuff, but when I'm doing all this other stuff, it's hard to orient.

But... it's such a wonderful challenge, and it's so successful when actually something responds and you go, "Oh crap, there's my bone! Oh, my goodness, where was I? What the hell was that other shape?", and then we're back to the lineage of going, "Oh my goodness, there is something to shape shifting and it's not... it implies something when it's written in a book or told in a group, but when you're actually doing it, it's like, holy crap, there's something to this!" That's just getting to know your own shape.

What I find hysterical is, as homo sapiens, we do everything to go everywhere else, and to try everything else on, and to get all of this external stimulation happening, which I think is fabulous. I'm going to advocate for that too. I think that's just lovely, but with that same ability, very few people seem to be able to find their own organs or even know where their own organs are, to know where their own bones are. They don't know how different their one leg bone is from the other leg bone, and to actually feel that there's two very substantial leg bones in the lower leg, tibia and fibula, (although personally I call the second bone... 'Ribula'. My dark humor is that 'fibula' is the worst possible thing to call a bone that in our language because it implies 'fib''. It implies that it's not substantial, when this other bone, the 'ribula', is robust and substantial and powerful and, and it does this amazing job of mediating load in the system and making it useful and expressive.) So, to do this kind of exploration brings me great joy and the humor of it is that, after all this time, you think I'd be good at it, but we're all very alive and slippery!

Then I sound like Pema Chodren, you know, it's like when she says she has the worst meditative mind ever. And she teaches thousands of people, and then she giggles. It's my favorite of all the stuff I've heard Pema talk about. The only thing my poor little brain remembers is this one most beautiful, honest statement that's now embedded in my soul. Like you'd think after all this time, I'd be good at this. You would think I'd found all my bones. I'm on a good working relationship with them and I'm good to go. I'm a good example for my clients. No, no. I need to be in my office all day long playing with bones so I can feel my own bones. It's funny in a very dark way.

The bones are *that* alive, and because those bones don't have a sensory nerve in them, (It has a sensory periosteum around them which has nerve endings in it, but these are not proprioceptively active like the skin is. They're a different kind of stimulated nerve.) it's just funny. It's just a funny thing to try and do. And yet when I do it, when I watch other people do it, the context of their consciousness changes. Now all of a sudden they have a contained sense of self.

Then some other aspect comes in and tries to take advantage of that. And that's hysterical to me because it's like, aha, there ARE sock puppets. There are sub-personalities, there are agendas, there are concept models that ride us like a donkey into habituation. It's true. I watch it every single day and I have no way to express myself around it except to run my people ragged! I'm going, "Oh my goodness, there's something to this!", which is probably my bumper sticker: "Oh my goodness, there's something to this!" Um, inevitably, in that delicious moment, something shows up, and inevitably, there's also a cultural piece to it.

Like right now, everybody's really addicted to grounding. I think it's hysterical and sets me up for work for the rest of my life. I was already good working with people driving cars and then bumping into each other. I was already great with people at computers being fixated for more than 20 minutes at a time. I will see them because they'll twist themselves up. I'm always already contented with what the world has given me. But now we've got the people stressing grounding. So now, the Jellyfish Brain, who's a reaching organ, who's a 'reacher', reaching for the cookie jar (thank you, Ida Rolf), reaching into the next moment, the next space, even the next dimension. The Jellyfish Brain's a 'reacher'. She loves it. It's what she is. Now with the grounding, she's trying to reach her senses into the ground. So now she's straining her energetics to gather yet another sense of self that has nothing to do with the self, literally.

So, they've created a different strain pattern in the other direction as a counterpoint to all the people saying, "I'm just in my mind. You know, I'm so in my brain. I can't feel my body. I must not have one." Oh, my goodness!

So... So finding bones, and sensing bones, orients all of our layers, WHEW, because all of a sudden you're not reaching. In fact, your Jellyfish Brain has to do something, as I've said before in earlier talks, um, your Jellyfish Brain has to do something counter-intuitive and counterproductive from a Jellyfish Brain's perspective. She has to soften her tendrils to sense her own bones. She can't reach, but her whole design is to reach, so she will try to reach her own bones that are giving her the ballast for her capability to reach. It's all these funny little things with language, but the act of doing the non (mechanical) doing is the hardest exercise.

Yet people will do yoga till they strain themselves. They'll do Pilates till they pummel themselves. They'll do sitting until they get bedsores on their butt. They'll do all these other things to get a sense of self, and then in the process they make that body stronger to withstand the very sense of self that they are trying to attain.

To interrupt that, we come back to bones. So it's, I like feeling my bones. It's taken a long time for me to anchor/establish that feeling. I still can't express it well after all these years. A lot of different, previous *Michael*s have grown and given me these current bones so that I can have the leisure with all of this as comical interaction and darker humors. Now I actually can go get senses of bones, and there are still bones I haven't met.

And it's different because I can do practices where I go through and find every bone. I can find every bone, I can name every bone, I know where they are, I can go do that, but it has a mechanical neural dominance to it. It has the Jellyfish Brain with a pointer stick going, "There you are, there you are, there you are. There you are." And I've got a cortical homunculus that's got them all mapped out, you know, and there's times I can actually remember all the names and times I can't. Um, but I can, you know. On a good day I can actually name all of them, and I know where they all are.

But that's different than going in and talking to them and feeling them and sensing them and letting them coordinate their own neighborhood, and then expressing that coordinated song of theirs to/with me. It's different to meet them with the respect of a feral cat, on their terms. But when that happens, is a completely different orientation, a different relationship!

**Christie**  ...and that's all the way through the bone.

*Michael*  It's 'The Bone' - that's allowing that matrix to do what it actually does, which is to orient and ballast all the tissues in its neighborhood... Hmm... Bones are space takers. They actually orient tissue to space, in space, giving space.

**Christie**  Okay. For me, who basically just started doing this in the last 10 -to- 12 years with you, it's easier feel the length of the bones. I mean I have to work with myself all the time around visualizing and taking away the visual, and then coming into other senses, which mostly have to do with weight and something to do with length. And I can't even tell you what that feeling is, but there's some quality of... but it's not even length because that's a visual again, but there's something in there.

*Michael*  So for those of you at home who can't see this, she's having as much of a dilemma at 10 years as I am at

30+ years. It's not any easier. That's how alive it is. It's funny now, but for a person coming into the office for the first, second, maybe the third year, it's not funny yet. And it's only funny when it gets funny. For most people It's terribly frustrating.

**Christie** Well... I... Yeah, I guess.

*Michael* I'd rather have them in that frustration because that can be integrated.

**Christie** You mean the frustration?

*Michael* Yes. It's an important part of getting comfortable with tension, you know, just them trying to find their own bones. It's so frustrating, because they can do all these other things, but they may not know or have a relationship with their own bones. If they can do that, then we can start introducing them to their organs, to their... to the Jellyfish Brain's sisters, without it being an esoteric practice but being a literal level of engagement, although you're employing all the other levels as well. You're letting the different layers of engagement feed each other.

Then you're using time differently or you're using your senses differently. You're making a whole different sense of self, biochemically speaking, tactically speaking, kinesthetically speaking. You're changing the diagram you have in your cortical homunculus. You're challenging your habits. All these things become a secondary process while you're just trying to find your own bones and developing and growing that sensory feedback, and getting to know what that flavor is.

It's not an easy answer if it's answerable at all. You know, it's easier to feel your own soul than it is to feel your own bones, and yet it takes a soft length of neural fibers/tendrils/roots stretched from head to toe, to feel the soul, but the soul can be felt, too. You can feel another's. You can feel it in yourself. Sometimes I think it is easier to do at times than finding a bone, roughly 206 bones. It's not like we don't have a lot of them to find without running and crushing ourselves against the wall to bruise them and then go, "There it is!" It is that difficult and yet it's not. It's one of those little funny quagmires.

**Christie** Yeah. Well, I think because you said, 'the matrix' to me recently and you said it to Claire and she repeated it in the course of saying other things, 'the matrix', it just caught my attention recently in the last two or three weeks. It's kind of like, 'matrix'...wonder how I could, wonder how I could feel that. I wonder if it's possible to feel that?

*Michael* Now if you could turn that into an open-ended question, you'd get engaged. I love open-ended questions. The brain and the brainstem love open-ended questions. Forebrains, prefrontal cortexes, they hate open-ended questions. Hate them. You get to feel contrasts really quickly. And, I think, there's something in handling bones, in looking at pictures of bones, having handled cadaver bones, handled just-found bones in their wonderful mineral content once the livingness has gone far, far away, years have gone by since that bone has seen a living tissue. It's just the remnants, you know, but it still has its history. It still can be read, it still can be handled. A living bone is so different than a remnant or ancestral bones.

Bones without a body are very different than living bones in bodies. Those differences and seeing how bone lays down its lines of force, and looking at them through normal eyesight, but then also microscopically, it's beautiful. There is a matrix to it. It does lay down lines of force and those lines of force are pliable in response to the tissues that surround them. You know, they give those tissues place and they give them an orientation and anchoring and a way to handle, move and direct the load (the living aquatic mass, the living aquatic weight of your actual body-garden) along their sinews, along their matrixes, you know, it's fascinating.

Christie  Wow, I hadn't gone there. So, it's like, oh, oh yeah, that's a whole thing!

**Michael**  Yeah. Bones have this 'tensegrity' where bones literally take up space and allow load to be dispersed throughout living tissue. Then when the bone gets to do something for a long time, it grows to the force put upon it, it grows from and into that experience, changing in relationship to that force. You see this in a triathlete, you know, these crazy, wonderfully passionate athletes who around 60 years old wake up and say, "I need a lifestyle change. I think I'll become a triathlete!", having never done anything their entire frickin' lives, and so the course of the next five to seven years, they grow a completely different body, and it's proven... you can garden a body. The Yoga people have known this for a long time. Do these things, give it enough time and enough consistency and you'll change the matrix of this body. You'll, you'll consciously garden something that's useful.

It's a shame it's turned into an exercise, but even exercise, even the PTs are right. You know you've got to get this stronger so it can take 'the load' so it can 'unload' the area that's in distress because every time you caused the area of distress to do something it doesn't want to do, it protects and disperses the load around the hairball to somewhere else and those other neighborhoods get strained, and the hairball stays protected, and nothing gets to integrate.

It's a marvelous thing and, for me, the feeling and sensing for the bone itself and getting to know its matrix pauses the system. Everything has to pause for that to happen. So, you have a functional pre-step step that a person has to go into in order to orient themselves before they take the next action. All the other systems are designed to take actions, to set up actions, but those bodies aren't oriented yet. They're coming from the habits of the previous 10 years of their life, and they're going into an activity - even if it's an exercise that they're devoted to - they're going to run into wonderful snags and hairballs and all that sort of stuff because no one's taught them to pause...actually orient their system and start from a pre-step. Their functional pause is that moment of orienting.

I like the challenge of that and in my practice it's ended up there, because in doing all the other things that I've done, I see all these other actions being taken, but still putting the distressed tissue into distress, even when they've had the healing "Ah hah!", and a place/space/hairball has let go. It's still going to take six to nine months for that to integrate. But in the person's mind, they're like, "I'm back to my previous usual." And they start to repeat the person they were two years ago, but they're not that person.

So that imposition all of a sudden sets up a new hairball, because the body's going to have to adapt to that new intention. Right?

**Christie**  Right.

# Chapter Six: *Interview #4*

**Christie**  You ready?  We're going...here we go...

**Michael**  It's hard to spell "laughter". Here we are. Here we are. Yeah.

**Christie**  So...well...I... it's hard to just dive straight in. It's like there are some preliminary questions that we've already done and so there's more specific things, like... how do you encourage clients to connect with root beds aside from the bones and the structural network? At least in my experience, I know that you have, but I don't really know quite how you did that. So, I just want to know what you might say on that subject?

**Michael**  That's a great question! Let me just get a sense of it. So yes, there's a way that I stage the session and surprisingly (someday it'll be written down... right now maybe, which is very funny), the staging of it is actually kind of particular for me in that, ultimately, it's how do you get a person on a table, and it came out of my work with Vivian.

**Christie**  How do you get a person on the table?

**Michael**  Oh yeah. Because this is a very interesting thing. It's like we've talked about meeting a person where they're at, right? It's one of these large umbrella ideas that practitioners whom I've watched over the years go right by, like they say, "Oh yeah, meet a person where are they at? Okay." And then they bypass that as an idea, a fine one, and at that they move quickly forwards to "Let's get to the juicy bits!" And then they go right towards the concept, the modality, or some little minutiae piece that they can get their hands or tendrils on, to get neural-dominant with, in control. Those little things, all those little things are interesting to me because what caught my attention early on was not those ideas, concepts, modalities. All those ideas/concepts seemed like the tools in the box, and it's like that's no problem, but if you've gotten a feel for them, the tools are just tools, and a lot of people spend a lot of time with those tools. The idea of meeting a person where they're at, of taking the time to try and figure out how you connect with someone, of contacting someone and feeling the relatedness that's there, right? You're getting a sense of your bones and then you get a sense of someone else's bones. You get a sense of your roots and then you let your roots get a sense of someone else's roots.

So, there's this interesting, almost formulaic way that I actually do approach it. You know, even though I'm trying not to be formulaic, I've tricked myself with these open-ended questions like, "Where's the bones?" In this case, we're going from 'there's a bone', to going, "Wait a minute, he's doing something else." Behind all the doings, behind the "Where's your bones? Where's this? Where's that?", is an invitation opposed to a territory or a position or a place – because the minute the brain has a place to get to, she goes for it. Everything else is disregarded, right? So, behind all that... how to meet a person 'where they're at', where are they... before you do anything? Where are they? Before touching their bones, can I get a sense of their bones? Before finding their roots, we're getting a sense, getting a sense of their roots... letting those questions lead, and seriously letting them lead, letting them float out in time, letting them float out in space, letting them do their job of inquiry.

And then there's this flippant little remark that came up a few times early on when working with Vivian, when she got frustrated, she would express that frustration with comments like, "Ugh... sometimes it's just about getting a person on the table."

I think what I love about our mentoring time together is that she gets to a place, especially with me because I don't have the same sacred interaction with language, she gets frustrated. I find language a big bother. You know, I don't... actually, it's not one of the first things I love, although I can orate, which we've talked about, and that comes out of some of these root practices. So, the flippant remark which has stuck with me ever since. Always expressed out of frustration.

I love frustrated remarks from old biddies because they're loaded, so full of expressed experience. She's doing all these things, but ultimately what she's doing as a sculptor of the medium of a body, as a tender of a human garden, she's really trying to get the person completely on the table. That may be the entire quest, because a person comes, and they lay down or they sit down in front of you. They might be sitting there with you, they may not be completely 'there', right, and then the 10,000 therapies arise. If they aren't really sitting in their body, then they're not really on the table.

So that meeting them, that trying to get it in time... well, it turns out different layers of a person aren't settled there in front of you, so, yes, you would like to work on this hairball or that hairball. Yes, the person came in with their agenda of what they want worked on. I always have my agenda of what I want to work on, let's be clear, but there's a space in between where they think they are and what can really happen. Sometimes when they lie on the table after doing the dance of entering the room, you are trying to figure out 'who' you're working on that particular day (which is also one of the open-ended questions: "Who's here?"). You get them on the table. They aren't on the table, and this is freak'n fascinating to me. Visually their head might be on the table... they might have a foot on the table, but the rest of them, their body's on the table, but the feeling of their body, the sense of their body is not on the table, right? And I know in psychology you can run into fragmentation and dissociation, those kinds of dynamics, as words to try and qualify where a person's psyche is. For me, I think the psyche's completely rooted and enmeshed in the body, so I don't see them as being so different. It turns out their physicality is the same thing, and then the quirky thing happens. I get the privilege of engaging them, so then I go for contact.

Well, I see that their leg is on the table physically, but I don't feel their leg. They're not occupying their leg. So, then my hand naturally goes, "What the hell?" And I go in for contact. Sure enough I got the leg in my hand, and of course that's not enough for me. I have to get my hands around that, so I have a leg between my hands, and still there is a quality of their leg that isn't there.

I've got them damn near clamped (have I mentioned Andrew the Anaconda?), and they still aren't there. So then the prompting starts. First question, "Where's the bones?", right? And I try to get them to feel that, as their psyche is going, "What???" My hands are prepped with, "*What*?!?! Come on!" Then, any response they have, I start tracking that response and start to prompt it towards where my hands are because I want to feel where their leg is, so we both have to participate, right? And I can do that verbally, and/or I can add some movement, and/or do some nonverbal cues, tease them in, tickle them a wee bit at their peripheral, you know, or I can go right into 'clamp' and go, "OH! You're going to be in your leg now!", which is the harder end of that clamping process. My tendrils start to go to work on their tendrils. My roots start to go, "Well, where ARE their roots?"

You know, you start rooting into the roots, trying to get them, their Jellyfish Brain, into their own leg. Um, and it has a great humor to it and there's a layer of it that doesn't have any humor to it. It's so literal what I'm saying. There's such a literal end to the metaphor, and I get the luxury of playing at that literal end.

So I'm sensing that I'm prompting the person towards the same place, because I want to know where they are and my sheep dog, that part of me, is frustrated with where the bleep are their sheep roots?

And then I start to find out where their perch is, where they like to hang out in their body, and I'm like, okay, let's not mess with that. But now I see where 'you' (they) are.

**Christie**  How do you find that out?

*Michael*  By this time we're in the session and all my previous agendas are set aside because I'm just trying to find them and get them on the friggin' table. This can take anywhere from minutes, to hours, to years, right? Yeah. This is where it gets very difficult for conversation, I think, because it gets tipped into symbolic and poetry, and in large batches of time, you know. Like in that moment, in the 'Now', you can cover 10,000 years pretty easily (definitely not what we 'think').

And then sometimes you run into their whole ancestral root, ancestral habit, and you run into all these other layers of them, because the bones didn't come from nothing. Right? Oh! The bones came from their grandma because they were developed in grandma's belly along with their mother. You know, the seed of the egg was being made and grown at the same time as their mom's body. So those two things belong to grandma (your mom's mom, your grandma). There's just this wonderful weave, and sometimes when you're trying to get them on the table, you're running into these snags, you're running into these beautiful other qualities, beautiful long threads of lives and roots.

Then there're the physical snags in those lovely roots and threads. I call them hairballs because it's the easiest way to describe them. They are attention 'eddies' that are hairballed somewhere else in their body, and every once in a while, not in their body. They're disassociated. So, they keep all this private, a very deep and sometimes secret privacy, saying, "Oh my Goodness, I can't lose this part of my soul. I will protect it and cinch it up somewhere just off the body, right?" Just off into the soul, a little bit, or off into the psyche a little bit, or off into some other layer. We all argue about those places, right?

So that's the first 10, 15 minutes of a session. That whole dynamic, trying to meet them where they are and trying to actually get them on the table, so that sometimes the session is just that, just trying to 'get them on the table', which can take a hell of a lot of time. And what is surprising to me is that a lot of practitioners that I know and have taught and all that... they, they disregard that whole engagement, and they just go after the musculature. They just go after whatever, whatever key word triggered them... "Uh, their leg is dysfunctional. We will make it functional", right? There's no engaging that. That leg's dysfunctional because of a lot of reasons. And there are layers of those reasons that are inarticulate, not reasonable, feral, beautifully intelligent and to counterpoint, can also be straight-forward mechanical, simple, basic snags.

So, we've oriented to the bones. We know that the bones are there, and we have the possibility of being informed by that contact. In the case of this conversation, we've put the person down on the table; so, there's a lot of bones on the table. So it seems, right? We know that between the bones and the table lie a layer of roots. Some of those roots are neural tissue. Other layers of roots are vascular tissue, lymphatic tissue, muscular skeletal tissue, and then wonderful mushy interstitial tissue. You know, there's just soup in and around this bag of bones and that's just that inch and a half to two inches between the table and the bone itself. I mean, it's so literal. There's this whole wonderful matrix of roots. I start to get curious if I can't find that sense of them occupying the space that I'm holding, then I start to go exploring for roots, right? Then I will prompt the person accordingly until I get a response from any layer.

**Christie**  So give me an example if you can.

**Michael**  So we're at the leg, got the leg on the table, I've got my hands gently placed around it and I've discovered that a part of their attention is up in a perch in their Jellyfish Brain's head, literally. People have different perches in their Jellyfish Brain. Last week, a certain perched person had an amazing perch behind their left eye. That's where every time they started to drop down into their body, they've sprung back up behind their left eye. Now, because one should have a little humor in a poetic sense, in an artistic sense, I think, for me that perch was very clear. It is a perch, a bench, a seat of sorts. They land on it like a freakin' bird and they've little clamps of their attention that clamp around that perch. It's a location in this person that happened to be behind their left eye and it was where they sit with their attention to track and map the world and look and interact, inside and outside, right?

It's a specific place. Not everybody's (perch) is so specific. This was startlingly really specific and makes it great for this kind of dialogue. This person, it was beautifully specific, so it's juicy. I'm down at the leg and I see that they're back on the perch and I'm trying to get them down where my hands are, so I'm trying to prompt them, "Where's your bones? Let's find this leg bone.", okay, and then, noticing where their attention goes. Attention doesn't quite go with where

I'm at, and so their attention then starts to spring back behind the perch. And I go, ah, okay, "What about your bones? Let's come back to the big leg bone." And I'll do several rounds of that, right? "Let's try and find this." But when you're tracking, and their attention starts to move through their body, interesting things happen. It's like, um, feeling when you're at your piano (Christie), you've hit a cord. Sometimes you can feel how it resonates through the other strings. (If you haven't done a lot of piano playing, just try to sense this, you at home with us.)

Um, there is, there are secondary responses, you know, because it's not a, you can't isolate the layers. And I think that's the joy of it. You actually can't isolate the layers. You may occupy them, but you can't isolate them. I think that's the joke. It's like the bones are alive. I don't need the person's attention to know or do my job. I just would like it because it adds a dimension of interaction. Ultimately, I'm trying to set up a place where the person can self-facilitate.

So now we're building this contrast of... I'm down at their leg, I'm trying to get them down in their leg, but they keep springing back to the perch behind their eye. So you name it, you say it, and this is the beautiful thing of naming, as a practitioner, is you just name the obvious, (and that'll be Mr. Obvious in capital letters when you're writing this), so being Mr. OBVIOUS, it's like, "Oh look, you just went to that perch behind your eye!", and then the person, "What?!?", and then a whole cascade of response has happened because their psyche thinks that you're psychic; "What? How can he see that?" You actually found something. That 'felt' feeling is acknowledged, mirrored, and named, all in less than a heartbeat, (which is saying something, because that's four beats to one measure of our heart music). So, you name that, and then there's the giggle, there's the uncomfortableness, a kerfuffle, and there's always a giggle of uncomfortableness, because that giggle allows other tissues to flutter and respond. (Hence why "Have your giggle ready!" is number three on our list because it's always number three on our, THE LIST). We do something, there's a response, and then there's a response to the response, right?

So, there's a whole cycle that happens, so we just named it. We just named where their perch is, after trying to coerce, entice, impose, invite them to come down into their leg, which for a myriad of reasons, they may or may not be able to ever do - right? Most of the time they do *do* it, but you know, you're opening a Pandora's box (originally, not a box at all, but a clay vessel full of mystery). You know a lot of stuff's going to happen between their leg and their perch. Most Definitely! They spring back behind their eye, and so it's like, "Okay, let's, let's try to come down here", and I'm finding that the bone thing works, but only sort of... you know. Now, now they're feeling a little exposed.

**Christie**  After you've named the perch?

*Michael*  After I named the perch, I'm still trying to bring their attention down into their leg (remember, it's a strange sea creature, our attention).

And so then we go, well, let's just feel for roots, "Well - can, can you feel the roots? Can you imagine your Jellyfish Brain with its roots/tendrils down here, through your legs? You've got these beautiful neural roots. They're in my hands. Can you sense that?" We know the perch is in their Jellyfish Brain behind their eye, so they might be, their Jellyfish Brain, might be willing to feel her roots because you know she could still be in her perch and feel into her roots... and a couple of funky things happen. One is that the Jellyfish Brain will use her senses to try to look at the leg from the perch behind the eye. A fantastic, beautiful, amazing thing about the psyche and the biology of the Jellyfish Brain is that her senses are designed to track and go get information, not just through her own tendrils, the actual physical nerve tissue, but the senses and organs in her face. Her proprioception is designed to scan space and go get information, no matter what room, state, planet, universe, or space the Jellyfish Brain is in. I've met some of the people who go to other universes and planets and many other dimensions, and they are trippy. Their senses can reach really into wonderful spaces, but it's from a perch. It will be from some part of their anchored biology.

Here, a funny thing happens. You'll see/feel a person (seems so invisible at the time) ...you'll see/feel a person use an aspect of their vision and proprioception to go down and 'look' at where my hands are, right? They actually partially disassociate. Technically it's a dissociative maneuver, but we're not using this disassociation as a negative thing. It's a fantastically complicated skill. Some people can disassociate and go look at other planets and then convince us to make NASA happen, right?

Oh, just a few people, really wanting to go do some fantastic dream, and willing to put in the 80 years to do it! One of my clients was just telling me about a friend of their father's got to see the whole cycle of his space program happen just a few weeks ago. One of the satellites, you know, one of the probes that were sent out into space came to the end of its life and it was sent off 30+ years ago. He had his life dream, his glimpse into the future fulfilled, just like William Sutherland did with cranial osteopathy.

**Christie** Yes, Stan and I saw it.

*Michael* Yes, I'm not prepared for details right now. But this is the beautiful, fantastic thing about this disassociation/dissociation and its positive attributes. It has a positive and negative connotation...positive connotations sometimes with very big dreaming, big seeing, big glimpsing! Fantastic! (That was a little diversion, kerfuffle we just did.)

So, I'm back at their leg, they've got a perch behind their eye and I'm trying to get them to, to join me a little bit just to see/feel how their attention moves through their body, through their root beds. Their Jellyfish Brain has already found a workaround to stay on the perch and come down and 'look' at what my hands are doing and 'look' at the bones of their legs, but they haven't had to go through their body at all!

**Christie** And they don't feel ...

*Michael* And... they don't feel it, but their Jellyfish Brain glimpses the information, and says, "I know where you're at." And then I'm saying, "You may 'know' where I'm at, but you don't 'feel' where I'm at." Right?

**Christie** Right.

236

**Michael**   The difference between jazz and elevator jazz is huge. It's huge. It's huge. Whew! So, I'm down with their leg, now I've figured out their work around, right, so I have to be in several places at once at that moment, I have to acknowledge what they just did and I use my giggle as well, usually. At this point I usually can't help myself because, not only are they having a giggle response or a flutter or an uncomfortable response, an awkward response, a response, a kerfuffle, but I'm tracking with my body and my roots and my psyche as well, so I'm going to have a similar response, my own response... now we're getting rapport with each other, right? My system's acclimatizing to their system because I'm using time. I'm not trying to do this all in the five minutes that they showed up and sat down.

**Christie**   Right.

**Michael**   I'm saying, "We're walking into this session." This is how you do it. This is elaborate; this back and forth-ness, is part of the session, whether it's verbal or nonverbal, absolutely both. The outline and almost formula is the same. The outline is the same. "Where are they, and can I get them on the table?" Right? Can I meet them where they're at, can I work in to get things on the table, so not only am I facilitating their experience, but I'm setting up a way for them to self-facilitate when there's not another practitioner around? We want to set up those pathways, so this back and forth, with their attention is very, very important. It also allows me to viscerally, with my hands on their leg, acknowledge and give my complete attention, going, acknowledging, "Hey Leg...I know they aren't in there with you.", right?

So, I'm having this conversation with their leg like, "Hey Leg... you see what they're doing, Leg... and I see what they're doing... Leg, and we'll see if 'we' can get the two of you to have a conversation.", because we're back to the advocacy thing. I'm the advocate for this garden. They're (the person's sense of self) up in their perch. Their Jellyfish Brain has found a workaround to go, "I know where my leg is!", and I have to hold down here with the leg next to me, and Leg and I both looking at their psyche perched at its 'usual'. I'm going, "Yeah. Right." And I have to find, depending on the person, how to do this. Their response could be in a range, either it can be very humorous, or it can be extremely frightening. It might be the biggest scare, the biggest overwhelm, for them to come into their leg. We don't know yet. We both may have our ideas. All three of us may have different ideas.

**Christie** Us?

238

**Michael** Me, their leg and them, in their perch behind their left eye (our current example). We have to keep going back and forth, right? This back and forth, this 'to and fro', is really important because we're going from neural dominance down into somatic dominance...Jellyfish Brain perspective, then mine, then Jellyfish, then garden, and back. But I want to be careful here because I don't want to associate this with another aspect of the neural net. (Ultimately this belongs down the hall with Jodi. Thank you, Jodi, who works with people's nervous systems from the Somatic Experiencing Peter Levine point of view.) I'm not a neural advocate. I'm the body's advocate. The closest thing the neurology has with that is the somatic branches of the nervous system, which are sensory branches. You know, they're not peripheral nerves. They aren't tracked in that way. You can't manipulate the somatic branches. You can only sense with the somatic branches.

**Christie** So the somatic branches would be the eyes and hearing?

**Michael** No, not even that. You might even say that, that it's, um, it's a sensory aspect of nerve as nerve information comes into it. There's a reaching peripheral aspect to nerves, neural dominance that goes out and gets information, "Oh yeah! Oh, Yum! Yum! Yum! Gimme!

Gimme! Gimme!", right? The stimulating response aspect, that neural-dominant aspect is of, "I'm in control. I want that, and that's going to make me very happy or it's going to scare me, make me pee my pants, but I really like that feeling, so I'm going to go get that."

The somatic aspect is the passive receptivity of that actual information, and this is, this is a problem in the Jellyfish Brain; one of the dilemmas of the Jellyfish Brain, is that she's got these two or more different aspects and it's the coordination of those aspects that builds her pictures and her interactions, her landscapes.

**Christie**  So it's just the getting of the information...

**Michael**  And then there's the actual receiving of it. Not the manipulation of it, not the 'coming out and handling of it', but there's a place that you actually get other layers of information... the quality, the feeling, the actual, the actual sense, of what's in contact. And this gets tricky because contact doesn't necessarily need to be physical. It can be proximal, you know, you walk into a room, you know who's angry, you know who's not, and the spectrum in between.

**Christie**  Right.

**Michael**  That's peripheral stimulation, and also that's limbic tracking and interaction that starts to breach into the somatic branches, the actual sense of quality, actual feeling sense, not just the grabbed information.

**Christie**   Right. Well, so... what is a felt sense that is not that?

*Michael*   So this gets really interesting because with neural dominance, you could grab, you could grab the leg, right? As a practitioner thing, I can grab the leg and I can work with the tissues, and I can feel the tissue being dense or not dense. Right? But I'm still in my neural-dominant proprioceptive activity, you know, "Stimulate. Stimulate. I got it. I got it, I got it. Stimulate. Stimulate. Okay. That's dense. That's not dense." So, it's that straight up information that I'm getting. I can look at the leg and see all the swelling. Okay. There's something going on there, right? There's that immediate information and the brain's 'on' saying, "Oh, delicious leg." If I stop, and I stopped palpating, I just have contact. I soften my nerve endings so that I can feel my bones, right, and then I start to let my bones feel their bones.

Here we go.

(As as aside: *You can't write what's happening in this room right now, but it's very palpable.*) *So we've both (Michael and Christie) just now softened our nervous systems. We've softened our nervous systems, and you can hear it in the voice. I'm starting to have to have more space in my words because I'm feeling at*

241

*the same time of talking, trying to. Yeah, so we're both*

*toggling back and forth in this, "There's my bones,*

*there's your bones, and we can actually let our bones*

*feel each other."*

And we are back...

That sensation is a somatic sensation because it

takes a whole body to do it, but there's no reaching

involved. It's almost purely receptive (our bones), and

there's a lot of information that's at a different

frequency than palpatory information, than um

adrenal infused, excited, alive nerve ending

information, right? There's another layer to the tea,

there's a bass note to the quality of space, and that

bass note takes up literal space and literal time, and

you'll hear this when you play this audio back. From

where I was a few minutes ago, which was very

excitable, and now I'm starting to drop, pause, drop

and now I'm trying to stay in a feeling of my bones

while I'm talking... very hard to do.

**Christie**  You also do it all day long.

*Michael*  I also do it all day long, which is true, so I can be in

that sensation and quality of space, and I've learned

the ability to talk. I can also start to practice what I

preach and start to slide into my own roots in the

same way I'm asking the person on the table to slide

into their roots. I also have to model some of that. It's

quite engaging, you know, and I'm having to start to track a lot of things which, as a practitioner, is terribly exciting for me. The joke is, is that it looks like (if you were to sit in the room and watch me work), you'd get that I'm doing a lot of things, but you may not see anything moving or you might see my body gently starting to move. You might see an aspect, um, of Tai Chi start to happen because I'm literally having to move my body so that the roots in my hands stay soft and receptive, (until they're triggered into doing some crazy maneuver of unwinding because I found a hairball and it's mine... now clamping of teeth because I've chewed into something, right? Like that octopus with the, you know, tendrils around the wonderful little shell and there's a clam inside and it figured out how to gently, strongly open the shell. So then 'I' have to slide inside and get the beautifully protected pearl of their experience!) (My afternoon is spent a lot like that, by the way. Truly.)

So, we're back on the table. I've got the person, who now has done some rounds of orientation to their bones, and we've named their perch, and they're uncomfortable, but now they've suddenly realized that it's not important whether I acknowledge them or not, that they've actually also now felt where they hang out and it's not in their leg. It's in this perch and it's a specific place in their head, and their Jellyfish Brain is starting to get disoriented right now because she's in a little bit of a panic because I found her place. (Jellyfish Brains don't like this, by the way, as much as they may want it. They never like it. They can get used to it though, which is nice.)

So, then we have to find a way to walk them from that perch back down to leg, back down to where we're actually working because we still haven't got their leg on the table. They're, they're still not occupying their leg, so now we're into the session. But we've done several rounds of going back and forth. We've created a circulation pattern. Not just the circulation of fluids, but also a circulation of neural information and a circulation of the...such a hard quality to decide to put words to but the attention has an awareness to it, and it moves. It moves like a little breeze, a little tidal pool of potency. It's very cool and we'll just stop there because that's full of wonderful, delicious tangents.

So, we found a way to work in. Now, we've gotten a little bit of sense of their bones. We've got their sense of their perch, so we start to move them away from their perch and get them used to migrating, to traveling, "All right, I don't have to stay on my perch." A big deal for a Jellyfish Brain.

Sometimes that can be a huge relief, but now we've got movement, so now we have to find some ways to give them some options. We always come back to the feeling of bones. Even the head's got 22 bones! We can have them feel their head lying on the table, so we can be near their perch, but we can drop them out of the perch. And then at some point along this road I'll introduce roots again, "Now we'll play with roots. You {client} know what bones feel like somewhat, but now let's sense for some roots. You've got all these vascular roots.", and two things will happen. One is they'll go, "Yes"... and their whole vascular bed will soften. Yeah... (Christie moves and *Michael* refers to that) here now it's just that she (Christie) has a history of being on the table... her whole vascular bed just softened. (You listening at home, yours may not. Don't take offense, don't email me.)

So, the vascular bed... two things will happen, just like most responses. The body either goes, "Yeah", and it softens (you can't make a body soften, by the way)... um, or it'll contract. I'm sensing for that next layer of responses. We found the perch. We're trying to get them into the leg. I kind of know where they're at now. We've found that, I know I got 'em now, right? But I still want to get them on the table. We're still trying to get them on the table, right? Trying to get them... just the roots to soften (hah... minutes, months, years go by). So, in this example, let's say that they don't soften when I go, "Oh, you've got this wonderful vascular bed!", right? And their body actually contracts, and they pop onto their perch again. There's my, "No, not that direction." It's very visceral. It's very clear. We're not okay. So, we, we toy, wander (wonder?!?!), explore around a little again, "There's your perch, let's find some bones."

And then we go, "Well, your left eye has a root off the back of it.", and then there's a little response. I've backed up into where I can stay in the response zone, right? I find the root bed we can do... (Note to self. Come back to vascular later, if ever. But it's in my little note, it's in my little notebook in the back of my little Jellyfish Brain's brain. 'Come back to vascular root. Won't happen today, maybe?' Right. Open-ended... maybe. We will try later because I'm a sheepdog.) We've got them. We're like, okay, let's stay close to their perch, but let's start messing with their perch. We know it's behind the left eye, so let's trick the Jellyfish into feeling her own tendril. Well, the eyes have their own tendrils because they're actually external sense organs (little sisters) even though they're right next to the Jellyfish Brain, technically, right? They're still extensions from the Jellyfish Brain, right? But, the Jellyfish Brain doesn't 'see' it like that. When she's neural-dominant, it's all functional. It's all coordinated in neural dominance, and she's going and getting information. That's how come it's called neural-dominant. When she's non-neural-dominant, she's disoriented (her side of non-neural dominance is a little disoriented) and then two things will happen. She'll go hyper-vigilant and get more dominant, or she'll go, "Alright, I'll trust you, but I don't like it." So, you trick her; you go, "Okay, we'll stay close to home. The perch behind the left eye and... the eye has a root.", and this is where it's fun about anatomy in that you don't have to educate a person on their anatomy. You just have to walk them through it.

I like anatomy, but I have to spend my time looking at my books and going over the words, and you'd think after 30+ years I'd have it all down, but I don't have that kind of brain. (So little insults of comments from previous teachers in my life, like, "Give this two years, you'll have it down. Just stay with it. At least spend time with it every day or every week... in two years you'll have it down." I'm on 30+ years from those little comments (of course I love little things) and I'm still looking at my books, (little tantrum) every single day! On average every day, on average we would say every other day if I was to be really honest... but I got my books, and, between peoples, I'm looking at stuff and, you know, after a while some names stick, but visually. It's the tactile part, the handling people every day, where those things have coordinated and gotten absorbed. When I look at an anatomy book, it's very alive. It's like looking at uh, the gardening book for a gardener to know what roots feel like. They know what the feeling of that plant is. They know... it's just part of rapport or a musician inside their instrument. I pull out my congas... I know my congas. I'm like, oh my goodness, I know what they feel like. The tones and the sounds all have a feeling to them when I engage the instrument. Piano, same thing. You get intimate and those who are good get very intimate with their instruments. The body's the same way, although not entirely an instrument, it's a garden.

So, I know that there's a root behind the eyes. I know that nerve. I know it intimately because I've spent all this time having to track it and find it because of people's perches in their Jellyfish Brains, and I have to find tricky ways to find it. In the early days I used to come up with all this stuff. Now, for me, it's Mr. OBVIOUS, Mr. *Name the Very Thing That's There!* Somehow, that's where my practice has gone, in that I then name this nerve, "Oh, you have an eyeball, it has a little sea anemone in it.", which is true. And right then you've got the brain in a snafu. She's like, "There's no sea anemone in my eyeball!", but there is! So, so you give a different quality. You name a creature that has all the same qualities, all the same attributes as the actual anatomy.

And it turns out, you know, if you go with an aquatic creature, chances are... (for some people you can't do this because the aquatic thing doesn't work. So, you say there's a lizard in their eye, or you say there's a little orchid, or there's...in their eye. Or you say something where their body goes, "Really?!", and the minute their body softens in response, you've got them!)

All this time I've got my hands around their leg, and they haven't, I haven't gone anywhere. They haven't really gone anywhere, but we've done all these rounds of engagement just trying to get them into the leg, so I can work on their leg. Hello! So, days go by, right? Just like this conversation.

Um, so we've prompted them into the neural net, and we've found a root that they can travel along, and then we do something crazy. We go, "Well, that root drops right back to where your head is touching the table.", which it does. It drops right into the visual cortex, which is along the line of where their perch is because they're trying to see everything, and they've been trying to do that all their life. It's not because I've discovered something, or I psychically have opened up the book of their soul to page 10 where it says they have been trying to see everything their entire life. No, that's not what's happened.

It's so literal. I'm just trying to work on how to get their attention to slide off their perch, which it'll do for a moment, but it'll pop back onto that perch because it's a stealth bird, their consciousness. We've now slid them into a root, they've softened their perch, they've softened their grip from their Jellyfish Brain, and now they've got a different orientation that they can work with as well. Then, we bring in the other eye and the other root and we drop them back into their visual cortexes, and then we do a crazy silly thing. We dupe the Jellyfish Brain. As a neural-dominant jellyfish, her job is to coordinate everything, and make everything even out into a singular thing, a coherent song. Her job is to make it one song...

**Christie** Because?

*Michael* Because that's her nature.

**Christie** That's her nature and supposedly there's one body?

*Michael* Supposedly there's one body, one world, one god, one thing and we all argue about these (everything, really, good bird banter). There's always one thing because neural dominance organizes to position, and she'll do counterpoint, do a counter to the counterpoint, creating a landscape until she can really anchor in that position. In this case, the perch behind the left eye is a 'position'. That's her central... we've discovered in trying to get a person in their leg where their particular perch is. (I hope this person never listens to this. There's no names to protect the innocent, and I'm sort of fussing with this because in this exact case, the perch of this person is too real, real and juicy because I was just there in that session. Oh!)

So, we've dropped them into their root bed. We found a small response. Their vascular system roots, no response. There's a little bit of neural net response because she'll give into that if I back up into her neural root bed. Bone thing's okay, but we want to start to get her from bones to roots so that she can discern the difference.

So, we found this little labyrinth. We've gotten the Jellyfish Brain to soften. She's willing to let me play with the roots of her eyes and drop back into her body. Her visual cortex (brain's perspective) is in the back of the head and the roots of the eyes go into the visual cortexes (somatic perspective, there's actually two visual cortexes!). What we may or may not tell them is that there's lots of roots that come off the back of the eye and each eye then shares a bundle, a bridge of roots. After their shared roots, they open up like hands and a chunk of the roots go to the visual cortexes, but other roots go to the vestibular and some other regions of the Jellyfish Brain to all do this amazing coordination of information which allows for movement. The Jellyfish Brain's primary reason for doing this is to move because she's an explorer, a dancer, right? So we've just duped her into her own nature, but she likes to have a certain amount of control, so she likes to be positionally based. Neural dominance organizes to 'position' (Somatic dominance organizes to 'quality' of space). It gives her that control, that ability to coordinate and that's her job. We've just tricked her to slide out of her job going, "I've got roots where? There's a back part of my eyes? Crap. The coordinated control, which is always forward field..." I've now tricked the person into their backfield, which is the feeling in the back on the table, right?

We're trying to get the person on the table, so we've at least got their Jellyfish Brain on the table. We got them feeling the oddest sensation. (Try this at home. Your eyes have roots that go into your visual cortexes. These roots are in the back, and then we keep adding in little bits. So, what we do, we're doing in circles, if you haven't figured this out at home.) (*I don't know how you're going to write this, Christie. Whew...!*)

**Christie** (Neither do I!)

*Michael* (Yeah. Pema Chodron talks in circles, and it seems to come out fine. This is different!?!? Maybe not?!?! Thank you, ma'am.)

So, their head is on the table. We've tricked them into their visual cortexes. Their perch around their eye has softened, and I'm like...bonus! We've got a softening. Let's just hang. Let's try to keep this tea steeping, and this is what steeping is. You add in more time. You try to keep them in a quality that has gentle motion, a gentle movement, and is safe for them. You're building potency, you're building trust, you're building rapport, not just with their nervous system, but with my nervous system, because I'm in proximity, so I'm doing this dance 'with them' (neural-dominant), 'during them' (somatic-dominant). I'm giving them a living mirror back to themselves because I'm letting my system be responsive, so I have to go through all this uncomfortableness, too, you know, because I just want to feel their leg on the friggin' table. (Sounds so simple...!)

So, we've got their head on the table. We've got them contemplating where their visual cortexes are, because it's touching the table where their head is touching the table. Literally. Actually, it's slightly above, but let's not get worked up over specifics. Hmmm... and then we do something really crazy, and this really does quirky things to a living Jellyfish Brain. There're two visual cortexes, not one. The minute...

*(There she goes. See? Every friggin' time! What you at home haven't seen is that Christie softens, and then the back of her head is doing it right now, again, it's separating. She's taking up 'width'!)*

You cannot make a human body take up 'width'. It'll do forward 'reaching'. It'll do back 'reaching'. It'll 'reach' above. It'll escape out some exit plan, from birth usually. (Yeah, see all that? You, Christie, have practiced.) For a person to soften and take up width (and it's a circular thing, it's not just side to side, but it's also other side to side). (It gets quirky in the conversation... um, it's quite something, it's quite gyroscopically tidal. GYROSCOPICALLY TIDAL!) Never mind, back to the book. Sorry folks!

So, you've got them into their visual cortexes, you've got them into some roots, you've got them entertaining the idea that their nerves are roots. You've tricked them to be there, and now they're taking up space, they're letting the Jellyfish Brain separate, and you're blowing the Jellyfish Brain a little bit. You're blowing some little fuses that are in the Jellyfish Brain, and then visual cortexes separate.

And then a couple things can happen at that point. I can have a great time at their expense, and usually I do, (which is what Christie's referring to from the beginning of this hour-long conversation). Then I start to have a little bit of fun with (with neural), during (with somatic) the person's experience, and it needs to be a little bit humorous because the morose technicality of it is too morose and technical (remember that's not what we're doing, this is experiential not technical). It's too sharp. It's too...into your Jellyfish Brain's turf, right? It's too aggressive. Without the humors, it's too aggressive, and the body really doesn't like imposition.

And then it brings us back to Marion Woodman, our psychological goddess of the north, the grandmother of grandmothers. One of her definitions for trauma is an arrested movement, an incomplete movement. Trauma is any arrested movement. She said a lot of things about trauma, but that one, for me as a body practitioner, is still on my mind, 30+ years later.

I do not want to start something and then aggressively force it to jump to another track unless I choose to do that, right? So, I need a little bit of humor. I need a little bit of time, and at this point, if I've got them into this part of their attention, their psyche and their biological landscape, and their physiology is starting to change, I want to have an enjoyable time. I better be enjoying myself, right? Because I can go into... (I'm feeling it now. I'm starting to get very emotional). [He's getting very emotional.] It's too easy to get really aggressive right there. This is a really tender... there's a lot of layers disoriented and reorienting. The person is having a sense of self that cannot be put into time, cannot be spoken, cannot be made into a location. And the Jellyfish Brain is at her wit's end. She's at her most vulnerable.

This is where many practitioners can get aggressive (me as well), and I have a whole part of my nature that is my sheep dog inside salivating at this point. My previous Michael Practitioners, they're going, "Oh, there's a bunch we could do!" There is, there are agendas that cannot be named that are historic and aggressive. There are ideas and concepts that want to come into this delicious moment and turn the whole thing into their donkey and ride the person for the rest of their lives. There's so much in the dynamic when more than a few layers get vulnerable. You've dropped this person into their visual cortexes, and this goes for any part, neighborhood of their/the garden body, but at this point in the session, we've got the person available to possible options, exploring, moving, starting to steep in 'their' actual motion, which is aquatic.        They're moving their perch. Something else is being allowed to circulate. Even though my hands are still on their leg (yes, still there), I've got them. They're starting to find the table. So, they're getting a different reference that may or may not be completely different than any other time in their life. They're vulnerable. Most people right there, if they get to this point, are vulnerable, but at this point then, then their agenda is ripe. My agenda's ripe, everything's ripe. Here, we have to get a little bit silly. So, we just bring them back around into another 'round of steeping, orienting'.

Then I'll say, "That's great, that's great!" You acknowledge what they just did. It doesn't matter how you acknowledge it, you just really go, "That's right!" You name it and you come back to the circle/cycle and name it. Name it, and then you orient: "There's the table. Yes, you have two visual cortexes, and they'll feel different.", and you give the Jellyfish Brain the ok and the understanding that both sides are different. When she's in neural dominance, they're even, balancing into a singular 'sight', and she's going to be wanting to 'even' out everything, to coordinate everything while you're in this moment. She can't help herself. It's her nature! So, you know you're right up against everybody's agenda. Everything's going to want to even out and to help, so you have to keep cycling at that, "Yeah, you've got roots coming from your eyes. Just feel the table, just feel those visual cortexes separate. Yeah, it does quirky things, right?" (We're doing it right now for those of you at home and it's quirky. It's making my... it's making my eyes do funny things and it does funny things to the neurology.)

This is the point: We're reorienting. When you have the person there, you're reorienting. It looks like you're reorienting their Jellyfish Brain and their perch, but really, you're setting them up to be able to soften their perch and to start to move around in their body, to differentiate their attention from their awareness which is being flooded 'Life-size'.

At this point, I'm also feeling responses in their leg. I haven't left the leg. I'm still doing everything on behalf of their frickin' leg. The neighborhood where my hands are is still my first and primary emphasis. I may have a lot to do to prep the soil. So, I'm prepping, but I'm also teaching. I'm also exercising, and I'm also getting a new dynamic and giving an opportunity for a reorganization, reorienting, an unwinding to happen. And, there's a global response to the root ball, 'global' just the domain of their body in this regard; although it's metaphor it's too juicy to resist, isn't it?

So, I've got them softened, got them on the table, got them starting to discern the differences between their perch and the table, and their Jellyfish Brain is starting to explore the different qualities of space. Then, I have a couple of choices. I can go, "Oh, and you know, it's not just your neural roots. Your Jellyfish Brain's also informed by your vascular roots." I introduce vascular again (right now your [Christie's] body just had her vascular response). Their body may or may not respond, but that's the testing of the labyrinth.

I take the next half step to see what direction in the labyrinth we can go. Where's the next "Yes"? Sometimes, you don't get to any other place. That's fucking good enough for the rest of a person's life really. Just, that's enough. Really! It's sacred, it's developmental, it's 'their' labyrinth, 'their' aquatic garden!

But I've got this leg who would really like to be part of things... inclusion. And I'm wanting to introduce that it's not just neural roots, but you have vascular roots, right? (Every once in a while, and it's a mood thing, I'll throw in, "You know, you've got lymphatic roots, too." But, lymphatic does something different, because it's a different system, you know? It's got a bunch of one-way heart valves in its own living root bed. The lymphatic roots and the heart roots actually have a lot to do with each other as co-mingled creatures, and there's a Jellyfish Brain co-mingled as well... so many beautiful living roots and tendrils.)

So back with the heart... and this gets difficult for me to say out loud because for me, experientially, the heart is not in the chest. Just four dancers of the heart are in the chest, held by their sister, the pericardium (have we talked about the organs being cisterns? Tea makers? Song hummers? Sisters!). The heart really is the entire vascular bed because there's no center to it, right? It could be argued that the bone marrow is the center for vascular, the heart, because the bone marrow makes, cooks, brews all the blood cells and the blood serum, so in that... [Christie shifts and Michael gets excited]

(Yeah, see! You guys, you (Christie) can't write this. You're going to try and write this all down, but there's a whole visceral, a whole global body feeling, a full body response to what I just said, right?)

So, you're playing with that as a practitioner, I'm playing with that back and forth-ness. This global response, softening of the tissue, or the contraction, yes or no? "Yes" will always be a softening. "No" is always a contraction, safety... and it's not about yes or no. "Yes" means there's more energy/potency, and they can take the next couple steps. "No" is there's not enough energy/potency. The next couple of steps can't be taken. It's purely a matter of attention/energy/potency. It's not the other implications of yes and no. "Yes" is a simple softening. Everything can respond. "No" is we can't respond. We can't handle that arising response. There's not enough energy to follow through. It's very cool. So that's a visceral piece, and I'm playing with it because ultimately, I want the person to be able to do this themselves, to self-facilitate.

"Oh, how do I include my leg?", or, "Where are the bones in my leg?" And then their questions become odd, "Well, where are my roots of my eyes. Oh, oh, that just changed my... wait... I was up in my perch again." Right. That's discernment. You've given them something to play with, to engage with, because I'm sitting there playing (musically, not like a game) with it in a way that gives them the option of doing this. Of course, by the end of this session, for some people it's really great. Other people, they nooo like it. Their Jellyfish Brain's like, "Screw this. I'm really gonna need somebody to pummel me into oblivion." That was too much. Even though I have my agenda that this is the first of many sessions or this is the middle of many sessions or "Oh, there's lots of work to do!", I have to hold that intent of, "Wait a minute, I'm gardening 'these' root beds with this person's garden today. We'll do what we can, today. What they do after that is none of my business." Right? How they integrate it, and the time it takes to integrate it, is a matter of time's nature.

So, we're back there. We've got them from neural roots. We've introduced a little vascular root again, several times by now. And we keep trying to find that, and then it gets interesting. If the vascular root bed doesn't work, and going into another root bed doesn't work, then I'll come back to bones, right? Right then! I'll go, "Oh yeah, there's the bone. Where are your bones?" So, then there'll be some response and I'll keep playing with where 'their' response goes. And then from the eye roots, if we get a response... (it's very rare I don't get a response from eye roots). If I don't, then then I'll jump muscularly. Then we do a crazy thing in that then we jump to the tongue, because by this time there's a little bit of guidance, you know.

The tongue is really an interesting creature because the Jellyfish Brain thinks that the tendrils of the tongue belong to her, because we can speak, as we are doing now. Um, so from the eyes, it usually goes to tongue. Because tongue is muscular, you know, the neurology thinks it has control over the tongue. Technically it doesn't. The actual roots of the tongue, which is a piece of wonderful anatomy, reach down along the esophagus into the throat and chest...literally the tongue's attachment. What makes the tongue so delicious is that it's a one-sided muscle. It's the only one-sided muscle in the body. The other side belongs to teeth and to air because the end of the tongue (right now as you [Christie] are getting an earful), is wagging and making all these wonderful sounds into words... musically... really! Actually!

The tongue belongs to an aspect of the Jellyfish Brain because she can control it muscularly, but the actual roots of the tongue go down into the throat and chest. So, this is another place to introduce a big, wonderful quagmire to the Jellyfish Brain because, somatically, the tongue has a literal location, a literal place, and it's attachment is literally into the esophagus, into the chest, to the throat. (So I'm having a problem right now 'thinking'... I'm feeling it.) And then the Jellyfish Brain goes, "Wait a minute. No,

the tongue is mine because I can make language."
You've set up an argument, a discord, which can be
terribly fun. Same argument you set up with the eyes
earlier, by the way, because it's very argumentative,
the Jellyfish Brain. She wants control! She's got
tendrils. Tendrils like to wrap around things, even if
they're ideas. It's a beautiful thing.

So, from eyes we'll go to tongue and throat. That'll
drop me back into the muscular, and the minute, yes,
*the minute* someone feels (try this at home) um, feels
their tongue and literally where it's attached, and feels
it into their throat, they're going into the somatic
branches of their neural net... and throwing the pre
and frontal cortexes into great disarray. It... you're
getting disoriented because the Jellyfish Brain really,
when you're talking especially, has control. It's hard to
not be neural-dominant and talk, although some of us
have tried for years to develop this ability, which is the
only reason I'm functional (That's funny in so many
ways. It's very private, too. That's for me and my
therapist. Thank you very much!). This is where it gets
very interesting because letting the roots of the
tongue fall back into the throat and chest also puts us
into a different quality of language where you start to
get into symbolic. We start to get into poetry. We

start to get to feel words in our throat and our chest, and then a part of our Jellyfish Brain softens.

Now, we've created an inclusivity with the body where the Jellyfish Brain and the body are more copacetic, are more co-mingled with each other. We're not so neural-dominant. We've gone into more of a somatic layer, even though we're staying functional. My hands are still on the person's leg and they're either with me on the table, or they are gone (asleep, adrift, steeping), and I'll still say this stuff out loud.    They don't need to be awake. I can still completely work with them because I'm talking to their body, a lullaby 'with' (neural)/during (somatic) their body, right?! I'm including all their roots in my conversation. My roots are still tracking for responses in their roots, and I'm in dialogue, a musical living jazz dialogue. Even though I'm saying it out loud, I'm still letting the visceral roots of my tongue, and the feeling of the words in my chest, still try to find that kind of sonar bat response in their body. The low-end sound/resonance in my chest 'during' the Lullaby, musical prompting, Naming... I'm still tracking where they are, and playing with it, you know, trying to get it to circulate, trying to get it to migrate, and then a quirky thing happens.

By this time session's over. Minutes/years have gone by, but they keep coming back, which is very funny to me because it's the same gardening no matter how many years, right? It's the same day, in a certain respect poetically, philosophically, viscerally it's the same thing. The advocacy still holds up. I'm still gardening this person's interaction with their own structure, their beautiful, hair-balled garden, from a living, gardening sort of way, you know, and, if I'm very, very lucky, one of these times, all of a sudden, they're in their leg with me. All of a sudden, their attention and the neighborhood in their leg are having a conversation and I get to be part of that, Right? Awesome!

I'm still a drummer providing rhythm, context, and quality of space for their song to happen. I'm still keeping a certain rhythm and keeping a certain like, "Here's the downbeat, here's your bones, here's the downbeat, here's your bones." The bass note is happening in your ankle. The base note is happening in your ankle. Today it's the tarsus ganglia providing the bass note, and the "why" (I don't like why's). "Why" the tarsus ganglia is the bass note is because, to feel the tarsus ganglia in the ankle, you have to soften all the roots of the entire body so they're responsive, like one big long plucked sinewed cello string, and then everything goes musically responsive as it is! You're the bass note. All the tissues go, "What? Life-size?", and you play with that, so it's still musical.

One day, maybe even that session, they drop into their leg and we're there together and the leg responds. So, I start to unwind and stay in the response of that leg, and I know that they'll only be able to stay there for a short time and they'll cycle back up to their perch. Then I have a choice, I can say, "That's great!", and start to swim towards the end of the session, "Hey, look what you did!" Or I can do several rounds of that, and then end the session and say, "Look what you did!"

**Christie**  So what do you mean by, "I start to unwind"? What... What are you doing?

*Michael*  When someone's dropping into their visual cortexes, finding the roots of their eyes, feeling the roots of their tongue, they start to feel roots. Then, at some point, they get that what's in my hands is where we're trying to move their attention. In this case, an example is I'm holding and working a leg, and all of a sudden, the leg responds, the same way the eye responds, the same way the back of the Jellyfish Brain responds, same way throat responds. All of a sudden, they are there in the leg, with themselves. They are

267

there in that leg with me, and the leg starts to respond accordingly. It starts to be able to move and have a conversation with the Jellyfish Brain, cuz in my hand is a neighborhood. The Jellyfish's tendrils are only one layer commingled with other roots. If I'm lucky, we can get them to entertain the idea that there's not just neural roots and bone, but there's vascular roots, maybe even lymphatic roots, and maybe even feel that there's these different layers of muscles, that there's fascia. There's a spider web, a Fascial web in there as well, and then, on a really good day, if you've gotten all those other things in place, the ideal is that you say, "And you have a joint. You have synovial fluid. You have a completely different creature within these creatures."

We usually can sneak it in at the end of the session when they're standing up and you're having to orient them so they can integrate and then walk out of your office somewhat coherently, and you'll get to talk about how joints negotiate space. Muscles are responsive. All of a sudden, a person's moving as if they've had three or four shots of tequila, a good glass of wine or has done Tai Chi for five years. They'll have this natural seaweed movement in their body, without collapsing and without imposing a shape. They'll take all the little efforts they do, all the habits they do, of wanting to fuss, and they'll let them drop back into their circulation, back into their bones. They'll orient to the contact of the floor against their foot, and they'll play with it. They'll have, all of a sudden, found this whole range of motion/movement that's not muscularly dominant, that's not investing all their effort and energy. They'll actually be able to play with the quality of their body, opposed to functionally pushing their body through space and throwing it to their next activity. And most people throw their bodies around. Very few people move their hands and can feel that motion/movement in their feet. That's a really rare thing, but by the end of a session sometimes you can get at least some of that to happen. And I'm a percentage guy, so if it's 5% more than when they walked in - ah! - and I don't just decide that. I make them decide that. "What's different than when you walked in?", and that's a trick question. Any response is the right response! That's somatic dominance!

And I know that their Jellyfish Brain's going to go, "Whoa mister...". And I'm not a psychologist, so I don't care how their brain responds, just that she is able to have her response! Their Jellyfish Brain has a response! Not any different, any more or less, than a vascular response or lymphatic response or a muscular skeletal response. Oh, and then there are all the Jellyfish Brain's sisters... the Organs! (they're all making Teas and singing for/with/to each other, all responsive! I get very excited!)

**Christie** So going back just a little bit to unwinding and what that means...?

**Michael** Unwinding is tricky. So, there is an aggressive manipulation of tissue, right? You find a hairball, a piece of tissue doesn't move. In this case, we've just got their attention finally in their leg, right? Which they've just been moving through and coping with... and their leg has just been doing habitual habits the whole time, the previous time. We finally got them into their leg. There's that visceral response, there's a, there's an, "Oh... yes.", response. Their leg responds to it by getting its own motion/movement, within its own range.

My hands are there. I've got them, believe you me! In my softest, nonaggressive way, I've still got them by the teeth. My sheepdog teeth are still right there ready to break skin. So, I've got them, but in a way I'm creating a container because I want to feel the response... what happens when their attention slides into their leg. There's an inclusion that happens, like your [Christie's] whole body just responded. It's that.

It's a motion, a movement you can't make happen. It's a movement they can't make happen. Honest to Goodness, it's the motion, the movement of that neighborhood. That neighborhood now has enough attention that the inclusion of the rest of the roots causes it to behave differently. We're banking on that. That's my job.

**Christie** And that's...

*Michael* That is the beginning of unwinding. Unwinding is the following through of that response.

**Christie** By you, by them?

*Michael* Good question. It's usually both. In an aggressive state, I may take advantage of the moment and, if that gate opens up, we're moving the sheep through, right? My sheep dog goes, "Yes, we're on!!" The person 's gone into unwinding, you know, and I'll move a root bed that is entangled. I will do it, or I will tie it into another root. I will find the 'through', a passage, from this neighborhood to that neighborhood, or that neighborhood to that next neighborhood, or I might even find a whole 'through' right up to that perch! OH...and I'll go, "HAH!"

I'm now moving along, starting to differentiate and that depends on what tissue is snagged, right? If I can find a 'through' for that snag, that part of the hairball, then we've gone into 'unwind', and that can look like

271

anything. It can look from very aggressive like, "I got you! There's no way you're ever getting your leg back the way you want it!", because the Jellyfish Brain has a picture of that leg that she's been using for a long time, since before she walked into that office. So, I'm up against the cortical homunculus, which is the map of the body used by the Jellyfish Brain.

She has chalkboards, I'm telling you...quite a few chalkboards. This is unconfirmed, by the way, but it is what it feels like. I've heard others are now also using this chalkboard analogy for when you get an injury and the overwhelm from the information of the injury itself smears the picture your Jellyfish Brain has of your body. Your body creates a shape to cope with that change, and that becomes 'normal'. So, the idea is to somatically reeducate the body so it cleans up that wash of overwhelm, the wash of trauma, and gets back to specifics, so it gets a cleaner map of the body. So easy to say, but they're using that analogy now, I'm here to tell you. They're using a single chalkboard reference, but I'm telling you, there're many chalkboards. The cortical homunculus is a very complex part of the neurology, and that Jellyfish knows where everything is. If you move her frickin' lamp that's in the leg, she's gonna put it back. You've got to convince her that the new position of the lamp is okay and will shed more light on the neighborhood. Yeah...which borderlines into the psychotherapy, just for the reference, but manually, you're frickin' moving a lamp that's in the leg and, Oh my Goodness! Jellyfish gets very feisty about where the furniture goes in one's house. So unwinding is the moving of that lamp. The unwinding is opening up those root beds, so they interact differently, and doing it in such a way that stays within the range of that tissue on its terms; and then you're back in the cycle/circle, you're back up against the neurology, the dominance, the habituated use of that neighborhood, and trying to convince it to do something else like, "No, actually your range is this. No, it's not two feet. It's this millimeter to millimeter.", because you're differentiating those roots so that there's greater function within that range of the whole neighborhood... not the neural-dominant picture of it.

There is a mistake I see a lot of practitioners do with this in that they again go neural-dominant with that. They watch limbs move through space in big arcs and big distances, but the tissues themselves don't move like that. You know the difference because how a piece of jellyfish tendril moves, an actual nerve root, an actual neural nerve fiber and its relationship with the surrounding fibers, the vascular roots, the lymphatic roots, the whole list, the fascial network, the muscular skeletal aspect, the intervention of those tissues, the co-mingling of those tissues... that range will be very small.

Yet when you free up a section of that, it changes the behavior through that neighborhood, and now you've changed this relationship to all the neighborhoods around it, and then we're back to the circulation of information. You change that position, so you've changed how the neighborhood relationally functions. You've changed the other positions in the other neighborhoods, you know. It's this wonderful... it's a... you wait for the global (body) response to the cascade.

Yeah. There's much drier and more technical language around that, that makes my mouth hurt, because it takes me out of, "Wait a minute...*this neighborhood is alive.*" It's been coping with this situation for a long time. I'm its advocate. Can I speak its language on its terms and help it move in a way that's within its own range? Within its range, which is not how we walk through the world, but how...This is the Vivian statement, "How we walk across the room is how we walk through our lives."

How one walks through a room is how one walks through their life, and there's a truth to that, but you have to feel how they're walking through a room.

And that was the gift of Vivian. Watching/feeling someone move is really important because you get where the hairballs are from watching/feeling the person move through a room and watching/feeling them sit and tell you their story at the beginning of the session. Then you have to go investigate, and when you enter into the landscape of that tissue, you have to be prepared to meet the behaviors of that landscape and that tissue on its terms, not from a translated neural-dominant view. And that's very difficult, but terribly challenging and very exciting for some of us. For those of us who like to watch grass grow, it's a beautiful time. Other people that don't like it, they can't stand it and they're just going to keep plowing through... which also has its place, also sacred!

So yes, that unwinding is noticing when the tissue finally gets its opportunity to respond in its own way on its own terms, in conversation 'with' the Jellyfish Brain, in conversation 'with' the neural net, and your job is to keep it there, steep it, add more time, and help it explore its range within its range. Technically, that's what unwinding is. You're helping that piece explore its options within its range, right? Not convince it to do something so the rest of the body can do its old dance again. Your job is really an advocate for that hairball, you know...how do you get it to have the confidence to explore and find its neighbors again and start to explore options, within its ability. Just that little bit... just that tissue even considering exploring its options is a big deal!

**Christie**  Well... I think this is a lot...!

*Michael*  Sure. That's enough.

# Chapter Seven: *Interview #5*

**Michael**  And alright. Alright, so October 16th, October 16, 2017. Here we go!

**Christie**  So this may seem like a very basic question, but I would really like to hear what you say, and that is, I was thinking last time when you were talking about 'getting on the table', you talked about sort of two, at least two ways that the nervous system tracks, and you said 'superficial' on one level, and then 'sensory'. You called it 'sensory something' on another level. Do you remember that?

**Michael**  Excellent.

**Christie**  So I was wondering if you can say more about what the differences are between the superficial and the deeper, the sensory, whatever, and how someone shifting their attention into that sensory thing, what kind of affect that has on the bones and the tissues which might be different. How does attention itself affect the bones and tissues, or does it?

**Michael**  Wow.  And here we go. Wow, that's a good, that's a good run.

We've got our daily attention, right? Our proprioception, our organs in the face, our sensors that are designed to track space. They literally are designed to, to mediate and be out here in the terrestrial world, you know, what's happening around me... what's that bird doing? Is it going to be a burglar? I don't know. Those types of situations... engaging in relationship lines... all that's done beautifully in that superficial, or that daily part of our awareness, or that proprioceptive part of our awareness, that kind of outer layer.

And then, we have an inner layer that, when the stimulations of the senses calm down, the Jellyfish Brain does an interesting thing. So, it's dominant, it's tracking, she's in her glory, and then she gets to rest. The Jellyfish Brain actually gets to rest. The Jellyfish actually gets to begin to just float within her own environment, which is aquatic, which is fluid. And she starts to disregard the outer world. She starts to not be so vigilant. She starts to calm that proprioceptive interaction, that reaching and tracking outwards, and she drops into that more somatic or sensate or sensory state where she's, um, starting to have the interactions with the more opaque, more abstract movements of sensations, feelings, and the more gentle motions of inner and outer environments.

**Christie** So what does that mean?

*Michael* That means that she's starting to drop into her interior environment. But the Jellyfish Brain does a funny thing when the body goes dominant or the brainstem switches into a developmental state where everything's all, "Yum! Yum! Yum!", soft, fuzzy, watery, you know, where curiosity and imagination are free flowing, circulating, and she's not managing any of that. She actually turns into an organ for a little while, just steeping.

Then, in that place, her actual tendrils are being informed from the interior. Information is moving a little bit more like molasses, a warm sap instead of electricity. There's lots of ways to talk about that step down that happens. And it's a step down that happens when one is resting right before one goes into napping, right? A precursor to sleep.

It's that kind of step-down process. When someone's in the office, they're walking in, so kind of an easy call. You know they're coming in their daily dance, their daily persona, whatever that daily dance and persona is that is their awareness, that is awareness, the quality of space they are/occupy. You have to meet that person where they are when they come into your space. It's just good manners, as well as the therapeutic necessity. Aside from all that complicated chatter, it's just good manners, very cordial. Meet someone, kindly walk them into your world, from their world to your world. You do the dance around that meeting, and like we've talked before, you're picking up the cues from that somatic layer, from their mythic layer, from their soul, from their bones. You're watching/feeling/sensing how they respond, how they move and express.

**Christie** They're not in that mythic place? They're not in...?

*Michael* Mostly they're not, because our daily senses when they are specifically engaged are too small to track that, that large quality of space and they may not have developed those skills yet, ever, right?

**Christie** But you as the practitioner...?

*Michael* Me as the practitioner, and the lover of such things... (those two things need to be, you know, they're coupled for sure. They're holding hands a lot) me as a practitioner, I'm wanting that information because that's where we're going. Ultimately, I want them resting on the table so I can have the freedom to have the conversation with the other layers of them, with that somatic layer, um, with that mythic layer, with their actual sinews and bones and tissue layers.

When that happens, what happens is the awareness drops out of that superficial proprioceptive vigilant "Ah hah! literal", into a symbolic wonderful dance that's also happening, the theater, the theater of our expression, and we start dropping down into those stocks, those soup stocks or the tea or the ingredients of that psychodrama of the daily, "Ah hah!". We start dropping into larger, different layers of landscape. That's where I'm going, that's what I'm interested in, that's what I'm there to palpate and work with, to gently move towards and into that place.

**Christie**   Into what place?

*Michael*   Into the place where they switch from that proprioceptive daily 'I'm on' sort of thing. In that 'on' place where the awareness is out in the field, is out on the skin, is out in the senses. Everything's tracking. The Jellyfish Brain is very happy managing all the delicious input, and making up her own when the gathered info doesn't satisfy. She's very clever, that Jellyfish Brain. So, in that place, a lot of the systems are in a secondary process. They're waiting. They're like, "Yeah, we'll digest a little bit, but we won't really break it down because this Jellyfish Brain is just gonna get up and start moving again. So, we'll just…. We'll get…" Anyways, all these wonderful things they'll do a little bit, but they aren't really going to, um, do reconstructive work because your body is too busy moving, engaged outwardly. The tissues can't really integrate and repair if you're moving, that's why rest is so important.

But you're out there, so your awareness is 'on' and it's out in your field and everything is just a little bit more alive, and it takes a great amount of energy to do that. The bones are just taking up space. They're literally in that daily upright place. The bones are in their element of taking up space, of giving a reference to all the other tissues who are active and 'on'. Our musculature, our joints... the bones are just orienting them in space. They're literally creating space... and... they're space makers.

**Christie** So that's true when you're walking around or...?

*Michael* When you're walking around and doing the daily stuff, you, your bones and a lot of your tissues are also 'on'; your joints are 'on', your muscles are in the parts of that superficial nervous system that are extremely responsive, you know, they're ready to go, they're in their patterns, but they're ready to go. They're ready to work, they're fired up, you know, those systems are 'on'.

As you stepped down from that, the awareness starts to flood into the body and after a little while, maybe 10, 15 minutes, at least 10 to 15 minutes, that first cycle, (these are also cycles), um, the Jellyfish Brain's going, "I'm not doing anything. I'm laying on his table or I'm just sitting on the couch, you know, thinking that it'd be great if he stopped talking." So, we're still 'on', but as we start to soften and not move around so much, that superficial, proprioceptive part of the nervous system isn't being stimulated, right?

Awareness is a very cool thing. The body itself is so freakishly, incredibly efficient!

Then the Jellyfish Brain starts going, "Oh, I don't have to manage all this mechanical response. Oh, I don't have to hype up and meet the drama of what's happening around me." She (Jellyfish Brain) starts to step down. As she does that, she starts to kind of soak or steep. The awareness starts to come into the tissues, and the tissues start going, "Oh great!" They're not going to move for a while. We'll start to reestablish our electrolyte counts. We'll start to kind of process out all the lactic acid from all the muscular movement. Oh, we'll start to feed. We'll do it quick. We have a half hour to go... Go! Pizza and beer for everybody! We'll start feeding the systems and we'll start recalibrating. We'll start reestablishing baselines. Marvelous really!

For a lot of people they're 'on' so much, they're so hyper-vigilant, the system never steps down, unless they're in really deep sleep. So, my interest in my job is that place of using my nervous system and learning how to move in a calm state (even when moving towards 'quick') and just acknowledging that I have these other layers.

Then, all of a sudden, the proprioception calms down and, not only am I paying attention to their interior or 'the' interior, but now I have to initiate another state of behavior, right? I have to do the very things I'm not supposed to do. I start at a more subtle form of coercion, enticement, invitation, manipulation, tracking. What I do is allow my system to start tracking their system, which, also in proximity, does a really interesting thing to the field awareness. The client's Jellyfish Brain doesn't have to track for saber-toothed tigers and burglars and love songs and people in the hall and the proximity, the surround because mine is (and I am). My vigilance has become a base for an orientation of their vigilance, and in proximity, the limbic systems talk to one another, the original cell phones.

For the first handful of years of life, technically the little one's nervous system is still regulated by the adult. Whatever that is, healthy or unhealthy, it doesn't matter. Biologically the tissues don't discern. It's like, "Well, that's the note that's being played so that'll be our bass note.", until the little one gets enough experience that it can start to displace the adult's song, and then that wonderful 'terrible twos' kicks in and the little one goes, "That is not my song... you are not my mom (well until I need you, so don't go far), but right now, that is not my song!" But, the little one can only say "No!" They can only start the interesting dance of differentiation, because that's what's happening in the system as well, just a little tantrum.

So, in the office we're allowing a person's awareness to drop out of the vigilant state or the active state, the activated state, the engaged proprioceptively external state, terrestrial state, (10,000 words later, which he won't try to say), and then we start stepping it down. My nervous system, because I'm in proximity and I'm tracking, starts to take over some of the jobs of the person's system and this is just part of our social nervous system.

As we step that down, softening, my system is becoming the dominant bass line. All of a sudden, their awareness is allowed to circulate inside/with the skin, instead of *on the skin*. The engagement becomes interior to the skin, in the nerves themselves, instead of being out at the superficial aspects of the nervous system like proprioception or hearing or seeing which are still superficial engagements, you know. Even though these nerves and organs (sisters!?!?) are in the head, they're all used to track outside the head.

So, all of a sudden those senses start to go, "I don't have to do that... Oh!", so 'surround' starts to happen. My attention and my awareness are sensing, tracking the space around/with the person. Then, their attention and awareness can start to steep, soak, become condensed into their interior. And that can be stated/named or not. Most of the time it doesn't need to be stated. But then I can do a wacky thing and I prompt, "Where's your bones?" So now, while the awareness is steeping, the attention has something to do.

**Christie**  Exactly.

*Michael*  Attention loves doing stuff, it seems! It's highly mobile. Fact is, it's faster than all our senses put together, I think. So that attention gets to go, "Oh, well, bone... bones!" And then something really cool happens that I find hard for words, but very engaging, just very satisfying, just extremely engaging. A person goes, "Oh my God, I have bones?", and something goofy happens...bones reply!

And this is a strange thing, which for me is normal because this is what I get to play with every day. To me, in my sheep dog aspect, it makes a lot of sense. (Other people are like, "My bones are just bones." I'm like, "You wish..!"). Um, so bones reply, and what made this significant early on for me, is that not all the bones reply. And that caught my attention. "Ah!" The person's attention trying to find their bones got my attention/awareness of the bones that weren't responding in contrast to the bones that were like little puppies and little cats going, "Hello? (A little purr, a little softening.)", like there was a response from the tissue. And that still...

**Christie** Now wait a minute... there was a response from what tissue?

*Michael* From the bone tissue, from whatever tissue was being prompted. Like the last time you and I dealt with legs. Um, it can be any neighborhood of bone. A bone sits within an aquatic environment with roots and all this wonderful seaweed stuff (and a bunch of technical words later), but that, but that neighborhood responded, and this is very cool because we think, oh, we're occupying our body, but even when we think we're occupying our body, it's kinda funny, you know, we're occupying our senses. We have specific sense organs, but we don't consider organs in our chest and our belly as sense organs, unless we talk about the heart, which is usually a symbolic reference, right? You know, unless something's so emotionally engaging that our feelings and our emotions create this amazing response, that our tissues have no recourse but to respond. And our Jellyfish Brain goes, "Oh Goodness, I'm out of control. I'm in love, I'm in total fear." It's hard to tell. Sometimes they can be coupled together.

So, we're holding this. My awareness is flooding and making a surround for the person. The room is not big, so it adds to that surround, to the safety.

**Christie**  And what about the music?

**Michael**  Um, the music is an interesting thing. I use music as white noise I think (as an aside, I've used the same piece of music now for close to 25 years. I've varied it in the early days and once in a while I'm forced to vary it by certain clients, but for the most part I've got the same hodgepodge compilation of music), but it just, it, it's gotten to be just background music and, because it's the same music every time, I've found that it has an inductive capacity... as when actual musicians are in dialogue with each other, it's similar and resonant with how the different root beds and organs sing to/with each other!

**Christie**  Yeah, that's what I would see in terms of the surround...

**Michael**  That's right. It's consistent. It's the same. Yeah. I try to stay consistent in the same way because I'm using my bones. My bones move in time differently, so I'm pretty consistent in the same repetition, a type of bass line. I try to use language the same, um, because I figured out (with lots of therapy and help) that I can use language kinesthetically and tactically. It's pretty much always the same language, and that can sound boring to those people who spend a lot of time in psychodrama, but I'm telling you, setting the surround and setting your own nature and your own therapeutic holding of the space can be very casual, very musical, and very vigilant. It can be a number of 'both-and' situations, and the consistency piece I find for a person's nervous system is essential, because I'm in the precarious position of trying to get their nervous system to soften in a way that we can unwind the environment that has caught the nervous system in its hairballs! Not so easy...good...and 'good' is seldom 'easy'.

The job is to get that nervous system calm enough so I can work, or distracted enough, which is a different form of calm, by the way. It can be highly distractive and highly entertaining (and some people get good entertainment value out of their dollar), and I have to get all the same work done. I learned that in the PT Office; that there's a certain cacophony of sound that, when that's normal, the person immediately will associate the sound with normal. So, if they walk into a PT office, they're not going to expect a spa, they're not going to expect Esalen, not going to expect serene.

So, awareness meets the space as well, floods the area. Um, the awareness has its own fluid state as well, for lack of a better way to say it, you know, and I think we all argue over this, so we'll just say that we can all argue over this. But, for me, when a person's starting to calm down, it's literally the field of their awareness that slides back into their body. It becomes congruent with their fluids and roots, and in that place the tissues get very responsive, in their own dynamic of responsiveness.

**Christie** Why?

*Michael* Because you start to talk their, the tissues, language. The tissues start to get an attention that they don't normally get. Remember, awareness tends towards tea, flooding and steeping, nourishing the 'quality of space'. Attention is the aspect that moves within the 'field' flooded with awareness. They, the tissues, may dream about getting attention, and our tissues are very alive and like to be interacted with. They're highly socialized, it's that disparity sometimes that can set off the myriad of things that, Thank Goodness, other therapies are great for. In my office, as we start to calm their external stimuli or make a consistent external stimulus, like a surround which includes music which is stimulating, that surround starts to create a buffer that the nervous system goes, "Oh, this is this. Oh, this is okay. Oh, this is..." And then, all of a sudden, their interior gets to express in a way that it doesn't get to in the day-to-day world... the neural-dominant world.

**Christie**   Yes.

*Michael*   And it's more akin to napping, deep rest in deep sleep where we just simmer ourselves. There's no reaching, there's no 'doing' really. And all of a sudden our attention, just because it's free to swim about... for most people in that place, their attention and their imagination will wander off. They'll grab their dream body, they'll get on a little dream body donkey, and they'll go wandering through the ethereal and dreaming, and they'll start wandering through the universe in the way that we do when we start getting near dreaming.

In the office it's really interesting because that part of the psyche does the same thing. It starts to drift, to circulate, and then I have a couple of choices of how I work with that. I can... sometimes I want them to stay in their body. I want them to find this connection with 'that which they can become'. There's still all this beautiful engagement happening in their biology, and they can be introduced to their biology in a respectful way, a playful way and, hopefully, a begin-to-self-facilitate-later kind of way.

This gets very tricky because you're having to add to someone's awareness of themselves and train their

Jellyfish Brain not to reach for their innards because the Jellyfish Brain will take her external relationships and education and training and history and experience, and she applies it to her interior, right? This may work in the ER, but it doesn't work casually in your home, or in the office.

I think this is one of the harder parts of being alive, in that our attention can be softened, but we have to be trained to treat our interior with the respect of treating a feral animal. And that's why I used the word 'feral' a lot, because people seem to understand that. They know feral cat, and they know you can't reach for it. And, if you grab it, you're going to get tooth and nail coming at you until that creature or aspect of us calms down, which may or may not ever happen, depending on the cat (aspect). Some feral cats are so good that they can smell you reaching for them. We know their limbic systems are really hyper-vigilant, that's part of the problem there. Yes. People have that too, you know when someone's sniffing you out at a party, you can feel it! The limbic system/sister has just sniffed a Saber Tooth Tiger, Burglar, Asshole (and, yes, a possible love song; but *now*... who's the Tiger?!?!)!

But interiorly, those are very real issues. They're as real as our external issues... the sense of safety, the sense of exploring nourishment, the sense of protection. All those things are there for all our tissues... it's hard to say 'concerns' because we start to use all these psychological or daily language in neural-dominant perspectives.

And this is why I love my job, and it's so frustrating for me personally because our awareness changes there. We start to step into the place where our symbolic use of language has no range...

**Christie** Has no range?

*Michael* No range. We, we start to move out of languaging.

**Christie** Oh...

*Michael* Right. As we get closer to the bridge between symbolic and mythic, we're moving out of language. We're, we're moving out of the ability to form... any linguistic ability, right? We're moving into that place where a symbology starts to move out of language and starts to move into its symbolled nature, into its containers, into its shapes, into its qualities, into the things that make artists salivate across the board (I'm salivating right now).

**Christie** Yes... so... so you're talking about the internal as being mythic, is that right?

*Michael* Not necessarily; but when our interior, when our awareness has softened, and it's just steeping with our tissues and bones in a way that our bones and tissues are allowed to be in their responsiveness as they are, within their range, on their terms, and their dynamics...our awareness changes. It does something that's really hard for words. And I don't know all the right words for that, except that it changes. It becomes a tea. It becomes a soup stock. It starts to interact with our actual bass notes and other baselines of the body. Our Jellyfish Brain goes from being this incredible dancing brain to being just an organ, with all of her tendrils on equal terms to all the other tendrils of the other root beds, co-mingled roots!

You know, the vascular system looks and can feel very tendrily, looks/feels very rooty, and those things in deep sleep are all on equal terms, and they're all moving and behaving in aquatic rhythms, in tidal rhythms, and they're all awash with activity like you would find on a calm day in a tide pool. All the little creatures have their time, and feel fairly safe, but anything big happens, they all scamper, they disappear... you know?!

Our interior turns out to be very similar. When I'm working with someone, those same behaviors happen. If I come in too quick, their tide pools are empty. The bones... the awareness moves out of the bone. The bones go feral, and you can be holding someone's neighborhood, including their bones and being right

294

there with them, and if I do something too quick, it's

vacant. It's so frickin' amazingly responsive!

**Christie**  It is!

*Michael*  The awareness will move. It will move off to safety,

taking the attention with it!

**Christie**  So what would you call mythic then?

*Michael*  Mythic is the motion/movement, mythic is the motion

of the movement... right? If I can get to a place where

my system's calm and I'm letting these other levels of

engagement or layers of engagement or interactions,

like symbolic language, literally, "We're doing this,

come here, you beautiful bone, you" - if I let those go

calm, then I can get into the dance. Then, all of a

sudden, if the person's awareness floods back into the

neighborhood, attention slides back in as well and

their bone becomes dominant, it becomes a dominant

intelligence in that neighborhood. The Jellyfish Brain is

just being held. She's being informed. She's not

responding, right? She's just one of the other tissues

(which happens). Then, all of a sudden, the whole

neighborhood gets responsive and starts to have its

own motion/movement in response to the person's

attention being calm, and my attention being calm,

but a part of me is not calm while I'm tracking all this

but allowing both awareness to flood and attention to

be responsive. So that system actually gets very

interesting. That neighborhood that we're handling has a couple of different responses. It's, it either goes, "This is cool, this person's talking our language, our non-linguistic language. We've got somebody's complete undivided attention, we feel their awareness... ", which adds to the dynamic, and then, when I don't mess with it too much, those neighborhoods get a little happy. And I don't mean happy like your response just now. But I mean there's, there's a "Yes" response, right? It softens and occupies, even gets curious.

**Christie** It's content.

*Michael* It's content. It occupies. The attention and awareness in that area are even. It's responsive. When I go quickly, or if there's a real panic underneath that protective interaction that has learned to normalize itself, then, when disturbed, that panic will come forward. And, and that, um, that's a trickier thing. It's like holding a salmon that doesn't want to be held. I mean, there's an activeness to it, but it's trying to get away, you know?

And then there's a whole myriad of choices to make at that point because by this time we've gotten the person very calm in some respects, or I've got them so distracted with their story that their legs are like, "Ahhh!", they don't care. So, I have this conversation with their leg. I'm having a different conversation with the person's Jellyfish Brain because their Jellyfish Brain just isn't going to come out of vigilance. I got work to do. So, I'm like, "Okay, that's great." I really concentrate my bones on feeling their bones. I concentrate my sinews on handling their sinews, and I start to stay within the movement of that neighborhood sensing for the motion underneath/within. At least we have that contact within contact.

So, I build rapport with that neighborhood, and it may not be congruent with what's happening in the Jellyfish Brain. It can split experience, right? We call that positive dissociation (If there is such a thing. There should be because dissociation is a beautiful thing we're capable of doing. Bad when the body suffers. Great when the body's nourished.).

Awareness/attention is this mobile, movable, living layer, an aspect of ourselves, and imagination is its own amazing movable layer and aspect of ourselves. Coping is an amazing, living, movable dynamic and so on.

**Christie** Right.

*Michael* When I work, they're not the same things, but out here, we all argue about all that, you know, but from the body's point of view, the body doesn't give a hoot.

So, when you start to calm and you bring and allow your attention to meet another layer of you, something really delicious happens. Yes, your bones will respond. Yes, your bones have their own type of attention. They have their own dynamic, they have their own rules, their own tendencies. They have their own behavior, their own steeping with awareness, which I find remarkable.

**Christie** Oh yeah!

*Michael* Anyways, for me, behavior has a certain layer of awareness and intelligence to it.

**Christie** So it sounds like you're saying that in a certain sense the bones then become dominant...?

*Michael* Yes, but not in a neural way; in a central to an oriented neighborhood way.

**Christie** Is that true?

*Michael* Yes.

**Christie** And dominant relative to the other tissues as well as... I mean...

*Michael* It's really tricky, isn't it? It's dominant in the fact that the neural dominance isn't taking over or has softened into a non-dominant steeping in the Jellyfish Brain's actual environment (sort of way).

**Christie** Right. So...

*Michael* The minute that Jellyfish Brain backs off, which is what your whole-body posture just did, your head went back. It's like that's what happens. The Jellyfish Brain actually falls back into a pool of deliciousness because she has her own ocean in there, and all of a sudden, the bones are dominant. But what makes a difference is I'm giving my attention to those bones. So, there's a response, there's an acknowledged response, but this isn't like the way the Jellyfish Brain responds, and this is where we get into lots of trouble because having these conversations is a little bit difficult because we're all translating into a neural-dominant terrestrial view, right?

**Christie** Right.

*Michael* Unless you've been a diver or, or a really stealth beautiful gardener, a non-species-centric gardener, you know... that end of the scale where you really are talking to your rose bushes and they really are talking back and you're like, "I'm not going to try to have this conversation with anybody because they'll take me away from my Rose Garden."

**Christie** Right.

*Michael* "And I won't be able to be in my intimate relationship with my roses." This kind of relating, this feeling, this contact can happen with any plant or any creature, anything. Yes, it happens all the time, actually. We get adopted by things, but those things... you'll hear people say in response, "Wow, I really feel that in my bones...!"

Well, it's a flippant comment, but it's a real feeling. You can slow somebody back down into their experience there, and if they're willing and are capable and skillful in dropping their language, they can go into that direct experience.

So, I'm having a direct experience with someone's bones, and I'm not so fixated. I also know that those bones are interacting with these other tissues, and these tissues are there. On my way to try to find a bone, I may have these other conversations, for lack of a better word. They, they literally are musical conversations with these different tissues, different layers, different roots, etc.

If we can get a person's nervous system calmed down enough, we can start to train them to prompt themselves or self-facilitate and go in with the same care that I'm using. I'm already there modeling it. Yes, I'm there to get the job done. I'm going to get my job done. No stopping now. How I get there and when I get there is a whole different set of issues. You know, it may take me years, it may take me a few minutes... doesn't matter to me. It's still a use of time. It's still modeling and rapport and trying to meet a thing where it's at, not just the person, but now we're getting particular parts of that person, and the respect of those living systems is very important.

In my world, it isn't a trite response. It isn't a neural-dominant, "Oh yeah, we're going to accept that they're living and, yes, the bones are alive and, yes, they're like coral reefs, you silly bugger you, but we're still going to come at... we're still going to... and we're going to get some gardening work done." Oh, there's that neural drive.

In my world, we get to work the awareness in a way that it can stay responsive. I think awareness already is responsive, but it can get, um, encapsulated through habits.

**Christie**  Habits... yeah.

*Michael*  Right. It's a big... heavy habituation of habits through training and through a family lineage. You know, a shape that's been handed down generation after generation, or socially. If there's a resonance between that familial shape and a societal shape, then you know that awareness is going to be that shape. It's going to only have that range, because I find awareness is a little more fluid, but it gets encapsulated, so there's all those issues.

But, when that's allowed to soften, then the tissues are allowed to respond, and you have that conversation with the tissues. Then our awareness is added, too, and it becomes quite potent, becomes a thicker tea, you know. The awareness is actually one really important ingredient of that tea, because that awareness is now being stirred/steeped into your actual fluids, amongst your tissues, your actual tissues, the area and field you occupy.

And those tissues are getting my complete awareness/attention, and also my contact and my pestering, really. You know, I'm definitely, definitely doing a little pestering... my sheep dog aspect is like, "Okay, here we go, back to work!", and then I just try to work with my interior questioning of that. "How are you guys doing?" You know, how to...how do I challenge my own agenda and turn it back into an open-ended question? How do I take that sheep dog drive and turn it into an invitation? How do I soften 10% without leaving, without setting up a whole different dynamic?? Challenging... deeply worthwhile.

Now, because I've sat there, and I've gotten the rest of the alleyway cleared away from all the hullabaloo, I've got the Jellyfish out of the alleyway, and the feral part of the person's coming out and saying, (purr?), and is coming out to check me out, so now I have to stay, because now I'm in a very tricky place of rapport. I have to hang out. If at that potent moment, if that dynamic, that feral aspect, pulls back, if I pull back or respond, we've made another dynamic, right?

If I stay there and have no response except an invitation (Taoist non-doing), just steeping in the invitation, and let that dynamic reach back out and check me out, sniff me out a little bit, then we've created the start of a cycle of rapport, right, and I may have to do lots of that. Lots of cycles, lots of steeping.

Then, at some point, that feral aspect, that traumatized tissue, will 'call'. I'll make a call back and say, "Are you going to pick up? are you going to check us out?"... so that tickle from that feral nature... if I stay with that and *feel* that, I can stay in a level that I can feel the tickle of what just happened in my bones. I can stay with that. The same thing you do with yourself or with someone if you're holding them, that self-facilitation going, "No, I really want to meet this. I'm neither going to attack, grab or reach, and I'm not going to pull away. I'm not going to add anything to the exchange. I'm going to really try and feel my way with 'what' shows up. I'm going to see what's really happening."

Does the bone actually respond? Do the tissues around the bone actually respond? Does the feral nature that resides in there respond? Can we get a different layer of circulation happening? Open-ended, invitational questions... Because that engagement is going to have to circulate in some way... whether the attention is the only thing that moves between that engagement or in that awareness. We can all haggle about that. I can still start to engage that neighborhood. That little exchange has a circulation pattern to it, a reciprocity, and if that has enough time, then time becomes an ingredient in that exchange, in that 'time' it does something to awareness. It does something to attention. It adds another layer of quality... and another layer of quality and potency. Soon we have a stronger sense of contact there... and then the tissues respond, "Well that's interesting. I don't feel defended from the... that's kind of cool." And then they get involved, all of those layers, and then, all of a sudden, something tips and I have a circulation. I have a response, right? And I have to hold through that. A form of engaged 'allowing'.

And there're many beautiful ways of encouraging that and stirring it a wee bit, and that can range from literally being perfectly still for extended amounts of time, which is at the Rosen methodology end of things where you just wait at the edge and the body cannot not react. The reaction is your information. So, you just hang out. It'll circulate through you, or you can pull a trigger and shake the bejesus out of it. Say, "Oh, I got you! I'm not going to poke you, but I got you... errr." You have those two ranges. Grab them and say, "I got you. I tricked you, you little buzzard. I got you!", and the little things in there go, "You do got me... Oh... Thanks for not being so still... it drives me nuts!"

So, you have your range of response, but you're responding to their response, you're responding to their bones, right? And sometimes, you have to add a little chutzpah, you have to add a little more attention... you have to bring in a little bit more, and other times you have to dissipate your attention. I might be getting like, "Oh, I'm going to get this!", and then, all of a sudden, that little thing goes, "No!", and I'm like, "Crap!". Then I have to take my attention and go for other bones. Without leaving the original contact, I have to include the rest of the body. I have to dissipate my immediate attention. Every once in a while, I have to take my attention to an object in the room. I have to *literally* get my attention out, which creates a void, which is a form of trickery because then that 'feral cat' cannot not respond, right?! The feral, overwhelmed, traumatized area cannot not react. Even if it goes numb, then there're ways to work with the numbness, right? Then you have to draw it out. You can't push it out, can't grab it out. You

can't sing it out. You have to do something a little
more clever. You have to take the kibble, walk away
ten feet, and go, "Kibble...", and the numbness goes,
"That might be far enough...", and you've got it.
Numbness is tricky to work with.

**Christie**  So you're talking about a response from the tissues.
So, there are tissues in there that are not part of
hairballs... yeah?

*Michael*  All tissues are part of everything.

**Christie**  Uh huh.

*Michael*  The hairball is just an overwhelmed, traumatized, but
mostly overwhelmed tissue (Marion Woodman would
say).  An arrested movement happened in that area,
and it had to re-accommodate due to a myriad of
responses. But those tissues in that overwhelmed
area, in that hairball, have had to change their
behavior in response to what has happened... whereas
the rest of the tissues didn't have to do that. And the
rest of the tissues get to decide whether they're going
to come in and support that area, or whether they're
going to disregard the hairball or... right... there's a
cascade of responses... they're not always congruent.
So, it creates something... its own dynamics, and then,
and during, sometimes even pre 'then' doing, the
Jellyfish Brain can, um, coordinate and, um, make a
hell of a coping response, because she'll coordinate

the whole thing. She (Jellyfish Brain) cannot not react! She will make an instant coherent song, to the best of her ability, at 'that' time.

And this gets tricky because you'll have individual tissues who are not neural tissues who are going, "Fuck...?!?!" Then, you'll have a response from the neural tissues in the neighborhood going, "It's all right." Tissues are going, "No it's not!" They'll have an argument. And then, that argument will get encapsulated, tangled. It'll adapt, and then the other systems will go, "Ahhh, bloody hell...", and they'll try to go on with their day. You know, you, we, they have such a range there. All tissues have their own range. And the awareness part of it is that awareness can move. Awareness can be reshaped; awareness can do a bunch of wonderfully wacky things. Meanwhile the attention is finding work arounds and new/other pathways.

**Christie** So, in your description of... it's kind of like... sort of slowly calming, settling, whatever. Are you doing that specifically in a place where you feel the hairball is residing? Or are you just doing that where your hands happened to want to go?

**Michael** I think it's both. So, we've stepped back away from the body for a moment. It's in that distance, on the way to the body that we're trying to meet the person where they're at. On the way, I'm letting myself be informed by their dance, in that their dance will show you right where their hairballs are.

**Christie** Oh, I see. Okay.

*Michael* Then, as you get close to those hairballs, a couple things happen. If they're vigilant, then they'll get defended. We may have to do a bunch of other stuff to tease that hairball back into relationship with the body... right? We'll have to do a bunch of things to help that neighborhood of distress, that neighborhood of coping, however long it's been there, to find its options again, because the minute it goes into distress, it'll be in a coping response, which will include vigilance!

That neighborhood of the hairball will come up with a new strategy to deal with the overwhelm and that the strategy will be unique. It'll have its own rules; and so you, you're going to have to tease that hairball back in and sometimes mediate between the areas that have been doing just fine, and, in fact, are pretty grumpy that this other 'thing' has happened; and then you have the tissues inside the hairball that, if they've been damaged, are re-growing, *literally* re-growing, so their behavior is changed. They've gone back to the beginning cycle of their developmental sequences, and so you have to mediate that edge sometimes.

**Christie** So their awareness is split?

*Michael* Split/multifaceted/fragmented/coping/vigilant/etc.

**Christie** Okay.

*Michael* Right. That's why... that's why awareness is an interesting thing. If you're neural-dominant, you think awareness is your attention, right? Or you clump it all together because it all works together. But, when someone's injured or there's been fragmentation or dissociation or all the myriad of things that happen, you have to mediate because that neighborhood of distress has its own awareness. It has its own attention. It has its own feral nature that has now pulled away from the rest of the community of cells. It may look like they're functioning, and they may be functioning. The rivers of blood are still moving through them, hopefully, right? Or there's been 'work arounds' which... everything's so adaptive, right? But it'll start to, um, cope, cogitate, congregate, commune with itself. It'll start to encapsulate and make a very unique neighborhood to deal with the issues of that neighborhood of tissues, of the experience of overwhelm. And it'll be in, in counter, or contrast, or different than the other neighborhoods around it.

So, it doesn't sound easy, but it's a pretty easy thing to spot when it's all you do all day, right? Right. So, you go in with some of your own curiosity and your own awareness and go, "Okay, what are you guys doing?" And then you're using other parts of yourself to set aside not only parts of your agenda, but their agenda also, going, "I hear you, but, but we're here for this."

So, you're bringing your awareness back, so that your attention (the little sea creature that swims around) can concentrate and be available and responsive to that area of distress. You know, in that neighborhood of distressed tissues, you're always keeping a part of your attention and your awareness on, because both these capacities can do different things. They're always keeping a little bit of concentration with the bone, the bone being the slowest moving, most concentrated part of that neighborhood. It's the home of that neighborhood, it's the coral reef. It gives everything reference in that neighborhood. So that section of bone or that whole bone in its entirety will be the reference for those tissues. The Jellyfish Brain doesn't like that. But, as a functional gardener, that's the truth of it.

**Christie** There're bones everywhere, so...

*Michael* Approximately 206, give or take...

**Christie**  The tissue always has some bone...

**Michael**  The tissue always has a reference, and it depends on the tissue and where that section of tissue is, you can get so retentively particular in it. I like to do a little bit more taking of those particulars and tipping them back into, um, from my justified position, a practical generality, and I'm going back and forth. But the beautiful thing about awareness is that you can move it! Can move with it! 'Both-And'!

**Christie**  Yeah. Yeah.

**Michael**  I can let my tissues be informed by my attention, but also by my awareness. I can let my awareness hold/flood the entire body, but my attention can go explore, be available to a specific section of tissue, a specific neighborhood, right? And if my attention needs a little help, all my awareness needs to do is pour gently into a little area, because we have to, and are able to, concentrate. We can concentrate that those things (attention and awareness) can be brought together and be made really concentrated. And then the tissues will respond in kind. They'll get very concentrated. It'll get to be a real joy fest or it'll be a real piss-ant. The neighborhood will respond, "Oh, fuck this..!" And you're like, "F-u-c-k... backup, backup, backup, backup. Start over, start over, start over. All right, well that's clear." Then, you've learned something, and hopefully, eventually the person also learns.

So, I'm doing a couple of things. My awareness is teaching their awareness how to flood, feel, sense, occupy and be available to track, right? Then things get particular... then they can bring their awareness and then create some attentiveness, and then the skills of that attentiveness, right? The Jellyfish Brain has its usual skills, in which it'll want to go in and do stuff. It'll want to wash dishes; it'll want to put the lamp back. It'll look at its history and say, "Oh my Goodness, that's not... put it back, just put it back... back where I 'think' it was before all this hullabaloo... before the overwhelm, before the accident, before, before, before...", even if it is/was a fantasy.

You have to get the person's awareness and their attention reskilled so that their awareness can flood into an area, give them a response and then their attention can come in and try and meet that the best they can. You know, with some skills like, "Oh, I don't want to go in here too quickly, even though it's my leg or my hair ball. Oh, I need to not go after my hairball because my hairball will respond in kind by protecting."

**Christie** How?

312

**Michael**  By bracing, kicking 'on' its' vigilance. It's going to respond in kind, and the title of the book should be, "The hairball always wins!" Hairballs can go on for centuries. They can outlast the person. In fact, the joke is that very often, if you get to live long enough, it'll be your hairballs that are holding you together.

**Christie**  It's, it's... more true than not... Yes.

**Michael**  It's more true than not. Then, at some point, you have to come to terms with it like, "Oh, that's really successful tissue. That's a really successful strategy. That really sucks. I have, I have to relearn all this stuff to go, 'Oh shit!'", right? It's a very funny thing. And at that stage of development, very appropriate, because now your hairballs are literally holding your garden together. They're literally giving you a place in space, right?! It's not all the healthy tissue, it's these gnarly old hairballs. Which, if you were fortunate enough to have some of them worked on in your life, you'll actually have some ease... or not, but...you get to learn about your 'actual' body garden.

**Christie**  Well, so if you don't mind, could you kind of say a little bit about what's awareness and what's attention like?

**Michael**  Awareness, I think, is a substance (and I think there're better people than me that can explain this). For me, my practice, awareness is the softer part of attention. It's a part that can flood. It can fill a room, if need be, right? Vigilance and our proprioceptive superficial daily attention, um, use the medium of awareness to fill a space, right? And then attention flies around within that medium to do really particular things, either to run back and get our adrenals to amp up and make more cocktails, or to go, "We got to get sleep now because we're going to pass out because this is taking up too much energy."

Attention is, is the more particular ability of focus within the awareness that involves beginning to use our senses. Our senses can take awareness and then, through our biology, through our capability, um, can make an 'attention'. In fact, attention can get so good, it can become a fixation. Our attention never leaves that place. We'll have awareness's in other parts of us, but we're not 'aware' of the fixation, right? Our attention can be held in a place and we're just not aware of it. Our awareness is just floating around, or it's being encapsulated and then so much attention and so much awareness have been focused into a single spot, that nothing else exists, you know? Those things can either dissipate or get concentrated, but I find that attention and awareness are different.

Attention is a more concentrated form of awareness. It's its own type of sea creature!

**Christie** Like a tool?

*Michael* It can become a 'tool'. It's what starts to shape change into that, a 'tool'... that's attention. And, once in a while, you can practice in a way that you can start to allow your attention to dissipate back into your awareness, so that when your awareness responds to a quality in the environment, it shape changes. Then your attention goes, "Oh, shape change!", and the two of them start to work together, you know? They can both be in a relaxed, responsive state, which sends a signal to the tissue saying, "Oh, we're cool!", or "Watch out!".

**Christie** So I assume that when people are getting more facile at moving between the literal, the symbolic, the mythic and whatever, that, that there is some... I don't know whether it's some fluidity...?

*Michael* Your awareness is informed.

**Christie** Yeah, that's so...

*Michael* Your awareness, because it's occupying all those layers, floods into your root beds, and starts to orient. And, as it gets responsive to what's happening, then it informs your attention, and your attention starts to become able to be focused. So, so you're sitting and, all of a sudden, you're going, "Ah, I don't know where I was, but I wasn't sleeping..." So, your awareness is all of a sudden popped out of a deep experiential layer, and then it triggers your attention like, "Wait a... wait a minute...", but with and over time, you'll have built up, steeped some rapport there. With some experience in that transition, your awareness changes, it shapes, fills, get satiated, or gets responsive.

Then, the next thing is that your attention gets triggered and it becomes more specific, but you don't do anything with it. Your, your cells and your tissues have learned to go, "Okay, well let's give it a few more... let's take in a little bit more." Most people can't do that. Their literal senses jump up and say, "Oh wait one minute... let's get a little prancy and dancy!", and then they write a play or a song, or they go off and, you know, get married, go back to the habit, the prancing and dancing.

**Christie** They leave.

*Michael* They, they take action.

**Christie** Yeah.

*Michael* So, that means that they just jumped, the minute their attention is triggered, right? Their awareness starts to do its sensing thing, and then the attention gets triggered and drives the person to do something. It tickles the Jellyfish Brain's tendrils and they'll respond, takes the attention and moves it into an action.

**Christie** Yeah. So, when you're teaching somebody to self-facilitate, which seems like you're doing most of the time in a certain kind of way...

**Michael** I'm always doing it... at a mythic level, I'm always doing it. Um, because we're engaged.

**Christie** Right.

**Michael** Right. So mythically, we're, there is always dancing, motion. There's no, there's no other, there's no 'not' dancing, our world inside and out is 'only' alive, VERY ALIVE!!!

**Christie** There's no...?

**Michael** There is no other dance than that...right? That's that. That's why that layer's so delicious... because the mythic quality is always in motion to movement, to motion, to movement... and it's life. It's always engaged. There's nothing you can do about that. You can satiate or not. I know that... see... Everything I say cannot have a standing point from mythic point of view. It is engaged. It is dancing, you know. And you 'are' involved. You 'are' being blown/breathed/grown alive, period. And... there's a motion/movement to that. Before/as the motion/movement takes shape, you're mythic. It's never out of relationship with anything. You're never alone. It's completely different than issues of aloneness or loneliness, but technically, from your cell's point of view, there is no outside, there is no other world. There's no... right... there's just lots of dimensions and lots of things, and lots of Aliveness. And it can be tracked. And... wahoo... minutes/hours/days/months/years/centuries go by!

Where tickles my interest is that, as mythic starts to get concentrated and your awareness starts to respond, then the living dynamics start to differentiate and get particular, and now you've got something you can do. You can respond with some attention, and you can be trained to slow and soften your attention so that it can reside within your awareness, within these dynamics.

**Christie**  So it can reside within the mythic?

*Michael*  Yeah, yes, yippee (everything has a Mythic layer, that layer is everything)!

**Christie**  It does... it does anyway...

*Michael*  Yes, but you can let those things start to, um, build an experiential response, so you spend more time there, so it becomes very experiential. You now know that you don't have to chase, you can't chase it with words, that you're... there is not a concept on the planet big enough to deal with that and, within the dance, we'll always try, the dynamic tickles us into a myriad of words and birdsongs, you know? If you want to do that, you can write a book, you can make a beautiful Greek mythic play that spans centuries. You can do that. You can come up with a religion that spans lifetimes.

And those are responses to the mythic... beautiful responses to it, but it will satiate, it will concentrate a little bit more. The dance'll get more specific, and then they'll pop you up and, all of a sudden, your awareness informs your attention. Attention goes, "H-e-y, that's like this!"

**Christie**  Symbolic.

*Michael*  Symbolic. Instantly. The minute it goes, "That's like this, this is like that!" You've gotten an association, uh, and you go, "H-e-y, that's not cool. It looks like this. But it feels like that!. You're not my grandmother!" But it's dancing a role at the moment that's granny-like, in all the myriad of ways.

Archetypes spring from that layer, that quality, like there'll be a certain tendency towards the mythic quality that informs everything. There'll be a certain way that the larger water, or that larger substance, moves, and a way that we all behave in response to those mythic waters. As those take shape moving into, towards specifics... our awareness gets tickled. Then, we'll start getting our attention involved and start tracking, get wound up in our specific responses and we'll start to play with it, because we have 206 plus/minus bones and with as many responsive joints,

319

a joint for almost every day of the year. And you know... I think I just started salivating.

**Christie**  Well, so...

*Michael*  Awareness co-mingles with all of it, but our attention may not.

**Christie**  Right. And as you teach people about...?

*Michael*  They start to engage their tissues, they start to go, "Well, where are my bones?" And they start the process of letting their bones respond, and now, they start to create rapport, friendships, or not friendships because some people don't like their bones. Um, you can never tell what's going to come out of that. But they start slowing their attention down so that their awareness can be available within a response.

**Christie**  And so, bones, you know...

*Michael*  As you become aware of your bones and start to become aware of the response of the bones, then your attention can go, "Oh... that was that bone...! That bone just responded to me!" Someone who's untrained is going to DO something about that. The Jellyfish can't stand the tickle. She'll have to go neural-dominant and do what she would do anywhere in her outer, daily world. And she imposes that on her interior world. All our views are imposed 'things' on our interior, and there's lots of things, you know, and then centuries go by. You can train yourself, or work

with someone, to start to soften that and not be
reactive, but to start to tip back into responsive, start
to tip and slow things down so you can steep longer.
So, your attention and your awareness don't have to
have any reaction, or action, whatsoever. They start to
steep until there's an honest response, a sober
response, a natural response, or all of a sudden, an
understanding.

**Christie**  And it's also... um, it's just increasing the capacity for
nourishment...

*Michael*  Oh, a huge one!

**Christie**  That's it. That seems like...

*Michael*  Because now you can take your awareness of
something... you can let your awareness start to entice
your imagination, um, and you can feel into food, "But
would this be nourishing for me?" You can feel into
your activity. It's not hard to allow your body to
experience, to soften and go, "Well, what does need
to happen in the next two hours?" And respond to it in
a way that allows the body to stay responsive. You can
allow your awareness to flood so that your attention
can start to get the particulars of like, "Oh, then I can
do this, this, and this. Oh, I can step... Oh!" So, these
things start to move within and with each other, and
you're allowing, training, and teaching your tissues
that, or you're growing a layer of response in your

system, your garden. It's hard to tell. It's a lot of 'both', a lot of 'both-and'.

This is where it makes it hard to have a linear conversation about this, because then your tissues start to get really responsive, which, if you're already in a hypervigilant, overwhelmed state, you don't want. You're trying to crash your system. You're trying to go into freeze response and dissociation, numbness, an overwhelm you can recognize and control. You're trying to dampen your field. If you're a dampened field, then it's a hell of a thing to learn that you can start to reach, and explore, and start to create a little fire; start to kind of get a little more life happening inside you.

It's just where you are in the spectrum, in your development. But, a person can be trained, and a person can learn skills. And all of a sudden, their interactions with that mythic, with the life around them and the life within them, starts to have a congruency, reciprocity. It starts to have an inclusion that's an actual inclusion, not as in certain areas finding a workaround to manipulate what *seemed* like inclusion. So, those particular concepts and ideas can (as sock puppets) carry on another moment, hour, week, season, another year. We have parts of us that help us persevere. They, your habits and sock puppets, are going to try and make it to next year. That's sacred! It's not easy learning how to slow down and pause.

**Christie**  Right.

*Michael*  Right. If we start slowing down and nourishing ourselves differently, those aspects aren't going to get nourished because a coping construct, and most ideas and concepts, need a certain verve, need a certain fire. They need a little adrenal cocktail or the myriad of other... I mean it's not just the... I don't hang it all on the adrenals! There are other biochemical responses that create a beautiful cocktail, but there're many things in life that need us as a donkey to get to the next cycle, the next year. We start slowing that down and start addressing what can be nourished, and start slowing down so that our tissues can be included in those decisions, those actions, more fully in our engagements.

**Christie**  Right.

*Michael*  Right. Then our awareness is allowed to really be interactive and really inform our attention like, "Oh, my attention just got pulled here. Just, let's just... Oh, that's all right...", right? We start doing that. Then all of a sudden, biochemically, we become different. Cellularly, we become different. Our tissues actually get to, some of them for the *first* time, learn new behaviors, learn new responses, and then they start to grow differently, and to the best of their ability.

**Christie** I would think it might affect the hairballs, too...?

*Michael* Well, this gets... this, for me, is what gets even more interesting, that some of the hairballs change.

**Christie** They do?

*Michael* Oh Goodness, yes! Well, how much have you changed from the previous women you've been?

**Christie** Have I changed? (chuckle) Well, yeah!

*Michael* (That was for you and your therapist to decide). Yeah, so you start, but here's the nice thing about softening awareness and attention is that you can, you can actually start to go, "Well, what about the 'me' six months ago? How is she different, actually. How is it different? And then how isn't it different?" Because there'll be layers that aren't different. Then you jump to a year ago, feel what changed; and then you do two years, feel what changed, and then from two years to five years, feel what changed for contrast sake. Two years to five years... that's a different person. It's a different period of time. It's a different ethos. It's a different season... even if you're just seeing a person in the same place, doing the same thing forever and ever, it's still a completely different thing. Even though all the behavior is the same.

If you learn to let your tissues respond (this is one of the fun things about that particular timeline modality technique), you aren't going to your memory in your brain, in the way your neurology houses your memory. You're letting in your biology's memory, as well as your bone's memory, who actually took all those steps, literally. You start letting those inform you as well. You get this myriad of responses, and you need your attention soft. You need it in a place that it can reside and free float in your awareness, so those things can move around and be responsive because their response to your inquiry is information. It's opaque, it's abstract, it's damn near mythic in its response, but there's this larger,

**Christie**  (he's [Michael] chomping his lips, making sounds. slurping sounds)

*Michael*  (slurping, water at the edge of a lake sound, lapping sound.) You get into that watery exchange before it starts to build and concentrate and then pop into a specific, into even a general specific. Some shapes, they abstract... they can, they all interact. One kind of engagement doesn't just go forward into another engagement, it goes the other way too. The literal can get very exhausted, and then you go, "Oh, fuck it. It's like this." Then 'like this' goes, "Oh, fuck it, I'm taking a nap, you know. Oh fuck, my eyes aren't closing... but being in a nap state watching trees is really cool. Hey, I just saw a tree breath. I'm moving at the speed of trees... well!" (Thank you, Ellis Paul!)

And you can train people to do that. I've been trained to do that. You can train people to do that, and you're both training them through the literal and the symbolic, the specifics. But, biologically, I train them by trying to stay in those states myself, and letting my awareness flood a little bit, letting my attention move around and between those states that I'm modeling, and, in some cases, maybe even some entrainment.

And then that person's got to integrate and digest and make it their own, just like I had to do, you know? This isn't how the grannies (a term of endearment for all my influences) talked to me. They had a very different use of language. It wasn't so comfortable for me. Some of it is their language, but it's been re-formed, because I've had to practice this, you know? Um, but yes, it's totally possible.

And that's what I do in my practice. I am training people, and that's different than doing a therapeutic thing where you're just doing 'it' for the person, 'to' the person, or 'at' the person.

**Christie** That's the thing that feels like the whole question of nourishment...and you nourishing and then me learning to receive that. But then, me learning how I might nourish myself, and how then I can receive that. And you know, it's... so it's not just the unwinding of particular hairballs or particular issues. There's a shift in relationship to... to self-growth or to self-facilitated nourishment, growth, whatever... not in a particular Jellyfish Brain dominant set of goals or directions, but more listening in a different kind of way. For me it's taken a long time, and it probably takes a long time for a lot of people, maybe, but it feels like there's just this weaving, you know, between what you're doing and what you're teaching, and how those things keep winding in and out of each other.

**Michael**  Do you wanna sit over here (teacher's seat)? That was beautifully said. Yes. That was beautifully said. There is a growing of self-tending that is spoken/sung and modeled/danced.

**Christie**  That's true.

**Michael**  Right? My goodness!

Um, it takes a long time to grow a human being. It takes centuries and centuries to grow a human being. I think it's 'becoming' human beings. You know, you're always growing and becoming a 'human being'; and it's gardening. It's, it's growing!

So yes, I'm undoing a hairball, but in the way that I undo it, I'm also training that tissue and helping it explore its options, right? I can, I can undo a hairball, and, at times, I will grab my rototiller and I will torture someone to get the friggin gruntzky gristle shit out of my way. Sometimes, I've got to do some pretty interesting things to get a tissue to be even close to a responsive state. And it's never pretty. But, even in that, my intention is, as I'm handling the body, I'm handling it as a garden even when I'm rough and gorilla-like. I'm still handling it rough and gorilla-like, my attention and my awareness is still, in a slightly possessive way, going, "This is my garden, these are my bones, this person can have them back when I'm friggin' done." And that's the truth of it. And it's some of my limbic system overcompensating for all their craziness going, "Okay, that layer, that's for some other therapy, I got work to do." I just go to it. And the surprise is that *that* tissue's expressing, "Oh, thank frickin' Goodness, you didn't buy entirely into the story because we need to start to move.", and I'm like, "I know... I know!"

**Christie** And then, because they've been met, they have the memory or the consciousness or whatever...

*Michael* They have the experience...

**Christie** ... the experience that they've been met.

*Michael* Whether or not the other things line up with it is part of therapy. That's what makes it therapy. The whole thing is meeting the person where 'they' are, but how I meet them and how you the reader, or you the Practitioner will meet them... completely different, but the *attempt* at meeting them, that's now in their experience. That's what elevates it from the mundane into ceremony, sometimes into ritual, or takes it out of the literal and drops it into symbolic, into mythic.

**Christie** ... into the mythic, yeah.

*Michael* However you wanna... You know, you take it out and you're, all of a sudden, instead of just getting through time, you're completely devoted to time. Everything becomes a devotional process. Language is secondary, you know, so it makes some Zen teachers really feisty, and they'll tap their students, but it's done out of complete devotion...or you make other people like the Dalia Lama just sit there. Everybody's crying, he's laughing. He's not laughing 'at'. He's laughing because, Oh my Goodness, honey, he understands. You know, you can only take sooo much... so you friggin' lose it, you know? He feels and holds, "I'll be right here with you."

So, it's that type of... all of sudden it tips into you're, you're using time or devoted time, you're modeling, or you're willing to be in that compassionate companion piece of, "I'll walk through this with you for as far as I can. I can't say how far that is. We'll see." Honestly... We'll see/feel/sense how far... and when 'it' shifts... we'll pause and... REORIENT!!!

**Christie** And you're teaching simultaneously that there is something that is continually being walked through and that it's all connected.

*Michael* That's right. And, technically, we have to slow down for that, which is the hardest. To slow down is hard for neural-dominant behavior. When neural-dominant behavior starts to slow down, it tends to slip into sleep or disengagement.

**Christie** Yeah.

*Michael* That is true for neural dominance, but for the rest of the tissues it's like, "Oh, thank Goodness! We get some time with this." Even if it's hellacious, you know? "Oh, how great... They aren't going to add fire to fire and..."

**Christie** Yeah.

*Michael* (Oh, as an aside, we'll just put this on the tape of it for the heck of it)

As an example, a plane flying 40,000 feet drops 20,000 feet. The stewardesses panic and are screaming through the plane... adding fire to fire. Everybody's already freaked out because they just dropped 20,000 feet, right? That's not something I want to be a part of, but the issue is that the people who were supposed to be calm and in control and understand these things well... They're not doing that. So now everything is doubled up, right? Fires added to fire. Panic is added to panic.

**Christie** Yeah. We don't want to do that.

*Michael* No, it buys time. It gets you through time, but in a not very nourishing way.

**Christie** No.

*Michael* There'll be repair work to do. So socially, that'd be a big repair work over the next few weeks. The airlines will have to do this and it'll cause this ripple of repair work, and then we'll all have our reactions and responses to it, and it'll be repair work that's needed. Can we do the repair work along the way? Can we start to slow things down? To model that, it's a hell of a thing, because now you're an attention/awareness field that involves all the living things around you so you're tipping into mythic. You're tipping into letting that tension in the field start to inform you. You've stopped being reactive to it, and even if you are reacting to it, you go, "Holy crap, that field is still alive and well."

Heck, you let those parts of you have their responses. You start to not correct your hairball. You start to not go after it, but not to counterpoint it! You start to include your hairball and say, "Okay honey...

'Oh', you now have your developmental sequence, and the rest of the systems/neighborhoods are really cranky because they've been doing all the work. Oh honey, I know." So, you start to do this inclusion piece, which takes (it turns out) a big chunk of awareness and attention, and that brings us full circle. Does that answer your question?

**Christie** It certainly does!

# Chapter Eight: *Interview #6*

**Christie**   I've been holding a question about something for a while and that is... What about the umbilicus? (Lots of laughter from both Christie and Michael).

*Michael*   Pure conjecture. Supposedly, everyone's got one...

**Christie**   Well, you've done some work with mine I know.

*Michael*   I have.

**Christie**   And at least you told me once that you were doing that, and you said it was very interesting and seems important. So why is it important and how, or how is...

*Michael*   How is having an umbilicus even necessary when one isn't in a womb?

**Christie**   Well, yeah. Yeah. So, what do you have to say about umbilicus's...?

*Michael*   Umbilici

**Christie**   Okay. Yes. And how would it be an important part of a session or...?

*Michael*   I was all prepared for almost any question, but that one. Yeah... there's so much, and it's all conjecture on my part. This is one of those funny places that it's, um, I want to say mostly in my experience. It's not... I don't know a lot of research. I've heard other people's conjectures and, and ideas. But for me, um, I find it still very alive for people.

**Christie**   So what's the 'it'?

*Michael*   The umbilici.

**Christie**  Okay.

**Michael**  Further to be known as 'it'. Um, no, our umbilicus is still, it's still a tube. It's still going into the body. It's still sensitive. You know, the umbilicus still has its memory, its neighborhood of experience. It's not a dead tissue, right? It's a very living tissue, and there is something about working on someone, you know? We talk about these centers, and there's all these other ideas and concepts which are fantastic, um... but I find umbilicus is one of the truth centers, because of its construct, because of how it spirals into the body, and at one time was our lifeline, our first mouth! When we were an organ in someone else's body, which for a while we were, we didn't have autonomy. We were basically another organ, another thing growing and living within the other person, Mom. So, there's...oh man, it's really hard to put words to it. You... I think you've may have stumped me.

**Christie**  Oh no!

**Michael**  I know... this is so good. Makes my brain really have to go, "How would I even begin to put/pour 'that' into words?"

There's something that happens when you're working and someone's in their trip (and we're all in/on our trips), and you're starting to work around the abdomen. We've got all these ideas about stomach and liver and intestines and gallbladders and spleens and you know, and uteruses and lack of uteruses and all our wonderful belly neighborhoods, serpentine intestines, etc. So, when working, you can tune into those neighborhoods. Something really different happens when you go for the umbilicus. There's, there's an access into a different behavior of the belly, and I don't have anything to substantiate that except that's purely in my experience, and it's been fascinating to me for 30+ years.

**Christie**  Wow.

**Michael**  It's one of those places/spaces. There're a few places I don't have a lot of... um... there's not a lot of resources on it, you know. It's like a handful of the medical establishment saying, "That appendix ... you don't need it!", "The cranial sutures are fused...", there're no sutures. These statements are not true, but are still considered true, back and forth, to and fro we go. So for me, when I'm working with/on someone, I have my list where I'm orienting to their bones, orienting to 'them', and feeling/sensing/looking at the neighborhoods directly in my contact, and then the subsequent neighbors... and I kind of move out in ringlets into the body from wherever I'm at with contacts. I'm always setting up being very local and then going distal (away from), outwards and then back to local... to see what responds and what doesn't respond. There's always that bit of fishing, curious singing, that bit of, "Okay, what's going on here, in there? What, what is this garden?"

And there isn't any literature about umbilicus. I've read some energetic stuff, but there's not, there's just like, well it gets cut and then seizes up and then it just becomes a cap. The tissues change, adapt and regrow into the surrounding systems, so incredible, definitely magical.

**Christie**  So there's a belly button...

*Michael*  In some people... belly button or belly cavity.

**Christie**  ... but that would be the remnant on the external.

*Michael*  Exactly. But internally, you still may have a memory, a feeling of the original tube, the original throat, the first cord (chord).

**Christie**  Okay...

*Michael*  It's not pliable... it's not active in that way; but I think experientially... I know the biodynamic people would have a whole lot to say about this, because they love the embryotic process. They love that, the developmental-ness of it... but it was still a tiny esophagus. It was this wonderful tube that brought one part of the world into us, into our part of the world. The umbilicus, the first throat, then after birth changes, adapts, regrows into new supportive weavings, regrows into supporting the surrounding neighborhoods.

Medically, we know a lot about this transformation; but experientially, when working with all these other organs, these neighborhoods, around this wonderful belly center, um, all have these wonderful characters and wonderful qualities, um, wonderful behaviors.

This belly button piece is really interesting because there's, it's not void, but still has a little void (confusing, huh?). There's a sense of space. It's not allocated to the intestines, the interstitial (the space between tissues), almost not relegated to the quality of how an organ takes up space. There's this quality of this little touch of void because it's not an active tissue in the way neural dominance considers 'active'.

So, it's really interesting when prompting someone, either out loud or from my interior, I'll prompt even without saying something sometimes just to play with that responsiveness. We get to the belly button.

When I prompt people, it does... it's like finding your bones. It does something so strange to the Jellyfish Brain that it drops the Jellyfish Brain into this really vulnerable state because She doesn't know what to do. The forebrains go, "It's there!", but it's a superficial response. It's a proprioceptive, superficial feeling oftentimes in the field, which is also relegated to eyes and proprioception. There's a mapping.

The cortical homunculus says, "I know where that is." And it goes there, but the rest of the Jellyfish Brain goes, "What?", because we don't talk about belly buttons. We have jokes about belly buttons, but it's not a thing. It gets left aside. Now we come back to this beautiful central vessel, there's something sweet and tender that happens when someone takes their attention and their awareness and starts to go, "Where is that belly...?" Oh, my goodness! "Where is that belly button, that umbilicus?" It changes the shape of our responses, but in a completely different way than any other prompt.

We actually come in, in a way, yeah...like what you're starting to do. There's a funny thing that happens. We get very interior. With other things we go inside, but we don't get into that funny dimensional interior where the field goes, "Oh!", and it doesn't collapse. It comes in to sense something that was extremely vital for nine months, give or take a few weeks, as vital as our eyes or our other senses of the head and body.

**Christie** Or more so because it was survival... yes?

*Michael* More so. I don't think it's even survival. It's natural, deeply intimate and nourishing... you know? It's the nourishment. It's the primal river, so to say and it's that connection that allowed us and leaves us with the fantasy of not having to do anything to exist.

So, there's something special about that. And clearly even for me, very hard for words. But, when you're palpating, contacting that neighborhood, then, every once in awhile, bring someone's awareness/attention there, there's something really lovely that happens. And sometimes a little jarring, because, for some people, their Jellyfish Brains just don't go there. It's like finding their bones. They just, they almost go dissociative, you know? Or they freeze. Or they have a myriad of other responses, which are nice things to get to know. Oh, sure they can adapt all these other parts of themselves. But get to their umbilici...

Also, for me... because I'll give homework once in a while about really paying attention to their umbilicus and returning it to a rightful orifice. It's still an orifice. It still has its tendencies, although it doesn't have its dominance. It doesn't have its necessity, its original job, but it's still, it still has its sensory, its memory, and it's really different because we really go there.

It's like sensing for the push of the floor with the bones of the feet. It does stuff to the Jellyfish Brain that just drives the Jellyfish Brain nuts. Yet, at the same time, once you establish that relationship, it then orients the Jellyfish Brain in a different way. I think there's something about giving the neighborhood of the umbilicus a little more due that, once you get over a little bit of nausea sometimes (as I am, playing with mine now) um, it gives another layer of experience.

I think that layer is harder for words because it gets, gets coerced by all these other layers right? These layers, "Oh, that's a great. Oh, we can take and do..." And the other layers, the other parts of us start to fuss with that quality. But to really bring the awareness/attention back there... and I know there's some literature in Taoism that ... just contemplating on the belly button, on that particular neighborhood/center can increase vitality. There's, there's many things that they'll concentrate on just by accessing the feeling of the umbilicus neighborhood.

So, I think that's curious. But I'm not a Taoist. I refer to it. It definitely informs me, but I, I don't know some of their particulars except that on the table it seems to be true. It changes part of their (the client's) consciousness. It changes orientation. And walking around in the world with a little sense of belly button, it changes how you move. Add some feet into that, and throw some bones in, soften/orient without collapsing, and you've got, you've got a completely different orientation, and then all of a sudden your head starts to behave differently.

So, it's one of those little tricks I would say, or, or little curiosities on my end. For me, it's such a vital place, a vital neighborhood, but when tuned into specifically, the behavior of the umbilicus, interiorly, is so different from organs and tissues and intestines and how it relates to the body. What it does to the field, what it does to awareness, the way it gently brings it, kind of pops it in a little bit. Even within the skin, you know, it does this, this concentration piece that's not, um, 'the mind', it's still an awareness. It affects the mind, but it's still in that awareness/attention dance.

**Christie**  Well, is there any particular timing to introducing that to somebody?

*Michael*  No, it's pure feel. Sometimes it's really specific. We've been working on stuff and sometimes you can't get a person into their legs. The feet prompting doesn't do it. The bone prompting doesn't do it. They'll slide in for a moment, and then pop back up/out.

So, landscape wise, the umbilicus is really interesting because it's also sitting where the femoral artery splits, coming from the body of the descending aorta and splits off into nice little tree trunks and then

341

splits off into its next set of roots, um, at that layer/neighborhood of umbilicus. It starts to bring a person's attention down and gets them to move into a space they can't control. And from there, you can start establishing a sense of belly as a whole and then slowly encourage them to find their way through to their legs, you know, using the umbilicus as a kind of a location. And then, in a way, because again there's something funny about the way it pulls the attention in, they start to get, "Oh wow. I just plopped in!" And then you name that a little bit.

And then you're like, "Oh, let's get to your legs. From here, can you just get to the top of your legs?" Then, we might do some psoas work or trying to find some long lengths of roots and try to get that part of their awareness and their attention to be able to start to slide into their legs more gently. For some people, it's terrifying. Any reaching is just... they just don't have that ability, so they don't occupy their limbs, they just function mechanically. So that can be a good use of the umbilici.

For some people, um, they're really good at shape changing. They really like these little games. Their psyche really, really likes it. The umbilicus gets exciting for them because there is a place they didn't ever consider, you know? I might just toss it in as a wild card just to mess with them. They might be out here in this one shape, holding an experience, and we might be doing an animal shape or they might be steeping with/in their bones and they're starting to... their Jellyfish Brain's starting to go, "Oh, I can play with this and I like this!" And then we'll just throw in a wild card like, "Okay, where's your umbilicus?" Then lastly, and I don't know about this...this is my curiosity and there's something palpable about it, I think that tuning into that umbilicus and feeling that there's still a cord inside, that there's still that wonderful tube, that wonderful root umbilicus still there... it affects the Vagus nerve in a funny way. So, I'm curious about that as well, about bringing attention below the adrenals and to the end point of Vagus nerve as it moves out into the intestines and starts to have its interaction with that part of us. There's, um, I'm still exploring it, you know. I definitely like exploring with people, and some people are just fun to play with. I mean their Jellyfish Brain gets this funny kind of excitement, but their biology also really likes to have dominance, to have our attention. It really likes to play. So, it likes wild, little wild cards. I have a number of people like that. I'll be doing something, and they'll be just right there, which becomes too many people/peas in the pot. I'll be working on an area and then they're helping me and tracking me...and there's just way too much going on, so I'll just redirect 'em somewhere else, like, "Well, how does this relate to your elbow? Or a big toe? Or toenail? Or umbilicus? Or... Hey there! Go find something else!" So, it has that whole spectrum, you know, it has that whole spectrum.

**Christie**  Well so if you were teaching somebody, a practitioner/client, to find it or feel it, how would you...?

*Michael*  Oh, my Goodness!

**Christie**  How would you teach that to them?

*Michael*  Oh my Goodness. Simply, but complicatedly. Most likely I'd have them have a hand on their belly, and I would ask them to just sense, sense for that tissue and what they're noticing. To really pay attention to how the body responds to them finding their umbilicus.

The practitioner has to do that as well as the client. The practitioner has to kind of find their own so that the sensation can resonate, so that they start to get a spectrum of sensing the responses. How and what are they sensing? Either the client asking that of themselves or the practitioner asking that of the client.

So, you're starting the dialogue. I mean, here's a blanket statement. Ultimately... (I hate that

'Ultimately') ultimately, you're asking permissions of the neighborhoods. You're trying to get to know their language. From a practitioner's point of view, you're using your senses to invite a response, with both hands on, if you can have that. Or, in our case where we're across the room with a table (coffee table) between us, you and I are still tracking each other. You don't have to do this hands-on directly, but you use your senses as you would your hands.

So, so you explore that neighborhood, you explore that song, you explore that quality, um, either verbally or non-verbally. You're using not only your palpatory senses like hands, but you're also, again it brings us back full circle... you're always, um, tuning to your own bones as practitioner so you can sense the client's bones, just as you would have the client sense their own bones. Your bones sense their bones. So, your umbilicus would sense their umbilicus. You could gather information that's experiential, and you stay with it until it starts to sing, and it'll have a spectrum. It'll have a 'fuck off' song, or it'll have like, "Oh, thank Goodness you finally showed up! No one pays attention to me! Everybody, everybody else gets attention, but nooo not umbilicus, we had one part of us cut, but now we're not viable?!" You know, you'll have a whole spectrum, "Piss off!", or "Thank goodness, you arrived!" (Oh my, now we're just getting silly.)

But as a practitioner, I would be encouraging the person, if I was training them, to really go for the spectrum, you know? Don't try to pre-know. Go in with what you know, but don't try to get ahead of yourself there because you're asking questions. You're trying to ask little open-ended questions to encourage a response, which is a form of circulation or a form of reciprocity.

You get one of the layers of response moving and the other ones will usually come along for the ride or they'll... tissue cannot not react. It cannot not respond, even if it's a freeze response. That's a lot of information, or there is numbness. That's a lot of sensation. It's a lot of non-sensation sensation but that spectrum is very important, especially with someplace like an umbilicus because there's no social context for it. We don't talk about it. We make jokes once in a while. We'll talk about someone's belly button, but it's never about the umbilicus, right, unless you're talking about so and so just born, and someone got to cut the umbilicus and that's a pretty huge exceptional ritual, so there's, so there're little snippets that hold for a short time that this umbilicus has been just this, you know, 'the giver of life'.

And then the transition of life when we cut it, that's a huge initiation. It's beautifully violent and necessary, and messy, and awkward, and glorious, and there's all these things. Start with getting a little weepy.

**Christie**  It's big!

*Michael*  It's a big deal.

**Christie**  Well, and it's also in itself, a big thing. I mean, relative to... at least my experience of feeling it is, you know...

*Michael*  It's not, it's not a little wimpy tissue.

**Christie**  No, it's, it's...

*Michael*  Ah, it's an esophagus transformed!

**Christie**  Yeah.

*Michael*  It, it's a robust, strong, thick, fibrous unique neighborhood.

**Christie**  Yeah, yeah, yeah

*Michael*  So yes, we can definitely enter into that part of it by just cheerleading the umbilici for the next 10 minutes for sure. We can move into that category, but it's not a casual conversation. It's not something we'll have over dinner. Not many people talk about their umbilicus at the dinner table. I've, I've never heard of it. Talked about it. It's talked about around birthing.

**Christie**  Right. That's the only place.

*Michael*  ...or in therapy if your cord was wrapped around your neck, which in my case was true. Maybe my fascination with the umbilicus is that. For a while the cord was very intimate with my esophagus, and caused, actually initiated, my birth process. So, for me it's a very alive topic for my personal process.

**Christie**   Right. Yeah.

*Michael*   But as a practitioner, it's beautiful to include it when I'm working with someone's abdomen, and I always work with... 90% of the time I work at least a little bit with someone's abdomen, either directly or indirectly, because it's an essential landscape. There's so many beautiful, huge roots and beautiful organs that are there that outweigh the Jellyfish Brain and give counterbalance and counterpoint to the Jellyfish Brain's dominance. And I think there's something beautiful in that. So, I always want contact.

Also, the other end of the Jellyfish Brain's trunk is in the sacrum. So, you've got the wonderful, beautiful spinal cord moving through that neighborhood, an essential part of the neighborhood, to the lumbar and into the sacrum, and then you've got the cranial nerves that are moving on the outside of the spine, inside the body cavity, that are going into the abdomen, and the whole aquatic garden! You've got a lot of Jellyfish Brain tendrils happening in the abdomen, so it's good to include those, because all those little tendrils are going to all these beautiful organs in the belly, and there's some tendrils that go to the umbilicus neighborhood. Wow, all this about a neighborhood (I feel put on the spot)!

Yeah, if I were training a practitioner, I'd want them to include umbilicus, and give a moment to feel the responses of their inquiry... again in your mind... just an open-ended question, "Where are you?", "How are you?", "What's going on?", you know, just a little whatever your inquiry question is, and then giving it that time to respond... steeping there for a few moments, a few rounds, and then going with... because something will talk back, and you have to be prepared to stay with that, you know? One of those little abdomen salmon aspects comes to the surface. You want to grab it with your bear claws and kind of meet, hold, create a space, because it will respond.

**Christie**  When you brought umbilicus up with me, when you were working on me, you verbally addressed it. You may have been working with it before, but at that point you also talked about the void space. So, do you use the word 'void', because it's not that? That's what you just said in this discussion... and is there a void space aside from that?

**Michael**  Yes, yes, yes. Maybe. Yes. Most definitely Yes. So 'void' gets curious for me. Voids can be felt in our totality. The best ones are right after a dear one passes away, right? So that's a fascinating thing. Um,

349

it's void. Someone passes, and a space opens up, right? Especially when it's fresh, even when it's not fresh. But when it's fresh, it's best. Not necessarily for the person going through the loss, but that void changes the quality of space, the weaving of relationships. It starts a very visceral, biological change, and a significant change it is!

The juiciest ones are when the other end of the umbilicus passes. That's very funny because the matriarch, that weaving of the umbilici, that weaving of genetics goes back through the maternal line. There's some paternal messiness in their wonderful little ringlets, but the maternal lineage is so palpable. When, when the Mama goes, no matter what the relationship is, something changes. You, the person, male or female, starts to inhabit part of the familial tree or the family mind or the family's space of the family. Whatever, we all argue about that. But biologically, all of a sudden, that holder of your lineage isn't alive and now your soul, your biology starts to take up space differently. And that grief process is really essential.

'Void' is just that quality of space that implies that there is no space there, but it's a change of space. It's a really different type of quality, and it's not something we can do. It's something we can remember, and we can incur, but we can't, we can't make it happen. It's our connection to things, and when that thing isn't there, and it's been really juicy and nourishing or horrific and awful, whatever that is... when that's gone, it leaves this space that we will naturally move into and occupy. So, that's a wonderful place to work with people because, again, it's another place our socialness doesn't spend a lot of time dialoguing. It's like another umbilicus. We don't talk about it. We'll talk about grief, sort of.

**Christie** Sort of.

*Michael* And then our grief is usually usurped by our emotions and feelings. And I think grief is a little bit larger than that, you know. I think it's a larger fluid in some ways. Certainly the grease that gets things moving that never wanted to move in the first place, for sure, and, um, void will accompany an aspect of that. So, grief and void can be intimate with each other.

Um, and then there's these, these funny little voids, which aren't like The Void when a loved one passes, or when someone significant passes and leaves a quality of space open and the biology actually starts to fill that space, or our freneticness starts to fill it. With that, we start to panic a little bit, you know, and I've watched it mostly with mothers and daughters over the years. There's something really palpable when the

mother passes, especially if they were close. It takes a
couple years for the biology to settle from that event.
Then, all of a sudden, that person becomes the family
tree holder, you know, as you (Christie) specifically
know. So, you have that as well. And it happens with
men too. It's not as structured. There's a different
quality that lies in the garden spectrum, for sure. Um,
it takes about the same amount of time though, in my
experience. So the little voids are like an umbilicus,
something happens and it changes the quality of
space when we spend time there, both as practitioner
and just as a person exploring the sense of the
different neighborhoods within themselves. Also, just
as a quick wildcard... armpits are a funny void.

**Christie** Oh...

*Michael* (Those of you at home try it.)

Um, and it's a funny feeling because it's a place
that's not a place. It's just, it's too tangled with words,
but it's the craziest thing to try and find, because
there's little void there, but you can find a place but
it's not... it's a... and it starts to tickle. Um, so that can
be played with. Belly buttons can be played with, can
be 'their' own experience, 'their' own experiential tea.
Those are two good ones. Sometimes there're some
spots in the foot that can be a little voidy. Whatever
else? Where else? Yeah. I think I'll stay with those

because the other ones start to get convoluted. You start to get into it because a person doesn't occupy a part of their body. That doesn't mean there's a void. It means it's unoccupied.

**Christie**  Right. That is completely different.

*Michael*  It's a completely different quality.

**Christie**  Yeah.

*Michael*  But again, people mesh those together. You know, it's like talking about blockages. There's really no such thing except when there's an actual physical blockage, and then to the emergency room you go. But there're places where things don't seem to move because the person's not 'in there', right? People sometimes call that a 'blockage'. Then it gets semantically nutty.

**Christie**  Well, so how do you... If it's... I don't even know if you can communicate the difference in sensate feeling between someone simply not occupying a part of their body, and a void?

*Michael*  Oh gosh, yeah, I can try. Um, void is an open quality of space, and it will usually affect your entire field. For a moment, you'll be able to feel your field, you know, the space around you, the literal space, and that space is not thick or full or any of those dynamics. There's a, a wispiness to it, an openness to it. Um, but it's, but it's defined. It gets very nutty to talk about. But um, but the senses go for it. They just kind of open like,

you know, it's almost like a blustery day and then the
air goes still really quick. There's a gap, there's that
openness to it.

Um, in martial arts, you can touch into void and it's
a similar thing. You touch into a really large quality of
space. So, you're allowing all your tissues to disperse,
or be open, or be passively engaged, or be soft or... I
think there's lots of qualities. Lots of words can be
thrown at that, but it's a specific sense, and um, some
people can step into that. They've practiced. And
there's some martial arts or meditation that um,
specifically works with void as a way to take your
senses and, for a period of time, let them all be equal,
all be open and be responsive. You know, it's almost a
non-action action. It gets really funny to talk about.

**Christie** It seems like there's a quality of aliveness, whatever
that means, all the way through.

*Michael* Yeah.

**Christie** Whether the space is occupied or not. It's still alive.

*Michael* That's right. That's right. And again, that openness
feeling. When someone isn't occupying a part of their
body, it's sort of the opposite of void. There's a
density to that, that's not responsively alive, right?
They aren't 'in there'.

Void is more alive. Someone not occupying a
space... there's a lack of aliveness. And I think that's

where some of the current language around blockages and things like that arise, which are very prevalent in the bodywork communities and other communities as well. They rely on that word like, "Well, I don't feel something here, then it must be blocked there."

**Christie** Ah...

*Michael* That's very neural-dominant and linear thinking. Um, I don't like the word 'blockage' because I don't feel that. When there's a blockage, you're in the emergency room... that's serious stuff, because that can actually happen in the body. You can actually get blockages. I would like to see that part of language changed a little bit like here's the body's 'work around' or here, there is 'non-occupied' space (or a tangled density, or my favorite... a HAIRBALL!), because at least the tissue is still viable and doing its job, but the person's consciousness/awareness-attention/etc. has never been in there, or it was there and got tossed out because of some trauma, displacement, fragmentation, overwhelming experience. There're lots of descriptions, but the quality of the tissue and the quality of that neighborhood will be a little denser.

**Christie** Right.

*Michael* Right. Because there isn't that dance of engagement. The tissues are in their 'feral, taking care of themselves' mode. So, in that neighborhood, they're just in there doing their job... and that's all that's happening there. That part of life is happening, but the other part of the person's awareness/attention, their consciousness, isn't in there. With void, your consciousness and your attention all get melded together for a little while, you know, and that's a big gulp. And then we satiate, and then body comes in and goes, "What the... ?!" Or they're going into grief, or... you know, it depends on the association, the situation, what's happening 'in' that time.

**Christie** Yeah.

*Michael* And then in martial arts, they take away all associations and just go for that quality of space. Then they try to just stay with that. In some martial arts, then you're responding to another person in that space. So, you're trying to stay fully responsive, but you're really in void. It's an achievement. It's done over a long period of time to prepare to be able to just exist in that and be able to take actions and stay within that space.

**Christie** When you're working on somebody, and I assume it's your choice whether or not to verbalize what you're feeling or ask them if they feel it, or you know, 'whatever' would depend on whatever else is going on, right?

**Michael** On everything. But if I was training someone, right, I'd be saying that's one of the questions. "Where's their bones? Where's your bones?", right? They go together. As a practitioner, you know, what's supporting them? What's supporting you? Those go together, and what's your Jellyfish Brain trying to do with it? What's their Jellyfish Brain trying to do with it? Sooo... throw a giggle at both, whew, at both of those and see what happens.

When you're engaged with the neighborhood, and you're asking these questions and saying, "Well, where are you, Umbilicus?", or "Where are you, Bone?", or "Where are you, Liver, um, where's your neighbors?" Then there's the other questions going, "Should I prompt out loud? You know, wait a minute, I'm kind of in a stack... there's something else here... well, what's going on? What's got my attention?" You're asking yourself this little list of questions like, "Well, what and who has what feeling? What's that quality and where is this connected? And where's this not connected?"

You know, I've come to deeply enjoy these open-ended questions, and some of them are just years of doing; not just doing, but also feeling the same questions all the time. And now it's a little bit more fluid, a little more of a jazz exploratory, inviting quality. Hard to verbalize, but there'll be a place of, "Should I say something or not?" Sometimes I'm so in that interior of them, and tracking, that my voice will naturally be triggered. My question'll go out to one of those dynamics like, "Did I say that out loud?", which I may say out loud or not. I may just go off on the tangent a little bit.

The use of verbal modalities, which can be just as intricate as kinesthetic modalities, tactile modalities, the hands-on modalities... don't think the voice is much different than the tactile. For me, there's a tactile aspect of my voice, and I use it that way. So, it's a little bit like a bat using its sonar. Like I'll be working in some neighborhood, I'm like, "Ah, I need something else." So, I'll throw some words at it. Most of the time, I start off by naming, 'naming' the 'thing' I'm sensing. 'Naming' is its own magic. Then, I sense and feel what responds, feel how the Jellyfish Brain responds, how the viscera respond, how other things respond - or not respond, right? I'm sensing that whole spectrum, from a "No!" response to sometimes a very excited response like, "He named 'me'... OMG!", and the Jellyfish Brain's going, "What are they talking about? Leave us alone!" You start to have these very interesting conversations. Very jazz like, but that's the conversation. The Jellyfish Brain's left out of the conversation and the Jellyfish Brains hate that. They really don't like it. It's really foreign to our Jellyfish Brain to not be part of any conversation at all. She wants all of them, all at once. She likes that.

Depending on how the tissue responds, when I name something out loud, if I'm working on something, I'll name it, "Well what's going on? Where is this umbilicus? I can't find it. Where is it?" So, I'll engage that. Sometimes, if a person's getting too involved with me being involved with them, right? Only one human being allowed per body. And, when I'm working, I'm the human being, so I sometimes have to displace them into or towards something else, so I'll distract with words, because the ears cannot not react.

**Christie** Right. And the Jellyfish Brain cannot not react.

*Michael* Yes. So, you can take advantage of that. If I need to get some gardening work done here, I might have to get a person off on some other tangent, some other place or some other direction, or some other... and it's, it's that same type of thing. I'm feeling my way through my verbal as much as I'm doing with my hands. What's responding, what's not, you know, and I can drive people crazy a little bit and do, purposely

359

sometimes (possibly more now with this interview!), because I'm really wanting to give this neighborhood my full undivided 'attention', and their Jellyfish Brain's messing with it.

So, I get a little territorial, like, "I'm this neighborhood's advocate right now, and the Jellyfish Brain is trying to get all her tendrils in there with me while my tendrils are in there trying to work." It's way too much: So, I will send somebody off on some other tangent like, "Where are your bones? Where are your...?" You know, I'll pick a place to include that isn't where I am working, so let's try to make it functional. I can feel what I'm working on over here by their liver, but I can't feel their left elbow and, you know (here we go...) so, "Where's your left elbow?", or "Where's this or that?"

And sometimes I may need assistance in helping this area, again, like our earlier example of a person not in their legs, so while I'm working on this upper umbilici area, the liver and femoral arteries, and that whole juncture there at the beginning of legs, the top of psoas, (um, legs really start in the diaphragms/diaphragms reaches in the legs) (Oh, by the way, in somatic dominance, there are two diaphragms, in neural dominance, the Jellyfish Brain thinks there is only one diaphragm, don't get me started!). So, if I'm wanting to find that 'path through', I may help myself and help them by going, "Okay, let's find..." And I'll start to prompt, for example, "By the way, there's a Jellyfish in your ankles that lives as a tarsus ganglia, sending you aquatic bass lines, baselines created from your body's liquid (aquatic) mass, and your mass 'loads' or creates pressure from your different positions in space." So, lying down creates a lite jazz, inducing napping...or as in standing, a heavy rich opera. Every position has its quality, its load, its song. Tissues don't discern, they respond. Only the Jellyfish Brain discerns in order to coordinate and describe and make a 'cohesive' song from what's been experienced.

There's also the 'space' that informs. For example, you can sense when you're in the neighborhood at the foot and there's this space between your first toe knuckle and your second toe knuckle that is a wonderful acupuncture point (Liver 2), which has a little void.

**Christie** Right.

*Michael* There're little voids right there. Acupuncture loves little voids. In Shiatsu, they talk about different qualities of points like little mountains and little valleys. So, you know, you don't pummel at the top of the mountain. You get in the valley and explore; really

give it some attention, some movement, a little fire.
Build it up. Fill it up, you know? You don't pound at
the wall. You go find the little divot. You find a little
void and add some attention. That's a principle right
there. Same thing when I'm working on an area. I will
verbally start to prompt them and either do it to
distract them 'from' or distract them 'into' helping me
find something; find the root of what I'm working on. I
might engage them, depending on what our rapport
has been, to build rapport, or to just to keep them out
of my hair.

Christie So you can actually stay present in your hands *and* be
prompting them to distract them. I mean, you talked
about wanting to get your work done and not wanting
them in there so you would distract them. So, you
verbally can maintain that kind of attention to discuss
or whatever with them, and your hands are doing
something different?

Michael Well, awareness is flooding/responsive, attention is
finding/engaging. But under the auspices of training
someone, this is also how we would train them. In the
beginning, what I used to do is we'd have a contact
place, and then, you would just soften without
'leaving' and just stay with that contact place till both
of you were present with it, in it. And then you do
something really good. You stay in a place and then

you have your attention go either to their leg or their crown, and you let them feel and you feel what happens when you move your attention around. The practitioner's attention is staying in the spot of contact. But now you extend the 'awareness' to include the rest of their body. Very much a cranial idea (and I'm sure other modalities have that as well, but I know it from the cranial work, meditation work, and martial arts work), um, so you're flooding that awareness and you're letting a little attention be specific in your hands and contact, but now you're including and adding the rest of their bones, the rest of their body.

Now you're including that entirety. But now you're taking your attention and you're moving your attention within that awareness; you're moving your attention down to their feet, and you can get really specific. You can go for a specific spot, or just their legs, and feel how that affects where your hand contact is in that neighborhood. And then you simply take your attention, keeping your awareness flooding, holding the whole thing, and move your attention up to the crown, or over to a bone, or off to a rib, or with an organ, or... You start to play with moving your attention around without functionally/physically moving. So, you're again doing that wonderful Taoist non-doing doing. You're non-doing. It's not 'not doing'. You're not doing anything mechanical. You've softened contact 10% while 'staying with/in/during contact', allowing awareness to flood, life-size, the whole body (always 'life-size'), an inch equals an inch, staying with where your roots are on the 'contact'.

So, if I was contacting with both hands around their specific area (and I'm doing this in space, you can't see this at home, or you won't see it in the book). I have my hands holding an imaginary liver at the moment (for some reason today is the liver day). My hands are below and above their liver because I like a dual contact. It's very comfortable for me, lets me have the whole thing if I have to clamp...if I have to hold the salmon if it tries to move, it's mine! My liver!

The other hard thing to teach practitioners is to be territorial. You either got it or you don't. Some people are just way too frickin' nice. (You can put that in the book.) Practitioners have a really hard time taking that therapeutic license of holding the reins of their/the experience. That's terribly important, and you can be just as goofy or as morose as you want with it, as long as you know that's part of the 'job'. Hold the reins!!

There's a whole spectrum there. I've gotten goofier. I started off very morose, so I've the whole spectrum in my experience. But, when I've got someone's liver, that liver creature is mine, and I'm treating it like a salmon. I'm treating it with the respect of the living thing that it is. So, my contact is there. Part of my attention is there. I have allowed my awareness to also include the rest of their body and mind, so there's a little bit of global context (the local 'global', of their/our garden, of course).

And then the attention... you start to play with the reality that you can actually move your attention around a body, and feel what happens in your hands, feel how that organ responds. In this case, you can do it with anything (remember the beginning of this endeavor?), but right now, we're sticking with the liver to keep it not so abstract (which is not easy for me to do. I like the abstract.) So, in training practitioners, it's a big moment for them to have that experience of holding something with their contact, realizing that they can stay with their contact and let their awareness then include the rest of the body, stay there as well, and then start to move their attention within that field.

**Christie**  And then notice how that affects...

*Michael*  ...how that affects the contact and anything else they/you can possibly be tracking. Everybody's different. For some people, just that little bit is mind blowing. Other people, that's just the gate, the beginning. Some people have very complex, multidimensional Jellyfish Brains, and their Jellyfish Brains get really happy when they get permission, "I can do this, and that and that and this other thing, and I can play with it?" Yes, yes, Dorothy, you can... all of them at once if you want. I can't do all, but I can do a chunk, and that's the jazz of it, that's the engagement of it, that's the quality.

You're gardening that person's root beds. All that attention you're giving them... they don't get that in the daily world. Very few people have it within their own personal practices to spend/be with their time in this way. I know, because at home the practice is different, private, more quiet, and then it's my turn to go and be tended, gardened. It's just as precious to have somebody else do it, which will be this afternoon for me because I go to my practitioner after this. It's very important for me to be handled so I can feel how that feels. I already have my sense of wanting to garden. I'm already engaged that way, whether alone, being tended or tending... there's now a continuity in my experience.

So, when training people, it's a big deal to have them learn how to soften their hands, just 10%, without retreating. To stay in contact without leaving contact. To allow their awareness then to flood the area, because you're aware, you don't need your awareness being held in one place, and that there's a difference between awareness and attention, you know?

**Christie** Yeah. We talked about that last time.

*Michael* Yeah, we did. It's our circular conversations.

**Christie** Yeah, it's great.

*Michael* So this is another place for that. When training someone, especially a practitioner, it's really cool to watch them watch their own Jellyfish Brain and get the permission that they can do these layers of engagements, and that they can really have these conversations with another human body (not just humans), and they don't have to do the esoteric/energetic of being careful and putting up shields, etc. etc.

When I mentor some clients, I'm still doing some of this type of teaching. Um, to get a person to track themselves, and prompting helps with that. And part of verbally prompting someone not only educates them, but the prompting helps them learn how to prompt themselves.

They can stay with their hairball if I'm not there or another practitioner isn't holding their hairball (today, it's the liver's hairball), and they can stay with their liver, have some steeping, nonverbal, non-neural-dominant dialogue with it, understand that their Jellyfish Brain will want to interpret... and learning that it doesn't have to. They just have to keep circulating their attention back to their liver, their hairball... they can learn to do that. And then, get to know their own awareness, that it includes the whole of their body, always flooded life-size, while their attention, the marvelous sea creature aspect, gets to explore.

So, we've tricked them up to this point because I've already had them find their bones (#1, *always #1!* Where are they, your bones?), and I've already had their bones find what's actually supporting them (#2, *always #2!* Where's the push of the world?), I've already been prompting their Jellyfish Brain. They've already got that they can go into a non-neural-dominant space and it's okay; but it's slippery as heck, and that layer of information circulates, right, and they can always have a place to step back to, slide back into, orient to... their own bones!

They can also always come back to engaging their own liver, or their own hairball, and then include the rest of their body. Their awareness is allowed to flood, and their attention is separate. It's a different thing. Then they can have these prompted dialogues. In that hairball, can they take their attention and keep a little bit on their liver, but then go down and feel for their ankle, or feel for a leg bone, or feel for their bladder, or feel for their umbilicus, or feel for their crown, or a tooth, or an ear, or under their armpit, you know? Can they play with moving some of their attention around while their awareness is flooded within their whole field and feel what happens? That is the same 'devoted time' that they're getting, steeping, being prompted, encouraged, in the office, either as a client or a practitioner being trained, and there's something delicious about giving a person skills and being straightforward with that, and sometimes silly, you know? And sometimes, the silliness is to keep them from doing all the habituated tendencies, so later, they'll have to self-facilitate because they weren't allowed to do it in the office. And it creates an amazing tension. And some people, all that's enough to have them go, "To heck with him!", and go find a different practitioner who doesn't make them work, but at least it's been seeded.

**Christie** Yeah.

*Michael* Right. That session, with a client or a practitioner or a... even if I only see a person once, we've seeded some things. We've tried to meet them where they're at and give them a little bit. Some people want that. Some people don't. Some practitioners want to learn this stuff, some of them don't. So, it's just feeling your way through it, modeling for them and yourself... going through it 'with' them, 'during' them, steeping an experiential tea, not a concept.

In a way, some of this stuff that we're talking about gets a chance to also be a metaphor. It gets to have its social engagement and its other beautiful interactions. It gets to circulate out, you know, and it's precious to watch that; both to watch a body respond even though the Jellyfish Brain's going, "What the heck are you doing?", and then, a couple of moments/hours/days/months/years later, they're going, "Holy crap, there's something to this!" Then you look at them like, "I know! It was done with/to/during the grannies. It was done with me, and now I'm doing it with/to/during you. And you're going to do it with/to/during someone else!" On the outside, it may be completely different in how it's danced, practiced, sung, shared... Yeah. But how it's 'felt' is congruent. Oh, it's very deliciously devious. The dark humors get some 'time'!

**Christie** So part of the holding the awareness and holding the liver, and part of the attention shifting, can also be the verbal stuff that's going on.

**Michael**   It very much can be the verbal, and nonverbal, both-and, always swimming towards both-and! If you sense it... Pause! Steep!

**Christie**   Okay, I can see/feel the nonverbal, but then the verbal...? I mean, we started this because I was asking whether you can do your work between your hands and have a verbal conversation with the client or verbal dialogue with them in which you're distracting them from this.

**Michael**   It's the same thing. So, think about you're holding this liver, and you found the client. You and they have found their way into their foot, while holding the liver. That's pretty big, but some part of them gets fixated. They start to anchor.

**Christie**   In the foot...

**Michael**   In the foot to the liver, making a unique shape of, with, and between those neighborhoods.

**Christie**   Right.

**Michael**   So they get... it's too intense. It's too, like their Jellyfish Brain has just figured out it can hold the/that shape. You don't want a shape held. You want the/their experience circulating. So you have to say, "Nooo." You have to distract them. You have to take their attention and encourage it to go somewhere else, while encouraging a bit of softening, just 10%, for awareness to 'flood'.

**Christie**  I see.

**Michael**  So, you have to come to, "Oh honey, no, no, no." You're always playing/experiencing in the dynamics, but the palpatory sense is keeping it circulated, is keeping a sense of salmon still in the river moving, you know? Even if it's staying still, it's not still, right? And that's different than the liver going into freeze response. Like all these doings (and non-doings) get us into a labyrinth, and each turn sends into another length and turn, and, pretty soon, it's an hour and a half later and we gotta stop and say, "Okay, that's enough... that's enough." Which is a whole different conversation of how things cycle, the little rhythms. But there's a rhythm to that, too... cycle/rhythms, satiation/maturation, dynamics/experience.

But yeah, your teaching can be in these spaces, these dynamics. And then teaching a practitioner to add in their verbal style is another layer of trickiness, trickery because some people can do it, some people can't. You know if their voice kicks on, they'll get formal and very intellectual, right? Doesn't work. So, you might have to train someone that they can be in that field and let the roots of their tongue soften into what they're doing, and they can talk from that space/place/sensation. It's a difficult thing to train because some of this I have a propensity for.

**Christie**   Right.

**Michael**   Now I know that. In the early days, I tried to be intellectual like, "Okay, this is this, and while the umbilicus is..." Now, I'm not so intellectual about it. It's like, I don't know what their umbilicus is. I've run into umbilici that have a whole different sense of things. I've run into livers that have a whole different sense of liver, and things that aren't always what, you know, what we intellectually or typically find. The character of a neighborhood in the body will have its own distinct character, and you have to be available to that in the same way when you're adding in the verbal layer of engagement.

The verbal layer of it you have to be prepared to kind of stumble your way through a little bit. Sometimes you can just nail it, and that's really exciting, but sometimes distracting... it's a, it's a stumbling thing. I think when you get used to stumbling verbally, then it sounds natural and stays in the field, still in connection with the roots. I'm doing it right now. I've been doing it since this interview endeavor began. This whole thing is a stumbling into technology which will end up as chicken scratch or deer tracks on a page somewhere that people may or may not ever see, which is fine. But that's the thing... How do we stay in the feeling, just like in this dialogue, and let pour, toss words at it, build a verbal teacup enough to hold the quality of the experience, then let the words stumble and wrap themselves around the feelings held within one of the qualities of the shapes of the experiences?

**Christie** And humor.

*Michael* And humor... and sometimes humors cover grief, you know... being willing to name that layer too. Then, sometimes when you're in something, you're like, "Oh fuck!" You know the person has never verbalized this. There's a feeling in the tissues. It's not circulating. It's entrapped. It's encapsulated... the overwhelm in that experience that had that tissue react and go into a protective coping mode... feral mode... self-protective. Just you hanging out there is a lot, *A LOT*! And so, sometimes I might have to just name that, "I'm just hanging out here.", right? I'll put words to the feeling because there's a sense that that hasn't happened.

That's an intuitive, educated zone. Then other times, you get the other upwellings, you'll get an emotional response. They're getting an emotional response, so you know you are...you've got a very charged area that has never had contact, or if it has, still hasn't been met. Someone got in there and tried to fix it and it went vigilant, so it encapsulated even more, and the person thought that that shift was a release. So, the practitioner went on with their agenda, their 'usual'.

There wasn't a release, there was a shift. Those are really different. Actually, I'm not attached to releases. I think they're just circulation. Not a big deal. Secondary processing... another book probably... and there's already 10,000 books!

So, you're in there, and so you name the quality and there's a response, and then you, you all of a sudden have your insight... the tactile, the emotional, the felt, and their intellect, your intellect... everything lined up for a few minutes. Then you name the distress, the feeling. You just try to name the quality there. Then, every once in a while, you can feel the event. For some people, you feel their traumatic event and it's so clear, but it was so early or was so averted in their experience, just those combinations of things are just so big, whelming to overwhelm, you know, there's just so much of a charge, so much held there, and they've been coping with it for so long that their whole biology doesn't know what to do with all that starting to shift, move, sense, circulate, whew... some type of strategy, some maneuvering has to happen to keep it all together.

So, the verbal stuff becomes terribly important, you know, as a distraction. But also, a naming and an education, and a support. You can do all those, sometimes all at once, simultaneously. And again, you're back in that "I'm using my body and my roots to resonate and be available to their experience." I'm not really in there to have my own experience primary. I have my primary 'experience', right? It gets interesting with words. Training practitioners is even more difficult in these ways because you're saying, "Well, you have to hold your experience. You can't go in to just enmesh with them and do your trip." But you're there, being honest with your trip as modeling that they can work with theirs.

**Christie** Right.

*Michael* It doesn't mean that you don't use enmeshment. As a modality, it's also known informally as entrainment.

**Christie** Right.

*Michael* It doesn't mean that you're not flooding them and yourself with your awareness as well, if for no other reason as a training for their nervous system. You have to use your nervous system because there's a proximity entrainment that happens, and you can use that. That can be done verbally as well.

So, you're letting these different layers learn to engage and hold/steep in the space and be available as a responsive mirroring for them. In doing that, you're educating their nervous system, and you're also doing some of the processing for them. Your stuff is going, "Oh! Hey, cool!", and their system inside is going, "What?!" and you got 'em! Their nervous system goes, "What?", you got 'em. What happens after that is what happens after that.

Christie  But you, but your practitioner or you would have your primary experience. You were, I thought, making a bit of a differentiation between your personal primary experience and...

Michael  You have to, um, you have to differentiate that. You have to stay in your own bones. But then, you have to extend, enmesh sometimes, to have some of the conversations/interactions available to try reciprocity in your exchange or allow other circulations to be responsive, but oriented. You have to go back and forth (to and fro) as well. In doing that, you're training them. You have to try and stay in your contact, and then, if you add words, that's a different layer. So, you let that be a different layer. You're always feeling the response... Be it to words, a different contact, or sound that's not even generated by either of you, you know, trucks and having an office downtown, it's essential.

Christie  Oh yeah.

Michael  You know, I like... the reason why I have my office downtown is because I want all those sounds there, because there's times none of those sounds are there. It ebbs and flows like our ocean, like everything in a person's body. And I believe the social part of the nervous system needs 'the opera' at large... and all that is okay... all that is part of the experience.

I will probably always try and keep an office upstairs because if a person can't walk up those stairs, they can't do this layer of work. If they can't walk up the stairs, then they need to go to a physical therapist. They need to go to a body worker/therapist who can come to their home, or has a ground office, you know.

For me, the layers of these conversations (verbal/nonverbal jazz), the layers of gardening I want to have and do with a person in my office, they have to be in a certain state of health. Or they have to have a certain layer of circulation, an ability to respond. Just because they walk up the stairs, uh, doesn't negate all their hairballs, but there's a certain function available. Their function has to be there so they can integrate what happens. If they can't integrate that, then what I'm doing is too much. These conversations I'm having are too much. There's a certain amount of motion to movement, movement to motion, that allows for integration.

For some people who are really healthy and all that... some of these conversations are also too much, so I won't see them again. And that's okay. We've touched into that and tended to their garden, and it gives them a contrast. So, they'll either go off and find other practitioners or not. Or they come back a couple of years later and say, "You know, that bone thing...?" (I've had that happen.) Like, I didn't think that session did anything. It was just a simple garden-tending session.

So yes, you can split/differentiate your awareness, your attention, and your contact, and you can use your voice as a modality. Then, there's another layer of just honestly naming what you're experiencing with someone, what you're tracking. Sometimes it works and sometimes you're just fishing. You're like a babbling brook singing to their salmon nature but that didn't go anywhere... "Fuck!" Every once in a while you say that word out loud like, "Oops..(admission) fuck!" (Did I discuss this?).

**Christie** But it seems like humor itself...because you talk about humor sometimes. I don't know whether it's just me that you talk about throwing a little humor at something, throwing a giggle at something. It just seems like humor, in particular, gets used in this process, by you anyway, quite a lot.

*Michael* A lot by me, a lot (It's # 3, *always #3,* in 'The Three Most Important Things'). Um, for me, the humors (plural) and the metaphoric cover a huge spectrum. Humors include grief and deep, deep dark humors.

**Christie** Okay, gotcha.

*Michael* Because humors allow tissues to flutter/ripple/giggle, to individuate. It allows tissues to flutter...um, no matter what the humors are. In general, for me, I think if I was to define without looking at a dictionary, which would probably be good, um, humors allow tissues to flutter. So many of our tissues are non-mechanical. They aren't engaged in muscular activity, and the humors seem to let them flutter. It gives them a moment of space; In that space, there's a response and the response can be a giggle. It can be a deep quiet. It can be even deeper grief, or it can be something really, really deep, which is really dark humor, where all of a sudden you get an insight that just shifts things, sometimes all at once, it's at your own expense, and it's just glorious. Then the whole body responds. You're like, "Oh fuck... that's it!" You know? And um, it's just that rich deep darkness going, "Oh goodness... of course... clunk... whew!"

You have a whole spectrum. Getting someone to giggle or being able to meet their Jellyfish Brain and start to track her antics, um, there's a pleasure in that, because the other tissues are now included. So, it becomes a pleasure, a type of satisfaction. All of a sudden, the hairballs aren't concentrated on, and for a moment there's something different.

It's not always pleasurable, but it's always deeply impactful, you know. Again, for me, although I use a lot of humor in humors, um, (wow, can I say this... it can be dangerous. We're moving into dangerous territory). I don't think joy and happiness and love should be the goal. I think they're secondary processes. I don't think giggling or humors are about that. I think humors are there to let something move that wasn't moving before. Sometimes that can be horribly traumatic and horribly, horribly, awfully, beautifully allowing!

If all of a sudden their trauma hairball... the one thing, the last place they want to go... and be... and it has moved... moves, you know, it's not exactly relief at the moment. But it's a shift and there's something rich, and dark, and important and vital about those responses. And it can throw the rest of the system into a disorientation.

So, it's not, it's not pleasurable, but it's terribly, terribly important because now that thing that's been held in place is starting to find its life, its motion, its movement, and its roots again. Otherwise, the person's going to bind back down, and then all their decisions, and everything they're maneuvering in their life is all around protecting this trauma hairball, whether conscious or not. It's incredibly constrictive, but highly intelligent, and they may not be ready for that to be moving, but it's been acknowledged and moved or shifted or contacted or engaged or...

**Christie** So do you do that intentionally?

*Michael* Sometimes.

**Christie** Sometimes?

*Michael* Sometimes we're like, "Nnn... no."
And I think that's where the rapport comes in. Learning to move your attention around. Learning that your attention and your awareness are different. Learning that you can use different things as modalities, different types of contact, different layers of your voice. You can use it either to bring someone really in and concentrate attention... or you can disperse it. You can make them nuts and crazy, and just want to start to dance and try to get off the table, and then you pin them down while they're squirming (terribly satisfying), and other times you're just, you're... you don't have contact, you have complete contact, but you aren't touching their body, you're completely touching their body (you can be across the room). Um, you have that whole range, and as you engage and explore with that, then you're starting to... model for someone (and always for yourself). So,

then there's an honesty there. You're willing to stumble around and explore in these other layers, and the tissues are in there going, "We know! We're in here trying to do that too!"

And then you come back full circle. And then you're training someone how to explore options, because you're willing to explore options. For the biology to have that opportunity's huge because, if our Jellyfish Brain's in charge, we're going to do it as if we're out here in the world in really big movements and really big activities and really big thinking and really large qualities.

Our interior doesn't always move like that. It has a really huge experience in very small ways. To have someone explore a little bit of its neighborhood may have never happened before, and the rest of the body will get very frustrated because they want to go off and dance, fuss, stretch, move quickly (which if you're not 'oriented' is 'habit'). And this little place we're tending is going, "You're frightening the hell out of us right now. This bozo working on us is giving us his complete attention and everybody, everywhere else is being told to back off." So, there's a little empowerment that happens. There's a little concentrated attention. There's a little exploring of an option, an acknowledgement, and a soft meeting.

Meanwhile, all those wonderful palpatory things are happening that begin to create a little bass note, then the psyche and the consciousness go, "Holy crap, holy crap!" They didn't know that they didn't know that they didn't know that they didn't have... that... 'that' didn't/couldn't move.

**Christie** Yeah, yeah.

*Michael* And you've stumbled into something, but you've done it with a flooding of awareness and a little bit of attention, you know? You've been inclusive of the rest of the body. So, it's not like asking them, "Do you want all this?"

This is another level and use of tenacity/aggression in responding to what's being felt, you're using your tenacity to help. These layers of response have subtle differences, yet in palpating someone, there are huge differences. You know, sometimes I can be extremely aggressive and very single minded. If my bear claws get triggered by that hairball behaving like a salmon, and that salmon's trying to move upstream and nothing's helping it, I may decide to help it. Or if it's moving way too fast and frightening all the other fish in the belly, I may have to grab that tenacious salmon and slow it down, pull it in and hold it until it shifts its freneticness, its habitual dance, just like holding a spasming child.

Sometimes you just got to clamp down, and be a grandma and say, "I'm so sorry. You want to do all these other things you can't, and you will submit because that spasm causes more freneticness with danger. You think you're squirming away, but you're actually causing the very thing you're screaming about being in pain from. So we're just going to stay right here (and bear-claw-clamp)." Then, you're using the tenaciousness that was probably in their overwhelm and their trauma, which abused them, subjugated them, did whatever the myriad of things that induce the overwhelm. You're using a very similar dynamic to help reclaim that neighborhood. It's the same aggression. It's the same tenacity. It's the same... It's the same mama bear thing, like, "HEY... This is your body, man! There's no fucking way 'they' (the original cause) get you back. Fuck those other clowns. Fuck them and their misuse of..."

This is good tenaciousness, you know, and you have to do/have that. Other times you have to be the opposite of that. You have to hold void. You have to make a complete invitation. So, it's a completely other end of the spectrum. You can't engage, you can't go after that directly. You've got to get everybody around that dragon/salmon really prepared because when that dynamic wakes, it's gonna have to have someplace to go. So, you'll sometimes spend chunks of time, days/weeks months/years, circling a dragon/salmon. It's that whole spectrum, and you can be working at it in layers because we have layers. Whew! And there's something to all this!

**Christie** Oh, so do you consciously know that?

*Michael* At this point, (unpretentiously) mostly. The previous Michaels... often. The previous, previous, once in a while. The previous, previous, previous Michaels... it was an amazing concept to chew on and see if there was any of it that was true, and sure enough!

**Christie** Well, it's just that I can imagine that there's a level of intuition that is not necessarily, well... not knowing where you're going, and then there's another layer of consciousness where you have some sense of what might need to be done before this.

*Michael* And there's two layers. So, yes to both of those, and more. We all grow in layers.

**Christie** Yeah.

*Michael* And, in this, I think, is where training is essential for intuition. A lot of people have this idea that training can squash and ruin imagination/intuition... that this part of our wonderful intuition is in our delicate bits of us. I disagree. I think it depends on the training, too. I think training gives more tools for intuition, and those aspects of imagination. But I always go in with an outline, you know, always go in with an agenda, because that sets my contrast. Always have an agenda, you know, because then you have something to set aside.

**Christie** Right.

*Michael* You know where your agenda is, so you can then go, "There's my agenda, but... I don't know." Then I have to practice that 'both-and', and what we're talking about is really that. It's these different layers. You can be in bits of them, at once, and you don't have to control it. Some of it you'll have to have a little control over, right? It gets very interesting to try and talk about, but it's definitely that place of going, "There is a developmental 'I don't know' that actually invigorates curiosity, and it invigorates imagination and allows for that intuitive reciprocity of exchanged songs, ideas and experiences between people's verbal and nonverbal."

And it's not for everybody. You know, people, I think, get caught in the connotations. "I don't know!", doesn't mean you don't have skills, but developmentally you have to come to the honesty of "I don't know!" And if you can hold both of those, you start holding 'both-and'. If you can stay in your bones and have your Jellyfish brain be a little off-kilter, and have a little giggle, and still engage in the rest of the world, you're in a 'both-and' place. It's not either/or. You aren't saying, "Let's get a batch of this experience and then we'll come over and deal with this experience." You're going, "Wait a minute. I can deal with a little bit of both of these because I have 'both-and'. I can have my 'I don't know!' and I have plenty of skills, but I don't know which ones to pick up, which ones will be responsive, because I'm not engaged yet. So, let's just keep those handy."

**Christie** But you have the agenda.

*Michael* But I have the agenda going, "We need to get to this part of the garden. I don't know how we're going to get there." Right? I have to get vulnerable, but I'm in proximity. As a practitioner, either training someone or engaging someone as a client, I have to go to the... I have to be in that place, because their nervous system is tracking me. They cannot not react, right?

**Christie** Right. So you have to be in what place? The 'I don't know' place?

*Michael* I have to be in a 'vulnerable' (which is also potent) place. I have to have my, "I don't know!"... and my agenda there and be willing to do both when I need it. I have my bear claws when I need them. They're actually badger claws. I like my bear part too, but my badger is a little more engaging. He's very happy. He's happy, practiced, you know? I have other animals, though, that have no claws, thank you very much. But I love the ones that've got claws. I just do ('specially the ones with retractable claws, 'both-and'!). So, you have that range. With that range, you're going in with your skill sets available. The 'I don't know!' allows there to be a responsiveness, to allow certain shapes, tools, modalities to be pliable and responsive and to come in and allow those responses, going, "Yeah, I know you don't like this hairball. I'm sorry your back hurts, you know, but we're going to go do this other piece first, because if we don't do that piece, there's nothing for your back to let go into." It can't 'let go' into nothing! I don't want to be pummeling someone's poor back... um, without this process being able to integrate... We can't let go into nothing! I'll say it again, "*We can't let go...into Nothing!*" That's a fantasy, a form of coping (very sacred, though).

The converse can be true as well. Same situation, next client. We can't do any of that other stuff because their frickin' back is in a tangle, and I've got to get out the rotor tiller and deal with this 'back' before we can deal with any of these other layers, right? We just can't go, "I really want to get to this other layer. I can feel it inside. I'm salivating... Oh! There's so much we can do... but... Oh, I gotta do that 'back' session!"

Nowadays I go, "Well, maybe I won't pummel their back. Maybe I'll do it differently and just try something (and piss both of us off)." And that's what I think the beauty of it is, that underneath it all, a body cannot not react, so find a starting place to go. And that's the agenda piece I think... to start with a starting place.

**Christie** Yeah. Yeah. I used to do that when I was teaching. I always had an agenda or outline.

*Michael* Yeah. Yes, absolutely!

**Christie** And, by the end of the teaching, usually I had covered a number of things, but how I got there was completely not necessarily at all what I thought I was going to do to get there.

*Michael* That's right. And that's how I was trained as a teacher as well. Get your outline down, map it out, be clear, this is your time, this is what you have them for, this is what needs to be covered. All that is really retentive, and parts of me like that, but when you get in there, there's going to be the living piece of it.

**Christie** Right.

*Michael* And I think that's the difference between teachers and instructors. Instructors are going to keep you to the outline... first this, then that, then... For me, the sheep dog in me wants to go, "Okay, that's our end point. Here's our labyrinth. Here's our outline, but how are these people doing?"

**Christie**  Right.

**Michael**  How can we get them to...? Maybe we just barely get to number one. Everyone's open here... can get way off into something else because that's where they are.

**Christie**  Right.

**Michael**  Right. You get to cover that information in a completely different way. Same is true on the table. You get what they're telling you because you're watching them walk in. You're asking them to express. Well, their words are going to say one thing. Here's the other side of the earlier question. Their words are saying one thing, but the body's gonna' dance something different, right? You can use both of those. They don't have to be congruent, right? I'm working on something. What I do verbally doesn't have to be congruent with how I'm working. I can throw in the discord. It's musical, counterpoint and explorative.

**Christie**  Yeah.

**Michael**  Right. That's good. How are they going to respond to a discord? Their psyche's going to want to coordinate the experience. It's going to want something that really ties in to 'its own' experience. It has to make sense... and then no it doesn't. We're going to just see. And then later you can try to do the repair work, which sometimes you have to do...in their cycle, you know, so it goes.

It's very interesting to challenge oneself to deal with stuff as a full spectrum living metaphor... to let stuff have an expression. Yes, we're doing this internal work, but out here isn't much different than... can we let those different layers just really be different, you know? They don't circulate the same. No, they don't agree. Yes, other parts of your experience will not agree with your mind or your Jellyfish Brain. Their experience was different. So, who are you going to advocate for? Well, in my office I get to advocate for the garden, the bones... get to advocate for the parts that don't have a tongue. The Jellyfish Brain's gotten them to the office, so the Jellyfish Brain's doing good. It may be in a tangled mess, but it's at least functioning.

**Christie**  Okay. So, I'm embarrassed to say that usually I remember because you've said this to me so many times, it's like bones, the only way that bones get affected or something is by the push of the world. They have their load bearing or they're...there were two or three things that you said, which I can't remember.

*Michael*  Oh.

**Christie**  So what I wondered is (and then I was playing with it this morning), it's like the bones are basically receptive, and there are only specific things that they pay attention to or that, that affect them, that cause them to grow or change. Does the sensate attention, you know, kind of the ability to go in there and actually track them or be with them, the bones, and feel them affect them?

**Michael** That's a great question. I think so. I think so. Not directly, because again what makes bones magical is the way they operate in time, um, differently than the other tissues, right? It takes their law, Wolff's law, which is that bones grow to the force put upon them. Our culture has been playing with those forces a long time. We can move the teeth around our face now because of the Invisalign products. You can order it on the Internet and put a little thing over your teeth and over time you can move the teeth because the Invisalign or braces put teeth in a specific tension, a force on the teeth, and that force sustained over months and months and months and months and years... the bones will start to lay down a different matrix in relationship to that force, so you can actually move your teeth around your mouth. It's grueling, because you're, you're putting a pressure and a force in place, and manually holding it there long enough for the osteoblasts and osteoclasts (which are what build bone and take away bone) to do their little dance.

And, over time the tooth will shift over, literally, you know. Frickin' fantastic. Same thing with, with exercise in that you put small weights on your wrists and ankles while you exercise, so your bones are getting more force. You're adding more load to 'their' experience, so they will build 'their' matrix in relationship to that load. You have to do it daily. It has to build up over a long time because, at some point, your bones are gonna say, "Oh, oh shit, she's not kidding!" And they'll start to adapt. They'll start to take that accumulated information, experience, and lay down their matrixes in response to that new force.

**Christie** Well, when the astronauts in space station...

*Michael* They don't have force put on their bones enough when they're in space like we do planet side, so their bones come back a bit more brittle. They have to build that bone matrix resilience back up. Now, they're very healthy people, and their circulation and their stuff is in great shape, so everything responds fairly quickly. So, over nine months to two years they've got their structure back because we, because we can play with this law.

We can come up with the Zumba, with 10,000 things, yoga, with 10,000 things, circuit training, 10.000 things, therapies, 10,000 things, Continuum, 10,000 things, etc. to change our relationships. And as we do that, as the bone changes its matrix, and once the bone lays down a new line of force, then the tendons and muscles lay down a different tension line. And so they grow differently. There's this whole cycle going deeply internal to widely external, this back and forth. By bringing our attention and getting involved with that, we start to become a part of that dance, the tending to ourselves, the Gardening!

And we can start to go, "Oh wow. I don't spend any time there." Then you start to spend time with your bones. Then, all of a sudden, the tissues start to respond. They've changed their behavior. Now the load moving into the bone is changed.

**Christie** Okay.

*Michael* So then the bone's behavior changes. So it goes, back and forth.

**Christie** Okay.

*Michael* It's very alive that way. It's just that it happens over long periods of time. That doesn't happen... you know, other tissue can regrow itself in a fairly short period of time comparatively.

**Christie** Yeah, well that's what I was... it's kind of like I've spent now, well I don't know how much time before I got really sick, but in the last two, two and a half to three years, lots of attention has gone into my bones and,

and what's interesting is when things opened up in my ankles this last summer, and the homunculus...

**Michael** The cortical homunculus, the little brain map.

**Christie** Yeah. The Jellyfish Brain map changed, and the Jellyfish Brain has been having a difficult time. It says, "Really? Are you sure?" Yeah. Really. And so now it's mapping, my Jellyfish Brain is mapping something different because I'm telling it...well, because it's obvious now because we're paying attention. So the ankles, the fibula and the tibia, actually... there're lines of force that go all the way down. They all... that's a trip. It's kind of like, well, where...? The bone was always...?

**Michael** ...has always been there, and it's a...Rib-ula! (not Fib-ula), Silly, it's a feeling, remember?

**Christie** It's always been there, and the ankle bones were always connected to that bone because it is the same thing.

**Michael** It's literal, it's...

**Christie** Yeah. But then the cortical homunculus, the map, has changed, and the actual experience is changing.

**Michael** That's beautifully said. That's said better than I did. That was beautifully said. Yes. That's a process. That's the process.

**Christie** What it's requiring, and what seems to be happening is that the actual attention... I spend a lot of attention in that place, you know, awareness, but also specific attention.

**Michael** Specific attention. So your attention and your awareness start to imbue those tissues differently. You start occupying the space. Before your cortical homunculus grew a leg, it just drew leg and then grew leg, and all that's fine. It had function. It had that wonderful, wonderful autonomic function. You know, your autonomic system is autonomic because it's autonomic.

**Christie** Right.

**Michael** But now you're in, now you're involved. So you reclaim a bit of landscape, so you get all the benefits and tragedies of engaging with that.

**Christie** Doing that.

**Michael** But what it also does is it allows a part of your awareness and attention to, um, really be ballast with your actual structure. That has to be gardened. Otherwise the world gets your attention, right?

**Christie** Yes.

**Michael** Before, your bones are still in there ballasting your tissues, but it's in a very opaque abstract way. It's functional. It's functional within a range that it has, and your cortical homunculus has mapped all that. But now, by you occupying it, it gets all the nuances, and then all the other tissues benefit because now there's this different line of force, line of attention. You described it beautifully. There's a different line of force all of a sudden, and you're like, "Oh wait, there's something there." Half of it's disturbing because the Jellyfish Brain wants to do what it did. Her habits want to hold and persevere.

**Christie** Right.

*Michael* And the other half is exciting because now you have another layer of engagement that's available to you, and you actually start to navigate space differently. You aren't scattered and out here in the world going crazy. You're actually starting to move and navigate through space literally, and you start to move at a different rate. You start to have a different rhythm. Then, all of a sudden, your biology's more included in your activities, if you want that. Some people want that. Some people don't want that. They just want to do what they want to do, push through the world. And some of that, that's their character, and that's their coping. That's where they were/are in their development.

**Christie** Right. What I was feeling this morning was (I don't know that I've felt it quite this way before), I was feeling like, "Oh, if I, if I...", (again, this is conceptual)... it, it's also honoring the force that is put upon them and, and that therefore the bones hold a kind of, I mean maybe more so than the other tissue, hold a kind of steadiness (obviously because they're providing structure), but because they're receiving and they're moving slowly, they hold something in relationship to the world that's different than anybody else... maybe...

**Michael**  Any, any body and any other body part... yes, bones are the ballast for our layers, all of our layers, inside and out. Even the layers we all argue about. The bones literally ballast, give a place in space for our experience; of course the bossy-pants Jellyfish Brain 'thinks' she's the center (Silly Jellyfish Brain)!

**Christie**  Yeah... the tissues. But... and then I was thinking, okay, so the Jellyfish Brain... I've been, we've been having discussions about how it could actually feel good to be inside that bone, you know, and, and so the orientation... it's kind of like, oh, the bones serve a function for, for the whole body, but for the Jellyfish Brain, in terms of orientation, it's kind of like, "Oh, there you are. Oh, okay. So, so that's a benefit that you have, that you get to have, Jellyfish Brain. You get to have this benefit of a kind of orientation that can serve you, Jellyfish Brain, by giving up some control or perceived control and relaxing into this experience."

**Michael**  Huh... yeah, you're hooked.

**Christie**  Yeah, I am, there's no doubt.

**Michael**  Beautifully said. That's why we do the bone orientation. That's why it's the first tenant of my office. It didn't start out that way, but this is what's been shaken into because everybody comes in, me included, with all these other agendas/habits/history, and we're trying to advocate for these other tissues, but we're doing it from a neural-dominant point of view.

That's fine for coping, and it's fine for function, in a certain layer of function, but it doesn't allow for what you just described. It doesn't allow for the Jellyfish Brain to all of a sudden be supported, held, oriented. She's trying to get it out into the world. She actually has it in Her interior, and the orientation does allow for the Jellyfish Brain to actually get what She's actually trying to get, which is more information... more options. She functions better with lots of information. Even if it takes Her to whelmed and overwhelmed. She still likes it, but there's a place in development where all that is externalized, and conceptualized, and idealized, and it's a very funny thing when all of a sudden all 'that' has to be set aside because She's full, satiated. You get to drop into the interior, and all of a sudden, all these relationships you're trying to have out here in the terrestrial world, you start to have in-house, in the aquatic interior, in-

400

body first. You begin to meet your needs first... you orient first, then glimpse what to nourish first and meet your needs before you've left the nest. Then, all of a sudden, navigating the world is easier. Not easier, but a layer easier. It gets funny with language, you know. The world is just as wacky. Your processes are just as wacky. None of the wackiness changes, but your orientation and your ability to navigate begins changing phenomenally, and it's not always articulable, although you just did.

**Christie** Well, it's just interesting because I've been seeing you for 13+ years... however long it's been... and the orientation I just got this morning, you know, something about the orientation I haven't gotten before and that's a part of the processes.

*Michael* It's a part of the gardening. It's part of the process. It's ongoing...you grow your experience.

**Christie** Yeah.

*Michael* And you, Christie, also put your time in.

**Christie** Well, yeah.

*Michael* That's the other thing. For a big part of the 'time', I'm putting the 'time' in, folding in 'time', steeping 'time', laying down these seeds. So if it takes root, it's got something to root within. If it doesn't, it at least supports, and it's being watered. I may not get this luxury of following through 13 years later or however many (I think it's been longer), but um, but I know that person's going to go on and live, for as long as they do, and they'll have lots of other inputs, but you cannot not react. You cannot not respond.

**Christie**  Well, so the question that arose in this for me is, in relationship to what we're doing, I wondered whether the tissues and the bone and everything outside of the neural-dominant place is actually occupying a mythic place?

*Michael*  There's nothing that's not occupying, residing in a mythic space. Mythic... It's a layer. I mean, we're talking about these layers...

**Christie**  ...but the... It just felt like if, if I take out the verbal neural conceptual thought process and sink into the actual, what I might feel like is the bone's experience of their world, their life. It just seems like they might be closer to experiencing the mythic or hanging out in the mythic or being aware... that's what they could bring to the Jellyfish Brain?

*Michael*  No, yes, yes and no. The bones are the ballast of the body. When the bones are allowed to take up their space, because they're 'space' takers, and they're allowed to be the center of the distributed load of the body's mass... when those two things are in place, that's orientation, right? You're in containment. You're your actual life-size. You're actual, really actually actual... Life-size!

When you have that, then a funny thing happens because all tissues love load bearing. They love, need that nourishing aquatic living responsive 'load', it's their definition of space. When they're allowed to actually have that, not be so contained or constricted or have to shape-change to do all the things that our body is so responsive and adaptive at doing - when they get that little bit of rest (and you can still walk through the world), it's really interesting because now the neural tissue is free-floating within her matrixes, within her root beds, so she gets lots of information. She's not relying on her very precise sense organs to do that. She doesn't always have to be 'reaching'. She has now developed, grown, a layer of responsive behavior throughout her entire root bed, so the whole length of cello string sinews resonate with the orchestra and what's happening, inside and out. She finds a layer of satisfaction that's not entirely about being stimulated, but she also gets it from being resonated, so she doesn't have to take action. She can actually work with what comes to her and be responsive in it. But those long lengths of neural tissue, from toe to crown, from crown to head of the toe, is what I meant to say. (Try to write that in a functional paragraph. I think that's very funny. Hard to write that kind of humor though.)

**Christie**  Yes, it is.

*Michael*  When that neural tissue is allowed to be softly held within its root-bedded matrix with all the other tissues... roots load bearing and dancing and co-mingling... then the Jellyfish Brain gets lots of delicious information, and her cognitive sense starts to be okay with 'both-and'. She has her felt somatic experience, which then leaves room for her emotional responses to those felt and somatic sensorial experiences. Then her cognition is free to cross-associate and correlate in the way that she loves to do, you know. Then, all that circulation and those songs have their place. They can interact, and they can be in discord or accord or... it starts to not matter so much (then you start to sound like a Buddhist).

Yeah... you are growing a capacity for your neural tissue to be in a more responsive state because she now has enough experience, life experience, in/with her tissues, mind, and matrixes. She also has enough words and dialogue, and the ability to go, "I can't have enough words or dialogue to cover my experience and that's okay". All of a sudden, information is allowed to circulate. It's not being held in the Jellyfish Brain. It's not being grasped in the tissues, not being anchored in one particular place or another, and for some people who dissociate/disassociate, a lot of that information is disassociated, pushed out into their psyche somewhere. They are actually displaced, you know, because their body is completely cinched down, unsafe. So now you've reclaimed all that landscape, hairballs and all, and now your roots have some room, some differentiation in there, and your Jellyfish is life-size.

So, the end of her tendrils get to be a little bit like octopuses' brains, you know? An octopus has her brains throughout her body, her tendrils and they don't all agree, but they coordinate, each sharing the experience. They're each gathering different information while sprawling through their landscape. Well, our senses get to do something similar. Our feet are giving us as much information as our hands, and the Jellyfish Brain's resting in that information as it circulates, as opposed to trying to grasp and hold onto it so that it can get off on some correlated management or feed just the 'habits'.

For the first part of our life we have to explore and feel because we're gathering, we're making sure that this world is what it is, and then all of a sudden we satiate, and go, "Well, the world hasn't changed for ten months, ten years, tens of years, 10 billion years.

Great. Maybe I can rest!" You know, we have access to food, we have access to clothing, we have access to nourishments in all different forms, and if not, we can begin to navigate towards more nourishing directions, even... ask for help!

So our nervous system gets to have some luxury our ancestors may not have, and so much of, but luckily some of them slowed down enough and had enough really big experiences to go, "Holy crap. I love dancing in the garden!", while the neighbor's going, "I hate gardening!", right? You get this nervous system that really is going, "I'm actually... my insides aren't much different than the outside!" Then it associates and correlates into really big concepts, able to gather, hold and integrate more nourishing experiences that you 'know', and you don't 'know' (yet).

This makes our garden a delicious moving target for things (concepts, ideas, habits, viruses, bacteria, etc.) which are looking for human donkey to ride into the next season. It's hard to tell, I'm getting ambushed by tangents... so back to 'concepts'. Some big concepts (or ???) are out there... and they go, "Uh, is this person ready for us? Is their... delicious Jellyfish Brain ready... let's saddle 'em up and ride 'em through time..." Sorry, just ambushed and saddled by tangents!

**Christie**  So that's where mythic comes in?

**Michael**  Mythic is the place below language, symbols, shapes (not 'below', in another layer… …) when the dynamics and qualities of space comingle and dance with each other, that's mythic! As they dance with each other, they start to take shape. At that point, they start to go archetypal, 'cuz this shape is in relationship to this other shape, the living qualities of/in space are in motion, in a dance, a relational motion/movement that, as it continues growing more defined, begins to flow into 10,000 archetypes, right?

   And then, these dynamics starts to get more related and matched entwining into an archetypical dance, however that dance is, whether it's struggle and, one dynamic, "No, I'm defined." The other dynamic, "No, I'm defined, but we're together." The first dynamic, "No, I don't want to be in a dance with you." Or both dynamics become enmeshed like, "Oh, we really like commingling." That whole spectrum, as these dynamics/archetypes continue to define, it'll go from that archetypal mother to son, teacher to students, etc., etc. …. and you know, whatever that set of relationships are forming.

   As it continues into more dance and gets more defined, then it pops up into symbolic. Then we can start to bring the softer aspect of language and art and poetry to gather it into a cohesive experience, and we'll become Rumi, poetically wrapping, steeping 10,000 words. You know, when we use 'this' to try and express 'that' (Rumi... "Don't ask me to write this down." Thank goodness his students did, despite his encouragement not to). And then when that has spent more time, and gets more specific, then it becomes literal i.e. this is this, this isn't like that, right?

These layers of engagement are all circulating with each other. The quality of space that begins to shape the felt sense of a bass note underneath the symbolic is mythic. There're these large qualities, these large batches of space interacting with space, right? The movement/motion of that is mythic, you know. The four-hour opera takes four hours because, for it to touch into its mythic significance, you have to steep in that operatic soup for at least a few hours. It has to be the whole thing, the 'whole' weaving of time and experience (unless you've seen it before and want to walk out in the middle of it going, "Oh right, I remember this. I don't need to visit the 'whole' experience again, thank you very much. I just remembered this one").

But for the first time, for that mythic theater expression of those qualities, you have to simmer/steep through/in the whole thing, and then, when we see enough of those, we begin to correlate to what's happening in our own life. Then we see our little arias, our kerfuffles, our hairballs. Then we've been able to step away from the part that totally broke down, part of it is totally broken down, and relationships all broken down and we're in the middle of our little opera, our own living aria, going, (Michael singing) "Well, what the fuck? I don't know what just happened but it's wrong. I don't know where I am, or who I am, or what's all going to be. And I don't like it. Oh, who's that stranger?" Now we go into the next phase of the opera, "I've been rescued." (Hopefully). That can take season after season, weaving seasons. Experiencing is growing tissue...growing both your personal opera within/of 'the opera' (social/nature) and The Opera (universal), Operas and Operas dancing/growing dying/tangling all within... within the medium of 'mythic'.

**Christie** Sure enough.

*Michael* It really depends on the opera. But our nervous system softening... more and more of our tissues get to be in that engagement, but, but this is all grown. We grow into reception, a receptivity of these layers, literally. Then we start to be able to slow down, or do like a sitting practice, or a martial practice, or any practice/tending space/place where we can get in touch and hold aspects of void, hold aspects of just being in space, and then, all of a sudden, our senses are like, "Oh!", and we grow the capacity to engage with that next layer.

At some point, outside of having little mythic experiences during our day that we can't verbalize what just happened, all of a sudden, we get really comfortable, and we know that 'that's' happening all the time, so we just leave that bass note there. By finding our bones, we're giving all our tissues orientation in space so they can all dance equally, have their individual dances and also be responsive, each in their own way and to each other.

**Christie** I'm going to ask you about this again and again and again, I think.

*Michael* Probably why you're going to write it down.

**Christie** That's right!

(Christie and Michael both laughing)

# Chapter Nine: *Now What?* (Christie)

Now that you have arrived towards the end of this offering, I'd like to point to some ways you can feel into what to do next with your interest and curiosity if you want to explore more with 'human gardening'.

As I have talked with Michael, written and felt into the progress of the conversation that we initiated about actually writing down his work and then following that creative path where it led, it has slowly become clear to me that Michael's intention has not been to expand his client base or specific teaching. His practice is full. The intention really is a sharing of his experience and his ideas that are born from doing 30+ years' work playing with bodies and consciousness in this way. The hope is that you, the reader, will take what you have learned from the book, what has piqued your curiosity, and absorb it into your own understanding, play with it, and if you want more, begin to seek out the resources that are available in your community for you to continue your own exploration.

By resources I mean those that offer ways to tap into not only what might be emotionally held in the body that is in need of some kind of easing, including pain, but also what wisdom might be available from listening to the body in ways Michael has found through exploring over the years. These resources focus on learning how to feel and be present to, and in, your body through sensation and the movement of sensation that is the body's language.

I came to Michael's work after spending most of my adult life pursuing health issues, including physical, emotional, creative and spiritual difficulties. I wanted to find practices I could use to understand the nature of my suffering and human suffering itself and what is possible to ease dis-ease. Most of the practices that I have found useful to me in this search are based in the body, which is part of why I have resonated so much with Michael's way of working. At the present this whole field of exploration is called somatic work, which has blossomed in the last 30 years.

I also was driven by my own curiosity and need to understand what life is, what reality is, what we as humans are. Most of the spiritual methods and tools I have learned are to that end. Those I have found the most useful are also based in the body.

I had been exploring for most of a lifetime, with immersion in many different practices, and, have been taught by many talented and generous teachers over the years. I want to name just a few of the most helpful to me to give you an idea of the kinds of resources that might be helpful to you:

**Bodywork**: Craniosacral Therapy, Somatic Experiencing, Michael's work
**Movement:** Continuum, Rosen Movement, Tai Chi, Yoga, Aikido
**Sound:** Improvisation
**Therapy:** Gestalt Awareness, Neo-Reichian work, Somatic Experiencing
**Meditation:** Buddhist (different lineages), Enneagram, Realization Process
**Diet:** Ayurveda

I know this is still a lot, but I wanted you to see that there are many different ways to approach somatic work. If you found that just one of these resonated for you, and you entered it deeply over time, that singular depth alone can be the way to go for you... or... you could let yourself be drawn into more variety as I did. There are pluses and minuses to both ways.

**Note:** Pre-covid versus post-covid: Most all of my exploring took place pre-covid when I could be in-person, which is essential with somatic work. Basic body to body transmission is needed to give and receive information in subtle and also ordinary ways. Covid has changed us all in the amount of in-person work we feel safe doing and with whom. There have been ways that online zoom classes have still made it possible to get quite a lot of intimate sharing and information that is very helpful with somatic work – YET – in the long run, we need that body-to-body communication in the flesh... in the very flesh that we are... so we will need to be creative in our safety... and... still do the in- person work somehow.

Back to this book about Michael's work and experience...

This book can hopefully continue to be a resource for you over time, something to read, put down, experiment with, contemplate, leave again and revisit as needed and as your curiosity pulls you in.

I've worked on this book with Michael for at least five or six years, reading it over and over as we have gone through its creation. I've heard Michael talk in sessions with me for over two decades. And still... a few weeks ago I read it again... and I got a big insight that was deeply meaningful to me... fresh... after all of this time already put in!  You never know what's going to blossom when! And... I know I will continue to reference the book for a long time to come. (Michael has teased me about this project being a way that I could fulfill my personal desire to get him to put his words into writing!)

I hope it will stay useful for you.

## Gratitudes

I will now turn you over to Michael for his suggestions and closure...there are more juicy bits to come!

However, I do want to speak my gratitude for the support, encouragement and suggestions I have been given by so many for my part in this endeavor. The process of turning audio interviews into a written book has been creative, surprising, fun, frustrating...and a lot of work. My community support has been critical.

I find it hard to express how much I've gotten from Michael in his willingness and vulnerability to keep going, step by step into this unknown process with me. I've learned so much . His generosity, honesty, humor, flexibility, insight....I could go on, but suffice to say I have received so much. Bowing to you, Michael.

Lisa, his sister, has been a miracle worker, taking all the pieces, clearing and packaging, with so much easy grace. This project wouldn't have come to completion without her. Thank you so much, Lisa.

Then there's Jodi, Michael's wife, who has done a remarkable job of helping when most needed and then stepping out at the right times to let the project find its way without input for a while. She has also supported and taught me much that I needed to understand over time of what I've been learning with Michael.

Family and friends have been essential for me and have been there steadily. Thank Goodness!

Bottom line with foundational holding and encouragement, occasional editing help and suggestions has been Stan, my husband. I couldn't have done this without you...all you have given means so much. Thank you.

# Chapter Ten: *The Last Chapter* (Michael)

## Creating Your Self-Facilitated Session

Well...

So let's do this last piece followed by my thanks to everyone. This chapter is a strong encouragement to create your own self-facilitated session. Yes, you have to do this! It will take time. You will get frustrated. It may make you nutty, but you have to do it. Play with it and make it your own!

There are many ways to record yourself and you'll be reading this recipe out loud, so go find one (most likely on your phone) and, please, give this a try. Now you may have to do this a few times till it feels right, let's really encourage this... Please read this out loud a few times to get the feel of it! That's what makes this such a living thing. Be gentle, don't rush, read as written and, after a while, you can begin to make it your own. Some little ways to feel your way through this... These will help with pacing, ready?

Three dots (...) = a good pause

Three commas (,,,) = a longer pause

A combo (.,,,.) = a full breath with body softened (silly, right ? but...)

Also, the feeling that moves this into a living thing is that it is felt as an open-ended, invitational question, like calling out to a feral cat, you can't reach for them, they'll scamper away. You have to sit, pretend you have a handful of kibble, open-handed, open-hearted (just imagine), inviting them over until they respond in their own way. You're just sitting, not reaching.

Remember to do some out loud practice runs (there's always practicing). Now have everything ready to record... and we'll begin.

Ready?!?! (.,.,.)

**Number one:**
Where are your bones?,,,
Your beautiful living coral reef bones,,,
Notice what bones respond...          just stay with
the first bones you notice...   notice the response, may not
make sense yet...       just try and linger...   gently keep
coming back to the bones that responded first...
your beautiful coral reef bones are so alive...
they get their information, their experience directly,
directly from the world,,,
Bones grow from the force put upon them...
that's their delicious law...      absorbing a 'push' from the
world, an emanated 'glee' expressed by this living planet...
Gravity pulls...          kisses us onto her belly...
then an opposite and equal response, a 'glee' is expressed
and absorbed...          through contact...

418

into your marvelous bones, right now while you're lying here,,,
gently swim back to that first bone response...
what do you notice?,.,.,.

**Number two:**
Where is the 'push' from the world?,,,
The contact supporting your beautiful coral reef bones, there's always a bone in contact, a bone touching something...   swim back to that first bone...
feel what's touching that neighborhood...    there's always a force coming to you...        there's no reaching...
just feeling the contact and the coral reef bone that lives there in its' neighborhood...      just linger there,.,.,.

now notice how your Jellyfish Brain may be trying to even things out, trying to balance the sensations between the sides of your body, so just bring your attention back into the bones, the place, the neighborhood you started, always swimming back to the beginning of this round,.,.,.

Remember you can always pause, soften and start over...        where is that first bone? where was that first response? gently swim back to that neighborhood, just linger and feel,,,
can you sense the contact there, feel a 'push' from what you're lying on?,,,
keep gently coming back...    do a few rounds,.,.,.

This begins to make an experiential tea, just a few rounds; *where's your Bones*, where's the 'push' of the world, the contact?    a few rounds, just feel...

what do you feel? Can you linger?... Bones are a bit feral, try to soften instead of reaching, just keep steeping your experience into a tea,.,.,.

**Number three:**
> Where's your giggle?...
> Have a little giggle ready...
> a little humor...
> Have a little empathy for your Jellyfish Brain, she'll want to do... something... it's her job, her nature to even things out, to balance everything...
> can you feel her trying to include the other bones?...
> now gently swim back, go back to the original place, the first bone that responded earlier, then notice what happens with your Jellyfish Brain... where's your giggle?... you'll need it!... it's her nature, her job, She has to coordinate everything... this creates a kerfuffle, a little disorientation, a little giggle helps... otherwise the Jellyfish Brain will start to "Hold on"... she'll try to "hold" through the kerfuffle, just give her... a little giggle, a little humor, a little empathy... she has to coordinate everything, such a big job, toss her a giggle and start over, back to your bones,.,.,.

back to **Number one**...
> *Where are your bones?*,,,
> what bones responded?,,,
> just stay there... stay with that coral reef, with that neighborhood, stay and steep, noticing the feelings, the responses,,,
> Number two, *Where's the push of the world*?...
> Where's that bone getting its' experience? Can you feel the contact?...

as you feel, have your giggle ready...
there'll be a kerfuffle...        a bit of wacky...
just soften...
after the ripples, just soften and gently come back to your
bones,.,.,.


        These three steps go together, they create an
'orientation'... *Where's your bones?* always number
one...*Where's the push of the world?* Where's contact,
always number two...        now...
        number three...W*here's your giggle?* You're going
to need it...
if you do the first two...        there will be a...
        kerfuffle...        a little wackiness,.,.,.


        this kerfuffle is sacred...        as sacred as your
coral reef bones...        as sacred as the world...
        as sacred as your beautiful, tenacious Jellyfish
Brain!,.,.,.


        to feel your bones, your jellyfish brain has to
soften...        she has to soften her tendrils...
to feel your bones, something has to soften...
when your Jellyfish brain softens her tendrils, it disorients
her...        there's no 'reaching'...
just softening...        there's no reaching to feel her
bones, her tendrils have to soften,.,.,.


to sense the 'push of the world' there's no reaching...
        OH MY...        the 'push' comes to her...
        no reaching, what a pickle!,.,.,.

between the 'world' and your 'Bones' are the tendrils of
your Jellyfish Brain...
tendrils comingled with your roots and tissues and bones
of your marvelous, very alive aquatic body, your living
aquatic garden...
and when a tendril gets tickled...      the Jellyfish Brain has
to do something,
Sooo, give her this gentle tender giggle, a flutter,
a softening, a moment...
and gently come back full circle...
back to your bones...
round and round...
round after round...
creating, steeping an experiential tea with time...
            devoted time...
now one more round,.,.,.

            *Where's your bones?...*
            *Where's the push of the world, contact?...*
            *Where's your giggle, your empathy?,.,.,.*

            rest...
            now rest...
            just rest,.,.,.

(turn off recording)

422

Now, it's time to set yourself up in a very private space to listen and feel. This needs to be to your comfort, with no distractions. When you're ready, play it back and feel your experience! If you feel the need to re-record... do so, until it's ok for you. If it's too odd, maybe ask someone with a talent to give it a try, make it yours!

∞∞∞∞∞∞∞∞∞∞∞∞∞∞∞∞∞∞∞∞∞∞∞∞∞∞∞∞∞∞

Dear reader, if you've made it this far, give yourself a treat of something delicious and nurturing. I would like to deeply thank you for wandering through my world, following these written deer tracks into territory that may be foreign and unfamiliar. This has been an aspect of my very private landscape and if you have people in your life that are dear, dear to you, ask them about how they navigate their world... use the same tea-making patience that you clearly had to use to find yourself here!!!

# The Final Chapter (Michael)

Well Dearest Readers... It's Jan 26th, 2023, (actually it's August 14th, 2024) and it has been over 5 (7) years or so to bring this conversation, this endeavor from one medium (verbal) to another (written). This has been its own experience! I've attempted this part so many times, 452, the amount of my tentacles needed to navigate through this world, the amount I clearly need to chew on things especially this endeavor! Oh and the number of beings I need to thank, so Thanks to all of you (you know who you are)!

This endeavor continues to be a conversation, a type of lullaby that doesn't quite lend itself easily to the page. My deepest respect to those who are able to leave their deer tracks so beautifully in the written word, so many blessings to them! But this monologued dialog that seems endlessly happening in my soul, this 'conversing' with my feelings of/with all of you, out there, in this wacky world, well... it's, it's all overwhelming and of course forces me to engage in another round of 'practicing what one preaches', so thanks to all of you!

The previous attempts at bringing this to an honorable close have kept me tipped into trying to give y'all 'my' story... it's been crazy making, honestly, really! This last part has been my trying to self-generate and organize my internal 'jazz' which is not a 'conversation' and it's not what I was asked! So imagine with me... 10,000 words later, Christie asked... so the most tender and awkward Thank You!

To continue my 'Thank yous': Thank you to Christie's beloved Stan. Thank you my dearest sister Lisa and her beloved Keith and his wonderfully tech savvy son, Jonathan. Thank you my dearest heart friends Kimberly and Joey. If Vivian could hear me (and she probably does!!!), all my blessings! Gaye and Donald for all the years of tending my heart. Helga and Franz for growing into the tenderest of friends. Wendell for seeing a feral seed back in the 80's, putting it in her pocket and keeping it safe until I could have my own roots, blessings! Kim and Bonnie, so many hugs for your tender support. Jami and Jimmy, your unwavering familial support constantly feeds my soul.

Now... My beloved Jodi, who hears me before I even have said anything, who, in a marvelous twist of fate, while I was at my lowest, flat on my back for months... SHE claimed me!!! Now, a ton of years later, I'm awkwardly and gratefully recovering from such a brilliant "Affection Ambush!!!"

Now for the pile of "just won't let me continue and get a decent night's sleep" (I've grown to really like sleep!) continued acknowledgements. There's a pile of Steves, the Rob, Doudi (Dave), JBH & Jeffery, a "J", Deirdre and Dragon sis Pawan. Robert & Michele. There's Ricardo, a pile of Sharons, Carrie, Perry and an amazing creature whose ability to tend the aliveness of words and language... Christina.

Oh, and speaking of which, there are members of the Fluid Community that have touched my Soul (left anonymous)... may they feel the Queer tears of gratefulness. Then all my teachers, my students, my run- ragged partnerships ,and all those who have cross-culturally pollinated my life into this odd sprouting of a human bean. My deep gratitude for the Q'ero of South America and the Incan tenacity of adapting and integrating with all the wackiness of what the rest of us think is important, my goodness! 10,000 words later... Blessings to all of you that have waded through this endeavor, Big Energetic Hugs and thank you for your patience! Then everything tips into the pile of 452 thank yooouuusss, so *Thank you!* to my beloved community.

So to everyone else... I invite you, almost insistent that y'all go ask your dearest, Dear ones questions, questions about what it takes for them to do 'what they do!!?' Pay attention, let your awareness flood so you can feel their responses and yours. Oh goodness, then go explore your community; if you need help... ASK YOUR COMMUNITY! Please! On that note... I'm more fragile than the people around me realize, so I ask that you deeply consider before reaching for me. I'm a very private and cave-like being and it's taken a long time, a lifetime, to get things in place to be able to manage my condition and my days. So the 'Practice' of all this and much more, whew, is my lifestyle. Christie not only asked, but committed to this entire round of gardening, neither of us quite grokking what it would take to grow! Now, now you've gotten to eavesdrop in a funny way, to read this book, to follow and mull over the deer tracks of my personal response to Christie's questions, and, subsequently, into our privacy.

So get to know yourself, as you is! And begin to nourish from what you discover; just know that it's a delicious bewildering tea and the world, inside and out, will rush in for a drink! Don't let it, it's not easy but good, good is not easy! But before you begin reaching... rest and explore your responses to the next handful of activities. See if you can learn more about your garden, your body, your beloveds, your community. It'll certainly be more nourishing than your computer or cell phone.

Soooooo...

10,000 piles of *"THANK Y'ALL"*

10,000 BLESSINGS

Big (energetic) Hugs

*M*

P.S. I think Martin Prechtel and Martin Shaw and so many others say it better.

www.ingramcontent.com/pod-product-compliance
Lightning Source LLC
Chambersburg PA
CBHW010937120626
46554CB00008B/2510